Strategy Instruction
for Students with Learning Disabilities

WHAT WORKS FOR SPECIAL-NEEDS LEARNERS

Karen R. Harris and Steve Graham
Editors

Strategy Instruction for Students with Learning Disabilities
Robert Reid and Torri Ortiz Lienemann

Teaching Mathematics to Middle School Students
with Learning Difficulties
Marjorie Montague and Asha K. Jitendra, Editors

Strategy Instruction for Students with Learning Disabilities

Robert Reid
Torri Ortiz Lienemann

Series Editors' Note by Karen R. Harris and Steve Graham

THE GUILFORD PRESS
New York   London

©2006 The Guilford Press
A Division of Guilford Publications, Inc.
72 Spring Street, New York, NY 10012
www.guilford.com

Printed in the United States of America

This book is printed on acid-free paper.

Last digit is print number: 9   8   7   6   5   4   3   2

Library of Congress Cataloging-in-Publication Data

Reid, Robert.
  Strategy instruction for students with learning disabilities / Robert Reid, Torri Ortiz Lienemann.
      p. cm.—(What works for special needs learners)
  Includes bibliographical references and index.
  ISBN-10 1-59385-282-7, ISBN-13 978-1-59385-282-5 (pbk.)
  ISBN-10 1-59385-283-5, ISBN-13 978-1-59385-283-2 (cloth)
  1. Learning disabled children—Education—United States.   I. Lienemann,
Torri.   II. Title.   III. Series.
  LC4705.R46 2006
  371.9—dc22
                                                                2005031508

To Karen R. Harris, who taught us what we needed to know

About the Authors

Robert Reid, PhD, is a Professor in the Department of Special Education and Communication Disorders at the University of Nebraska–Lincoln. He received his doctorate in special education from the University of Maryland in 1991. Dr. Reid's research focuses on children with attention-deficit/hyperactivity disorder (ADHD) and on strategy instruction. He has published more than 60 articles and book chapters and presented at national and international conferences. Additionally, he codeveloped the ADHD-IV Rating Scale (1998). Dr. Reid received the American Educational Research Association's Special Education Student Research Award in 1992 and the Balilies Child Mental Health Award in 1996. He currently serves on the editorial boards of five journals and actively reviews for several others.

Torri Ortiz Lienemann, MEd, is a doctoral candidate at the University of Nebraska–Lincoln. Her work focuses on strategy instruction and self-regulation, specifically in writing. Currently, Ms. Lienemann is involved in research on strategy instruction for students with ADHD and in creating new programs to assist students with special needs and their teachers. She has been a classroom resource teacher at both the middle and high school levels and served as a remedial teacher at an elementary school.

Series Editors' Note

S*trategy Instruction for Students with Learning Disabilities* guides teachers and other practitioners through the effective use of strategy instruction, proven by researchers to be a powerful instructional approach for students with learning disabilities, students at risk for school failure, and other struggling learners. The reader is taken through the what, why, and how of a classroom-validated model of strategy instruction—Self-Regulated Strategy Development—in conjunction with practical examples of how to teach powerful academic and learning strategies.

This volume is first in the series "What Works for Special-Needs Learners." The series addresses a significant need in the education of learners with special needs—students who are at risk, those with disabilities, and all children and adolescents who struggle with learning or behavior. Researchers in special education, educational psychology, curriculum and instruction, and other fields have made great progress in understanding what works for struggling learners, yet the practical application of this research base remains quite limited. This is due in part to the lack of appropriate materials for teachers, teacher educators, and inservice teacher development programs. As demonstrated in the present volume, books in the series will present assessment, instructional, and classroom management methods that have a strong research base, and will also provide specific "how-to" instructions and examples of the use of proven procedures in schools.

Strategy Instruction for Students with Learning Disabilities features extensive use of examples drawn from classroom teachers and their students. The authors also provide tools for organizing and implementing strategy instruction, guidelines for effective strategy modeling and scaffolding, sample lesson plans, and materials helpful in teaching students to use core self-regulation strategies (e.g., goal setting, self-instruction, self-assessment/self-monitoring, and self-reinforcement).

The authors, who have significant experience with strategy instruction in the classroom, provide detailed information on instruction in and the development of academic and self-regulation strategies across written language, reading, and mathematics. Each chapter in these areas includes a discussion of the prerequisites for learning, major problems experienced by learners who struggle with that area of academic learning, and research-proven strategies. Strategy instruction in the areas of study skills and memory strategies are covered as well. In addition, the authors clearly explain and demonstrate how implementing strategy instruction in the classroom includes the development of motivation, positive attitudes toward learning, and attributions for effort and strategy use. An invaluable resource for practitioners, this book is also suitable for use in a methods course.

Future books in the series will cover such issues as math instruction, word learning, and reading comprehension for students with learning disabilities. All volumes will be as thorough and detailed as the present one and will facilitate implementation of evidence-based practices in classrooms and schools.

KAREN R. HARRIS
STEVE GRAHAM

Contents

Strategy Instruction
for Students with Learning Disabilities

CHAPTER 1

Why Use Strategy Instruction?

Students with learning disabilities (LD) constitute by far the largest group of students with special needs. According to the U.S. Department of Education, in 1999 there were 2,789,000 students from birth to age 21 served in federally supported programs for LD. Students with LD constitute 46% of the special education population and 5.9% of the total school enrollment according to recent figures (U.S. Department of Education, 2001). Over the last 25 years the number of students identified as learning disabled has showed a steady increase. Since 1976 the numbers have more than tripled. Although the rate of increase has slowed, the overall numbers continue to increase.

A learning disability affects nearly every aspect of a child's life and is a lifelong challenge (Lerner, 2000). Interventions for students with LD cover many areas (e.g., academics, self-esteem, transition, vocation). Students with LD are often caught in a vicious spiral of school failure. Their learning difficulties lead to slower development of academic skills and abilities, which in turn impedes new learning (Stanovich, 1986). As a result of the repeated cycle of failure, they fall farther and farther behind. According to the U.S. Department of Education, students with LD are at greatly increased risk for dropping out: nearly 70% of students with LD fail to graduate from high school with a standard diploma. The academic problems also result in a lower engagement rate in postsecondary schooling, employment, or both, compared to typically achieving students (Murray, Goldstein, & Edgar, 1997). Thus, the need to address the academic achievement of students with LD is critical in order to improve their academic outcomes.

The purpose of this chapter is to provide background information on LD, discuss characteristics of students with LD that affect instruction in general and strategy in-

1

struction in particular, and provide a rationale for the use of strategy instruction. Readers who are interested in more in-depth information should refer to Swanson, Harris, and Graham (2003). In this chapter, we first present definitions of LD and briefly discuss the history of LD. Next, we describe some important characteristics of students with LD and how our conceptualization of LD has changed over time. Finally we make a case for the use of strategy instruction with students with LD. Note that the use of strategy instruction is *not* limited to students with LD. Research clearly indicates that strategy instruction is effective for the great majority of students who struggle in academic areas.

WHAT IS A LEARNING DISABILITY?

LD has been recognized as a category of disability under federal law since 1975. The current legal definition of LD is written into the Individuals with Disabilities Education Act (IDEA); however, as Table 1.1 shows, other organizations have proposed their own definitions of LD that differ substantially, and exactly how to define LD has been and continues to be a controversial area. This is in part due to the highly heterogeneous nature of the students who are defined as LD. Students with LD manifest a number of different problems in academic, behavioral, and social-emotional areas. However, students with LD may exhibit vastly different profiles both within and across these areas. For example, some students may have serious problem with reading but will excel at mathematics. Others may have difficulties in mathematics, but not in reading. Some students will have serious problem with self-esteem or depression while others have little or no problem in these areas but may exhibit serious behavior problems. Another factor that contributes to confusion in the area of LD is that the field cuts across a number of professional disciplines, such as education, psychology, medicine, and sociology. Each of these disciplines brings its own perspective on LD, and like the proverbial blind men and the elephant, each focuses on a different aspect of LD. As a result, there are differences across professional groups on the terminology that should be used to describe LD, and on what aspects of LD should and should not be included in the definition.

While there is a lack of consensus on how to define LD, there is a practical consensus on how students with LD are identified. Despite the fact that all of the definitions of LD contain references to causes of LD (e.g., disorders in basic psychological processes, neurological origins, central nervous system dysfunction) and that difficulties in academic areas are often described in medical language (e.g., dyslexia, dyscalculia, dysgraphia), these factors rarely if ever play a role in diagnosis. In practice, LD is a category of underachievement, and students with LD are identified based on chronic and severe academic difficulties. Historically, a discrepancy formula was used to determine if a child should be labeled as learning disabled. Mercer (1997) noted that over 90% of states include a discrepancy component in the identification process. These discrepancy formulas assess the difference between ability, as determined by the results of intelligence tests, and academic achievement, as assessed by standardized tests. If the difference between the child's presumed ability and actual achievement is large

TABLE 1.1. Definitions of Learning Disabilities

Individuals with Disabilities Education Act (1977)

The term "specific learning disability" means those children who have a disorder in one or more of the basic psychological processes involved in understanding or in using language, spoken or written, which disorder may manifest itself in imperfect ability to listen, think, speak, read, write, spell, or to do mathematical calculations. The term includes such conditions as perceptual handicaps, brain injury, minimal brain dysfunction, dyslexia, and developmental aphasia. The term does not include a learning problem which is primarily the result of visual, hearing, or motor handicaps, of mental retardation, of emotional disturbance, or of environmental, cultural, or economic disadvantage.

Association for Children with Learning Disabilities (1986)

Specific Learning Disabilities is a chronic condition of presumed neurological origin which selectively interferes with the development, integrations, and/or demonstration of verbal and/or nonverbal abilities. Specific Learning Disabilities exists as a distinct handicapping condition and varies in its manifestations and in degree of severity. Throughout life, the condition can affect self-esteem, education, vocation, socialization, and/or daily living activities.

Interagency Committee on Learning Disabilities (1987)

Learning disabilities is a generic term that refers to a heterogeneous groups of disorders manifested by significant difficulties in the acquisition and use of listening, speaking, reading, writing, reasoning, mathematical abilities, or social skills. These disorders are intrinsic to the individual and presumed to be due to central nervous system dysfunction. Even though a learning disability may occur concomitantly with other handicapping conditions (e.g., cultural differences, insufficient or inappropriate instruction, psychogenic factors), and especially attention-deficit disorder, all of which may cause learning problems, a learning disability is not the direct result of those conditions or influences.

National Joint Council on Learning Disabilities (1997)

Learning disabilities is a general term that refers to a heterogeneous group of disorders manifested by significant difficulties in the acquisition and use of listening, speaking, reading, writing, reasoning, or mathematical abilities. These disorders are intrinsic to the individual, are presumed to be due to central nervous system dysfunction, and may occur across the life span. Problems in self-regulatory behaviors, social perceptions, and social interactions may exist with learning disabilities but do not by themselves constitute a learning disability. Although a learning disability may occur concomitantly with other disabilities (for example sensory impairment, mental retardation, or serious emotional disturbance) or with extrinsic influences (such as cultural differences or insufficient/inappropriate instruction), it would not be a result of those conditions or influences.

enough, the child can be identified as having a learning disability. Discrepancy formulas, though commonly used, are coming under scrutiny, and concerns pertaining to their validity have been raised (Fuchs, Fuchs, & Compton, 2004).

CAUSES OF LEARNING DISABILITIES

The search for causes of LD has been the subject of research for more than 50 years. A number of possible causes have been put forward over the years with varying degrees of support. Table 1.2 presents some hypothesized causes of LD. No one has yet pre-

TABLE 1.2. Hypothesized Causes of Learning Disabilities

Cause	Example
Central nervous system abnormality	Abnormal brain hemispheric symmetry, nerve cell anomalies in areas of the brain involved in language
Central nervous system damage	*Prenatal*: maternal drug use, smoking, fetal alcohol syndrome, fetal alcohol effects
	Perinatal: prematurity, anoxia, complications during labor, injury during delivery
	Postnatal: brain injury due to stroke, high fever, meningitis, encephalitis, or head trauma
Genetic	Evidence suggests that reading disabilities may have a strong genetic component. Conditions caused by chromosomal abnormalities such as Klinefelter syndrome, Turner syndrome, or fragile X syndrome can result in learning difficulties.
Environmental	Exposure to environmental toxins such as lead or other heavy metals
Biochemical abnormalities	Imbalances in neurotransmitters (e.g., dopamine, serotonin, acetylcholine)

sented conclusive or compelling evidence to support any particular cause of LD, though researchers continue to make progress. In part this is due to the problems inherent in studying LD. Given the highly heterogeneous nature of LD, the differing theoretical orientations of researchers, and the problems with defining and accurately identifying a child as having a learning disability, this should not be too surprising. There are some clear trends in how LD has been approached that have direct implications for educators involved with instructional decision making for students with LD.

Medical Perspectives

Historically, learning disabilities have been viewed as brain-based disorders. That is, the learning problems evidenced by students were thought to be due to some specific neurologically based deficit or disorder. For example, James Hinshelwood (1917) coined the term "word blindness" to describe a child who had an inexplicable inability to learn to read despite apparently normal intelligence and normal functioning in other areas. Hinshelwood speculated that the child's problem was due to a defect in the angular gyrus. Another researcher, Samuel Orton (1937), noticed that many students who experienced difficulty in reading also tended to reverse letters such as *b* and *d*, or *p* and *q*. Orton termed this phenomenon "strephosymbolia" (twisted symbols) and attributed it to the failure of some individuals to develop "cerebral dominance" (i.e., neither of the brain's hemispheres was dominant). He hypothesized that reversals were due to mirror images of words or letters stored in the nondominant brain hemisphere. This work was continued by more modern researchers such as Kirk Goldstein (1936) and Alfred Strauss (1947). Goldstein worked with soldiers who had suffered brain injuries during World War I. He noted that these soldiers commonly exhibited perceptual problems, impulsivity, distractibility, and hyperactivity. Strauss noted that students with mental retardation exhibited many of the same characteristics and theorized that the problems were due to brain injury. As a result, terms such as "brain-injured child" and "minimal brain dysfunction" were used to refer to students we would today call learning disabled. Strauss hypothesized that perhaps some extremely subtle brain damage was the root cause of a child's failure to learn. These labels were, understandably, unpopular with parents, and their relevance was also questioned. The medical influence on the field of LD is still strong. For example, use of medical terminology such as dyslexia or dyscalculia to refer to problems in reading and math is common. Current research on the brain and LD now uses extremely sophisticated tools and is beginning to shed further light on the relation between the brain and LD (e.g., Shaywitz, 2003).

Learning Disabilities as an Academic Problem

In 1963, a watershed event in the history of LD occurred at a meeting of concerned parents in Chicago (Mercer, 1997). The parents met to air their displeasure with medical practitioners who described their children as brain injured or as having minimal brain dysfunction. Samuel Kirk, a psychologist with years of experience working with students with academic problems, coined the term "learning disabilities" to describe those students who had difficulty in learning to read. This resulted in a change in perspective on learning problems. Rather than being attributed to organic damage to the brain, these problems were seen as related to underlying cognitive processes. That is, the students were neurologically intact but had difficulties with psychological processes (i.e., perceptual problems, as evidenced by difficulties with visual and auditory discrimination) that prevented them from receiving visual and/or auditory stimuli correctly and resulted in difficulty learning. This perceptual–motor approach shifted the focus from the medical aspects of LD to the academic, resulting in the creation of assessment instruments designed to measure underlying deficits and intervention programs designed to remediate them, the idea being that if the hypothesized underlying deficit in perceptual processing was corrected, the child would progress academically in a normal fashion. Numerous programs were designed and implemented. Students learned to walk balance beams to improve motor skills, and trace shapes to improve perceptual skills. Unfortunately, the training programs designed to remediate process deficits were found to be ineffective, and the assessment instruments were not reliable (Hamill & Larsen, 1974). However, the perspective on LD as a problem rooted at least in part in *instruction* remained and served to change LD practice.

Behavioral and Cognitive Approaches

During the 1960s, '70s, and '80s, new, influential perspectives on learning disabilities began to emerge. The first of these was behaviorism. This approach developed by B. F. Skinner was based on the theory that a functional relation exists between behavior (e.g., reading) and the environment. Behaviorists stressed direct observation and ongoing collection of objective information. Learning was viewed as a hierarchical process in which a child must master skills in a prescribed order. In this approach academic tasks were broken down into their component parts, and each part was taught in sequence. The application to LD lay in the notion that academic problems would be best attacked by changes in the instructional environment. From the behaviorist perspective, a highly structured instructional environment that directly addressed the problem area was necessary for academic progress. Thus, if a child had reading problems what was needed was to directly teach the skills needed to read using appropriately sequenced, highly structured instruction. Several extremely effective instructional approaches, such as DISTAR (Engelman & Bruner, 1974) and Precision Teaching (Lindsley, 1964), were developed based on behavioral approaches.

In the 1970s, cognitive approaches to teaching and learning began to influence the LD field. The cognitive perspective focuses on the role of the individual in the learning process (Mercer, 1997). From this perspective, the key is the relation between demands of the learning environment (e.g., the task, instructional materials) and how the learner processes information. Learning problems may result from deficits in cognitive processes such as memory, failure to process information efficiently (such as failure to use an appropriate or effective strategy), or a combination of both. Metacognition (knowledge of one's own cognitive processes) also became important. During the 1980s, cognitive approaches became very influential, and a great deal of basic research was done on cognitive characteristic of students with LD. Memory researchers developed new models for addressing how cognitive processes work. Perhaps the most important of these was the information-processing model, which envisioned cognitive processing as analogous to a computer with input, storage, and processing components. The information-processing model was extremely influential because it focused attention on the processes involved in memory and learning. Curriculum materials such as the University of Kansas learning strategies approach that utilized cognitive approaches were developed and used effectively. The work done on behavioral and cognitive approaches resulted in progress in understanding the nature of the problems encountered by students with LD and in development of effective teaching techniques. The field of LD is still building on and refining the advances that occurred during this period.

CHARACTERISTICS OF STUDENTS WITH LEARNING DISABILITIES

It is important for educators to be knowledgeable about the characteristics of students with LD. Important characteristics of students with LD span emotional, behavioral, cognitive, and social aspects of development. We focus on the information that is needed for teachers—whose job is to successfully educate students with LD. For this reason, the discussion of their characteristics will be limited to characteristics that directly affect academic performance and that are thus relevant to strategy instruction.

Attention

Teachers who work with students with LD commonly note that "Things seem to go in one ear and out the other," or they remark on the need to "jog" students back after their attention has wandered. Attention is a critical aspect of successful learning. It is also a complex and multifaceted phenomenon. There are three important aspects of attention. First, there is task engagement. To succeed in school, students must be able persist at tasks. Students with LD are often off-task in the classroom. Research shows that, when left to their own devices, students with LD are on-task only around 30–60% of the time (Bryan & Wheeler, 1972; McKinney & Feagans, 1983). This has obvious educational implications. For example, students who do not complete practice tasks may fail to develop necessary fluency in important skills. Students who stop work when they encounter difficulty will learn less and are more likely to have negative classroom experiences. Maintaining focus is a common problem among students with LD (Hallahan, Kauffman, & Lloyd, 1996). Students with LD are often described as "spacey" or "not with it" or "distractible." Failure to maintain focus has serious consequences. Students whose minds wander while reading a passage will have difficulties remembering information. Students who are daydreaming and as a result don't attend to their teacher may not be aware of assignments or miss important directions. Finally, difficulty with selective attention—the ability to identify important or meaningful information—is also common among students with LD (Brown & Wynne, 1984). As a result, students with LD may attend to unimportant components of a task and ignore relevant information. Exactly why students with LD experience these problems is still unclear, but we do know that much can be done as a part of strategy instruction to improve all aspects of attention.

Memory

One common concern among teachers who work with students with LD is that one day the child can readily remember important information—they've "got it"—but the next day, for no apparent reason, it's gone. The ability to remember information is obviously critical to academic success. For example, if students cannot remember basic math facts, how commonly used words are spelled, or content-area facts (e.g., Civil War battles or the parts of an atom), they will have difficulty progressing academically. And, students with LD exhibit just these types of problems. Research shows that students with LD do have more problems with memory than students without LD (e.g., Gettinger, 1991; Swanson, Cochran, & Ewers, 1990). Research also shows that memory deficits are also linked to problems in academic areas (e.g., Ceci, Ringstorm, & Lea, 1981). Historically, these deficits were seen as due to a lack of innate capacity. To use an example, if we were to see memory as one of the "underlying psychological processes" with which students with LD exhibit deficiencies, we might use the metaphor of a bucket to describe the memory problems of these students. For these students it would seem, at least on the surface, as if their bucket is smaller (i.e., less capacity) and is very leaky (more forgetting, problems with retaining information). However, this is a case where appearances are deceiving.

There are a number of factors that affect how well a person can remember information. First, the amount of background knowledge, or the knowledge base, can affect memory. Individuals with background knowledge in an area will have an easier time remembering new material in that area than individuals without it. Being familiar with material can enhance memory (Swanson, 1996). This is a problem for students with LD as they generally tend to have lower levels of background knowledge. Second, the problem with recall exhibited by students with LD may not be related to a memory deficit, but rather may be a function of their failure to use processes that would allow them to remember. For example, if skilled learners faced with the task of remembering a series of 10 random numbers, such as 3014056488, they would, almost automatically, use one of several methods for remembering. They might repeat the numbers to themselves several times (i.e., verbal elaboration). Or, they might rearrange the information using "chunking" into fewer components that would be easier to remember (e.g., 30, 14, 05, 64, 88). Both of these processes will improve ability to remember the 10 digits. In contrast, students with LD are unlikely to do this spontaneously (Swanson, 1996). In other words, students with LD may lack or not use strategies that would help them remember information. Strategies for improving memory are commonly part of strategy instruction.

Attributions

The term *attributions* refers to the manner in which students explain the cause of academic outcomes. For example, if we asked a successful student, "Why did you get an A on the science test?" the answer would probably be that "I got an A because I studied hard." In other words, the student attributed the cause of the good grade to studying hard. Attributions are extremely important because they can affect expectations for success, academic behaviors, and students' reactions to success or failure (Weiner, 1979). Students who attribute a good grade to studying hard have a healthy attribution pattern. Unfortunately, students with LD tend not to exhibit this pattern. These students often attribute success to external factors that they do not control, such as luck or the test being easy. Moreover, students with LD often attribute *failures* to internal, uncontrollable factors such as lack of ability or task difficulty (Chapman, 1988; Kistner, Osborn, & LeVerrier, 1988; Stipek, 1993). Think for a moment about the ramifications of this pattern of attributions. Any academic success is outside the student; in contrast, failure is internalized. This is an unhealthy or maladaptive pattern that can affect students' academic motivation and performance. Strategy instruction is sensitive to this problem and fosters the development of positive attributions.

Learned Helplessness

Learned helplessness refers to a belief that efforts are unlikely to lead to success. In other words, students believe that no matter how hard they try they simply won't succeed, so therefore there is no reason to try in the first place (Dweck, 1975). A previous pattern of failure has led them to "know" they can't do it. For many of these students, the source of failure is perceived to be lack of ability ("I can't do this"). Even when they do succeed, they are likely to attribute the success to outside factors ("The teacher was easy on me"). This has a corrosive affect on academic motivation. Why strive for success if failure is inevitable? Research suggests that the problem of learned helplessness is common among students with LD. Kavale and Forness (1996) found that as many as 70% of students with LD may exhibit learned helplessness.

Lack of Coordinated Strategies

Imagine the following scenario. It's late at night and you are studying for an exam. You're reading a very difficult portion of your text, so you are reading much more slowly than normal. Suddenly you realize that you have no recollection of what you just read on the last two pages. You sigh, and begin to carefully reread the section of the text. Though this looks simple, there are a number of things happening under the surface. First, you knew that the purpose of reading is to understand the text, so you adjusted your reading speed because you realized that in difficult sections you need to read more slowly if you are going to remember important information. Second, you realized that you had experienced a lapse in concentration and had no recollection of what you just read. This occurred because you were engaged in ongoing monitoring of your comprehension. Third, after you recognized the lapse, you realized that it was necessary to correct the situation, because if you did not you could miss important information. Finally, you used an appropriate method (going back to reread) to correct the problem.

This scenario has probably happened to you a number of times; it is common among skilled learners. In fact, there is good reason to believe that this sequence of events describes a skilled learner. However, this scenario is rare among students with LD. Students with LD are unlikely to respond appropriately to the demands of an academic task by using an effective set of cognitive strategies. For example, they will spend less time studying and will not realize that it is necessary to slow down for difficult sections (Bauer, 1987; Wong & Wilson, 1984). They may be unlikely to recognize that they have experienced a problem because they will not be actively monitoring their comprehension (Borkowski, Weyhing, & Carr, 1988; Harris, Graham, & Pressley, 1992). And if they do realize they need to correct the problem, they are unlikely to use an effective method to do so. Students with LD commonly exhibit problems in four areas (Swanson, 1993):

1. They have difficulty accessing, coordinating, and organizing mental activities that occur simultaneously or in close succession.
2. Even when students have an idea of appropriate strategies, they use them ineffectively.
3. They fail to engage in self-regulation of mental activity (e.g., planning, monitoring, revising).
4. They have a limited awareness of the usefulness of specific strategies for a given task.

In short, it seems as if students with LD neither spontaneously do things that would improve their learning, nor in some instances even are aware that they are necessary or appropriate (Owings, Petersen, Bransford, Morris, & Stein, 1980).

WHY A STRATEGY APPROACH?

The federal definition in the IDEA notes that LD is the result of a "disorder in one or more of the basic psychological processes," and the National Joint Council on Learning Disabilities definition states, "These disorders [learning problems] are intrinsic to the individual, [and] are presumed to be due to central nervous system dysfunction." As we noted earlier, the cause of LD has not yet been clearly proven; however, even if we accepted these conceptualizations, they would provide very little in the way of guidance for educators who are charged with teaching students with LD. For example, we can do very little about central nervous system dysfunction. However, at least in part the problems experienced by students with LD are due to difficulties with effective use of strategies. Swanson (1999a) noted that poor academic performances across all ages in students with LD has been seen as a problem in the use of efficient strategies. Students with LD tend to develop fewer strategies and to use strategies less often than typically achieving students (Stone & Conca, 1993). Exactly why this occurs is not certain at present. However, what is well known is that strategy instruction can meaningfully improve performance among students with LD and other struggling learners. Therefore it makes sense that strategies be treated just like any other academic problem. If students with LD lack effective strategies for an academic task, then *we should teach them effective strategies*.

What about problems with maladaptive attributions or learned helplessness? Strategy instruction addresses these problems directly using an approach advocated by Licht (1983). In a very influential paper, Licht (1983) argued for a new definition of "ability." She argued for an "incremental" view of ability. From this perspective, what makes you "smart" is not some unchangeable entity such as intelligence, but rather "an accumulation of knowledge and skills that can be increased through effort. . . . The harder you try, the more you'll learn, and the smarter you'll get" (p. 487). From Licht's perspective, problems such as maladaptive attributions or learned helplessness can be addressed through instruction. If students have unhealthy patterns of attributions they can be taught appropriate, positive attributions—failure and success depend on effort. If students have developed learned helplessness, they can learn that success can be obtained through the use of effective strategies.

Swanson (1996) aptly summarized the advantages of the use of the strategy approach:

> A focus is placed on what is modifiable. That is, differences between ability groups are conceptualized in terms of cognitive processes that are susceptible to instruction, rather than to fundamental or general differences in ability. Thus, rather than focusing on isolated elementary memory processing deficiencies, the types of questions . . . are more educationally relevant. For example, a focus is placed on what students with LD can do without strategy instruction, what they can do with strategy instruction, what can be done to modify existing strategy instruction, and what can be done to modify existing classroom materials to improve instruction. It [the strategy-oriented approach] allows for the child to be actively involved in the instruction. Students can participate in the analysis of which cognitive strategies work best for them . . . [and] . . . materials can be developed which maximize strategy use. (p. 301)

There are several significant advantages of the strategy approach. First, it assumes that many of the problems of students with LD are due to the lack of or failure to use strategies. Thus, from this perspective, past academic problems were not due to an innate lack of ability or capacity, but rather to ineffective use of abilities. Second, it assumes that if students learn effective strategies there will be a significant increase in academic performance. Evidence for the strategy deficit hypothesis has been well documented. For example, in the area of memory, Torgesen (1984) found that when students with LD are directly taught memory strategies, there were no differences in recall between students with and without LD on selected tasks. Third, it assumes that strategies can be directly taught and effectively learned. There is now ample evidence that students with LD can be taught to utilize strategies (e.g., Swanson, 1990). Note that this *directly empowers* both students and educators. It places the control of learning directly in the hands of students and teachers. Students can always learn new strategies, and educators can always teach them. Finally, and most importantly, the strategy approach has a *20-year track record* of success.

The last point is undoubtedly the most important. In a time when there are more and more demands for accountability, educators can no longer continue to adopt educational regimens that are not evidence based. Recall the perceptual–motor approach, which appeared logical but was also a complete failure in terms of helping students with LD progress academically. Given the number of students with LD and who are at risk for academic failure, we simply cannot afford to use anything less than the best methods we have; and we have a very good idea of what methods are most effective at improving academic learning. Two studies (Swanson, 1999b; Swanson & Sachs-Lee, 2000) using meta-analysis evaluated the effectiveness of numerous teaching methods for students with LD. Meta-analysis allows researchers to combine the results of numerous studies and to test which instructional approach is the most effective. The two studies conducted by Swanson and his colleagues are the most comprehensive investigation into instructional methods for students with LD ever conducted. All told, Swanson's meta-analysis included a total of 163 separate studies with over 1,000 comparisons. This encompassed all the basic skill areas: reading, math, and written language. The results were clear-cut. The most effective methods were those that incorporated most of the following elements:

- Explicit explanations, elaborations, and/or plans to direct task performance.
- Verbal modeling, questioning, and demonstration by teachers.
- Students cued, reminded, and/or taught to use strategies, or procedures.
- Step-by-step prompts or multiprocess instructions.
- Teacher–student dialogue.
- Questioning by the teacher.
- Assistance provided only when necessary.

What instructional method typically incorporates most or all of these components? You have probably guessed. Students taught via the strategy instruction method showed the most improvement compared to other methods. Further, the degree of improvement was impressive. In sum, we can say with confidence that strategy instruction approaches are highly effective for students with LD.

PUTTING STRATEGY INSTRUCTION INTO THE CLASSROOM

By now you may be wondering why strategy instruction isn't widespread. After all, if strategy instruction is effective, and we've known this for two decades, shouldn't everybody be using it? Unfortunately it's not that simple for a number of reasons. Educators may choose to use one method over another based on a number of factors: (1) acceptability, (2) effectiveness, (3) time and resources, (4) theoretical orientation of the intervention, and (5) intrusiveness (Witt, 1986). Note that effectiveness is only one of the factors that influence what may be used in the classroom. Another factor could be termed inertia. In many cases, educational practices seem to develop a life of their own, independent of their effectiveness. As Heward (2002) noted, teachers sometimes become wedded to ineffective approaches and continue to use them regardless of whether or not they are effective. Poor communication between researchers and the classroom teacher is also a factor (Pressley & Woloshyn, 1995). Researchers often do a poor job of presenting the results of their research in a manner that teachers can grasp and, more importantly, immediately apply.

All these factors have probably inhibited the use of strategy instruction to some extent. However, we believe that there is an even more fundamental explanation. Few educators (either in-service or preservice) are provided with any degree of systematic professional development in strategy instruction approaches. This is a critical omission for two reasons. First, as Kauffman (1996) suggests, practices that are accompanied by systematic professional development are more likely to be adopted and used correctly. Unfortunately, few teachers are given more than a brief exposure to strategy instruction approaches. While strategy instruction is a very powerful tool, *effective* strategy instruction requires specialized knowledge on the part of the teacher, an investment of time and effort, and an effective model for teaching strategies that addresses the cognitive, self-regulatory, and motivational problems of students with LD. In short, strategy instruction can be demanding. Even locating and selecting effective strategies for instruction can be difficult. There are many strategies; however, some individual strategies are very limited, and the effectiveness of others has not been evaluated (Pressley & Woloshyn, 1995).

The purpose of this book is to help teachers develop a practical working knowledge of effective, proven strategies and how to effectively implement strategy instruction in the classroom. Note that although we focus on students with LD, the same basic approach can be used with *any child* who needs help mastering a specific academic task (e.g., long division, writing an essay, comprehending a story). The strategy instruction model that we will use—the Self-Regulated Strategy Development (SRSD) model—is based on well-established theory and has been validated in over 20 years of research. There are many models for strategy instruction. However, few are as well researched and "user friendly," and few focus on both academic and motivational aspects of students' learning problems.

In Chapter 2, we define a "strategy," present background knowledge on critical concepts basic to strategy instruction, and explain common misconceptions about strategy instruction. In Chapter 3, we present the SRSD model. Here we explain each of the steps in the model, present the rationale for each step, and discuss the importance of each step. We stress that the SRSD model is an invaluable tool for teachers. In Chapter 4, we provide an example of strategy instruction using the SRSD model. Some tips and useful tools for implementing strategies are presented, along with a discussion of how differences between strategies affect implementation. In Chapter 5, we discuss self-regulation. The four major types of self-regulation strategies are defined and explained. Chapter 6 includes examples of how each of the major self-regulation strategies can be implemented. In Chapter 7, we show how to combine strategies and self-regulation to enable students to be self-regulated strategy users. The following chapters cover strategies in major content areas and study skills. These chapters focus on well-validated strategies. Finally, we provide appendices with listings of strategies for academic areas.

FINAL THOUGHTS

The approach that we use in this book mirrors the actual instructional model we teach. We have discussed why strategy instruction is an important skill for you to learn. Next, we provide you with the necessary background knowledge to conduct strategy instruction. We explicitly explain the components of the SRSD model. We then provide examples of how you might implement various steps in the strategy instruction process in general, and examples of specific, validated strategies for use in major content areas. Our intent is to provide teachers and teacher educators with detailed, practical, step-by-step information on strategy instruction. Moreover, the model contains many components that are useful in and of themselves aside from their use in strategy instruction. In closing we emphasize that the method we present is *not* the only way instruct students with LD. No single method is that powerful. However, mastery of the techniques we present can improve instruction and academic achievement for all students.

REFERENCES

Bauer, R. H. (1987). Control processes as a way of understanding, diagnosing, and remediating learning disabilities. In H. L. Swanson (Ed.), *Advances in learning and behavioral disabilities: Memory and learning disabilities* (pp. 41–81). Greenwich, CT: JAI Press.

Borkowski, J. G., Weyhing, R. S., & Carr, M. (1988). Effects of attributional retraining on strategy-based reading comprehension in learning-disabled students. *Journal of Educational Psychology, 80,* 46–63.

Brown, R. T., & Wynne, M. E. (1984). An analysis of attentional components in hyperactive and normal boys. *Journal of Learning Disabilities, 17,* 162–167.

Bryan, T., & Wheeler, R. (1972). Perception of learning disabled children: The eye of the observer. *Journal of Learning Disabilities, 5,* 484–488.

Ceci, S., Ringstorm, M., & Lea, S. (1981). Do language learning disabled children have impaired memories? In search of underlying processes. *Journal of Learning Disabilities, 14,* 159–163.

Chapman, J. (1988). Cognitive-motivational characteristics and academic achievement of learning-disabled children. *Journal of Educational Psychology, 80*, 357–365.

Dweck, C. S. (1975). The role of expectations and attributions in the alleviation of learned helplessness. *Journal of Personality and Social Psychology, 31*, 674–685.

Engelman, S., & Bruner, E. (1974). *DISTAR Reading I.* Chicago: Science Research Associates.

Fuchs, D., Fuchs, L., & Compton, D. L. (2004). Identifying reading disabilities by responsiveness-to-instruction: Specifying measures and criteria. *Learning Disability Quarterly, 27*, 216–227.

Gettinger, M. (1991). Learning time and retention differences between nondisabled students and students with learning disabilities. *Learning Disability Quarterly*, 179–189.

Goldstein, K. (1936). The modifications of behavior consequent to cerebral lesions. *Psychiatric Quarterly, 10*, 586–610.

Hallahan, D. P., Kauffman, J. M., & Lloyd, J. W. (1996). *Introduction to learning disabilities.* Boston: Allyn & Bacon.

Hammill, D., & Larsen S. (1974). The effectiveness of psycholinguistic training. *Exceptional Children, 41*, 5–14.

Harris, K. R., Graham, S., & Pressley, M. (1992). Cognitive behavioral approaches in reading and written language: Developing self-regulated learners. In N. N. Singh & I. L. Beale (Eds.), *Current perspectives in learning disabilities: Nature, theory, and treatment* (pp. 415–451). New York: Springer-Verlag.

Heward, W. L. (2002). Ten faulty notions about teaching and learning that hinder the effectiveness of special education. *Journal of Special Education, 36*, 186–205.

Hinshelwood, J. (1917). *Congenital word blindness.* London: Lewis.

Kauffman, J. M. (1996). Research to practice issues. *Behavioral Disorders, 22*, 55–60.

Kavale, K. A., & Forness, S. R. (1996). Social skills deficits and learning disabilities: A meta-analysis. *Journal of Learning Disabilities, 29*, 226–237.

Kistner, J., Osborn, M., & LeVerrier, L. (1988). Causal attributions of learning-disabled children: Developmental patterns and relation to academic progress. *Journal of Educational Psychology, 80*, 82–89.

Lerner, J. (2000). *Learning disabilities.* Boston: Houghton Mifflin.

Licht, B. G. (1983). Cognitive-motivational factors that contribute to the achievement of learning-disabled children. *Journal of Learning Disabilities, 16*, 483–490.

Lindsley, O. R. (1964). Direct measurement and prosthesis of retarded behavior. *Journal of Education, 147*, 62–81.

McKinney, J. D., & Feagans, L. (1983). Adaptive classroom behavior of learning disabled students. *Journal of Learning Disabilities, 16*, 360–367.

Mercer, C. (1997). *Students with learning disabilities* (5th ed.). Upper Saddle River, NJ: Prentice-Hall.

Murray, C., Goldstein, D. E., & Edgar, E. (1997). The employment and engagement status of high school graduates with learning disabilities through the first decade after graduation. *Learning Disabilities Research and Practice, 12*, 151–160.

Orton, S. J. (1937). *Reading, writing, and speech problems in children.* New York: Norton.

Owings, R. A., Petersen, G. A., Bransford, J. D., Morris, C. D., & Stein, B. S. (1980). Spontaneous monitoring and regulation of learning: A comparison of successful and less successful fifth graders. *Journal of Educational Psychology, 72*, 250–256.

Pressley, M., & Woloshyn, V. (1995). *Cognitive strategy instruction that really improves children's academic performance.* Cambridge, MA: Brookline Books.

Shaywitz, S. (2003). Neurobiological indices of dyslexia. In H. Swanson, K. Harris, & S. Graham (Eds.), *Handbook of learning disabilities* (pp. 514–531). New York: Guilford Press.

Stanovich, K. (1986). Matthew effects in reading: Some consequences of individual differences in the acquisition of literacy. *Reading Research Quarterly, 21,* 360–406.

Stipek, D. (1993). *Motivation to learn: From theory to practice.* Boston: Allyn & Bacon.

Stone, C. A., & Conca, L. (1993). The origin of strategy deficits in children with learning disabilities: A social constructivist perspective. In L. J. Meltzer (Ed.), *Strategy assessment and instruction for students with learning disabilities* (pp. 23–59). Austin, TX: PRO-ED.

Strauss, A. A., & Lehtinen, L. E. (1947). *Psychopathology and education of the brain-injured child.* New York: Grune & Stratton.

Swanson, H. L. (1990). Instruction derived from the strategy deficit model: Overview of principles and procedures. In T. Scruggs & B. Wong (Eds.), *Intervention research in learning disabilities* (pp. 34–65). New York: Springer-Verlag.

Swanson, H. L. (1993). Principles and procedures in strategy use. In L. Meltzer (Ed.), *Strategy assessment and instruction for students with learning disabilities* (pp. 61–92). Austin, TX: PRO-ED.

Swanson, H. L. (1996). Learning disabilities and memory. In D. K. Reid, W. Hresko, & H. L. Swanson (Eds.), *Cognitive approaches to learning disabilities* (pp. 187–314). Austin, TX: PRO-ED.

Swanson, H. L. (1999a). Cognition and learning disabilities. In W. Bender (Ed.), *Professional issues in learning disabilities* (pp. 415–460). Austin, TX: PRO-ED.

Swanson, H. L. (1999b). *Interventions for students with learning disabilities: A meta-analysis of treatment outcomes.* New York: Guilford Press.

Swanson, H. L., Cochran, K. F., & Ewers, C. A. (1990). Can learning disabilities be determined from working memory performance? *Journal of Learning Disabilities, 23,* 59–67.

Swanson, H. L., Harris, K. R., & Graham, S. (Eds.). (2003). *Handbook of learning disabilities.* New York: Guilford Press.

Swanson, H. L., & Sachs-Lee, C. (2000). A meta-analysis of single-subject-design intervention research for students with LD. *Journal of Learning Disabilities, 33,* 114–136.

Torgesen, J. K. (1984). Memory processes in reading disabled students. *Journal of Learning Disabilities, 18,* 350–357.

U.S. Department of Education. (2001). *Twenty-third annual report to Congress on the implementation of the education of the handicapped act.* Washington, DC: U.S. Government Printing Office.

Weiner, B. (1979). A theory of motivation for some classroom experiences. *Journal of Educational Psychology, 71,* 3–25.

Witt, J. C. (1986) Teachers' resistance to the use of school-based interventions. *Journal of School Psychology, 24,* 37–44.

Wong, B. Y. L., & Wilson, M. (1984). Investigating awareness of and teaching passage organization in learning disabled children. *Journal of Learning Disabilities, 17,* 477–482.

CHAPTER 2

Building Background Knowledge

In Chapter 1, we noted that to effectively use strategy instruction in the classroom teachers need specialized knowledge. Strategy instruction is a powerful tool. But to gain any value from a tool you must know how to properly use it, and what it is good for. For example, a hammer is great for driving nails, but a hammer only works if you know which end to grab and which end to hit with. And hammers are not much use if you need to tighten a screw. One of the most dangerous misconceptions about teaching is that "anyone can do it" and there's no special knowledge or set of skills necessary. This is half right. Anyone can do a poor job. But to do an optimal job of instructing students, especially students with special needs such as those with LD, you need to know how to use tools—such as strategy instruction—correctly and appropriately.

Strategy instruction may fail if teachers lack critical knowledge of the theory or process behind it—if, in other words, they don't understand the "why" behind the activities and steps used in the strategy instruction process. Understanding why you do a step in the strategy instruction process sensitizes you to the need to do the step and helps you to do it correctly. To do strategy instruction well, teachers need basic knowledge about how students learn, because instruction will need to take this into consideration. Additionally, effective strategy instruction goes beyond the academic. It involves affective components as well. Motivational problems such as maladaptive attributions or learned helplessness must also be addressed. The best strategy in the world is useless if students won't even try to use it. For these reasons, simply sharing strategies with students is unlikely to result in any real improvement.

In this chapter, we provide you with some of the key background knowledge that you will need to effectively implement strategy instruction for students with LD in the classroom. First, we provide both formal and practical definitions of the term "strategy," and discuss major aspects the definition. Second, we discuss the information-processing model, which is useful for understanding the rationale behind some steps in the SRSD instructional model. Third, we continue the discussion of attributions and provide more information on why attributions must be considered when using strategy instruction. Finally, we introduce the concept of metacognition (literally, thinking about thinking), which is critical to successful strategy instruction.

INTRODUCTION TO STRATEGY INSTRUCTION

What Is a Strategy?

Everyone uses strategies. Adults write themselves notes. Students are taught familiar spelling strategies: *i* before *e* except after *c,* or in words like *neighbor* or *weigh.* In fact, strategies are so integrated into our everyday life that we are usually not even aware that we are using them. This tendency toward strategy use is a critical component of academic success. Evidence suggests that the most effective learners have a large repertoire of strategies that range from simple to complex, and that they can be combined to meet different task demands (Pressley & Woloshyn, 1995). Thus, the fact that you are reading this book suggests that you are an active strategy user. But what exactly is a strategy? The term "strategy" has been used in many ways. As with many terms, exactly what people mean by "strategy" may vary. In fact, there are a number of definitions of what constitutes a strategy. There are some differences across these definitions, but for the most part they are quite similar. Alexander, Graham, and Harris (1998) listed a number of important aspects of strategies.

First, strategies are "facilitative and essential." The purpose of strategies is to improve performance. In other words, we use a strategy to do a task better, more easily, or more quickly. In this sense, a strategy is much like a tool. Tools help us accomplish tasks to a higher standard with much less effort. Strategies do the same. We would stress that it is important to understand that, like tools, strategies serve a purpose; *we don't learn strategies just to learn them.* "Essential" refers to the fact that strategy knowledge and use is what distinguishes good students from the less competent students. Second, strategies are "willful and effortful." Students must make a conscious decision to use a strategy, and must commit time and mental effort to do so. The fact that the use of a strategy is a conscious decision is important. If students could not be made aware that they were using a strategy and control its use so that the strategy could be employed on demand when needed, then strategy instruction would have little practical use. To continue the tool analogy, if we can't learn how to properly use our hammer, or our hammer is never around when we need it, then it's not very useful. Finally, it is important to realize that strategies and task requirements are linked. Strategies must be matched to an appropriate task. For example, one strategy that many of us are familiar with is "ROY G. BIV," a simple technique to help remember the order of colors in the rainbow. However, ROY G. BIV wouldn't be too useful if the task was to write a term paper. Again, strategies are like tools, and some tools have a very narrow range of uses.

The term "strategy" can also refer to cognitive processes that occur inside our head. For example, while driving in a strange city, you might mentally visualize a map to help you find your way (a visual imagery strategy). Or, if you had to remember an address, you might repeat it over and over to help maintain it in your memory (a verbal rehearsal strategy). The act of managing your activities or monitoring progress, attention, or understanding can also be called a strategy. For example, making sure that you have all the materials you need before starting a task would be a planning strategy. Stopping periodically while reading to ask yourself what you just read and how well you understood it would be a comprehension monitoring strategy. Strategies are typically used in combinations. For example, in the comprehension monitoring example above, every time you stop to check comprehension, you might create brief summaries of what you just read, and then write them down. This combines summarization and rehearsal strategies with a monitoring strategy.

For our purposes, we will use a practical definition: a strategy is a series of ordered steps that will allow a student to perform a task. For example, Figure 2.1 shows a very simple strategy used for subtraction with regrouping. It provides a four-step process to follow to solve a subtraction problem. The strategy serves to help structure the student's efforts (i.e., to do the steps in order) and to remind the student what to do at each stage of the process. Now look at Figure 2.2. We've added a new wrinkle. Now the student is asked to *track the use* of the strategy by placing a check mark on the appropriate line. This combines a self-monitoring strategy with the subtraction strategy. Note that strategies aren't limited to describing steps to use in performing a task. Strategies can also be used to cue students' cognitive processes. For example, the last step in the "4 B's," remembering basic facts, serves to cue students to activate prior knowledge, and requiring students to check the line after performing each step serves to cue them to monitor whether they've performed the steps of the strategy.

This looks pretty simple and straightforward, doesn't it? If a strategy is just a series of steps, all you need to do is break a task down into its component parts and teach the steps directly to the student. This would actually be fairly effective for some students. Unfortunately, as we will see in the next sections, the students who

---

To subtract, remember the 4 B's:

Begin? In the 1's columns.
Bigger? Which number is bigger, the bottom or the top?
Borrow? If the bottom number is bigger I must borrow.
Basic Facts? I need to remember to use my math facts!

FIGURE 2.1. The 4 B's subtraction strategy. Adapted from Frank, A. R., & Brown, D. (1992). Self-monitoring strategies in arithmetic. *Teaching Exceptional Children, 24*(2), 52–53. Copyright 1992 by The Council for Exceptional Children. Adapted by permission.

To subtract, remember the 4 B's:

Begin? In the 1's column.
Bigger? Which number is bigger, the bottom or the top?
Borrow? If the bottom number is bigger, I must borrow.
Basic Facts? I need to remember to use my math facts.

Remember to check off each step in the 4 B's as you do it.

- Begin	- Begin	- Begin
- - - Bigger	- - - Bigger	- - - Bigger
- - - Borrow	- - - Borrow	- - - Borrow
- - - Basic Facts	- - - Basic Facts	- - - Basic Facts
8 7 6	6 2 3	5 6
− 3 9 8	− 1 5	− 3 5

FIGURE 2.2. The 4 B's subtraction strategy with self-monitoring. Adapted from Frank, A. R., & Brown, D. (1992). Self-monitoring strategies in arithmetic. *Teaching Exceptional Children* 24(2), 52–53. Copyright 1992 by The Council for Exceptional Children. Adapted by permission.

might profit from this approach are the ones who would need it the least, because they are already good strategy users. For students with LD or other struggling learners, simply teaching the steps would be unlikely to have any meaningful effect, because cognitive, metacognitive, and motivational problems of students with LD haven't been accounted for. In the next sections we provide you with additional information about these areas.

INFORMATION PROCESSING

One of the reasons the strategy instruction approach is so successful is that it incorporates knowledge about how our memory and cognitive processes work into the teaching process. The information-processing model uses the computer as a model of how our mind works on new information or attacks problems such as academic tasks. It's not an exact comparison for many reasons, not the least of which is that our minds are infinitely more complex than a computer! However, at a very basic level it is both useful and informative. In the next section we discuss information processing and its implications for strategy instruction. We draw our discussion from Lerner (2000) and Swanson (1996).

Figure 2.3 shows a simplified model of information processing. As Figure 2.3 shows, the information-processing model divides the flow of information into three stages. This is analogous to how a computer is divided into different components that perform different operations:

Information processing

Sensory register—Hearing, vision, touch.

Short-term memory—Information from the sensory register is stored here for a brief interval. Unless the information is acted on in some way it is lost forever.

Working memory—Information is stored briefly to be used in some task. This store is limited and temporary. As soon as information is not being used it disappears.

Long-term memory—Information is stored permanently. Information stored here may be transferred to working memory when needed.

Executive functions—Control how information is processed and stored.

Computer

Input devices—Keyboard, mouse.

Random access memory (RAM)—Temporary storage. Unless transferred to permanent memory information is lost.

Random access memory (RAM)—The portion of memory used to process information.

Permanent memory—Hard drive, optical disc. Information stored here is permanent. Information may be transferred to RAM.

Operating system—The code that tells the computer how to transfer information and allot memory for various functions.

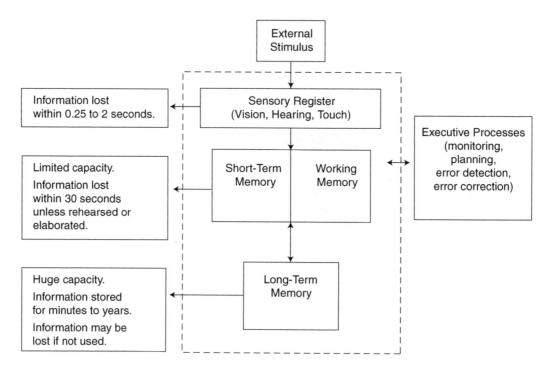

FIGURE 2.3. Simplified information-processing model.

Here is how it might work in practice. First, our senses perceive a stimulus. For example, we might see a printed word or hear a sentence. This information is stored in the sensory register. It is stored for only a very brief period of time—a fraction of a second. Our sensory register is bombarded with information, so information can't stay too long. From here, the information goes to short-term memory. There are two important aspects of short-term memory. First, short-term memory is quite limited. Estimates are that short-term memory can hold only around seven "chunks" of information at one time. Second, short-term memory is a temporary holding area. Information will remain in short-term memory for only a matter of seconds. When information is in short-term memory, we are consciously aware of it. For example, you are consciously aware of the sentence you just read. It's in your short-term memory, but it will be replaced with the next sentences you read and will fade from your memory. We want to remember information such as the sentence we just read, but it doesn't happen automatically. Our memory isn't like a videotape that faithfully records an exact representation of everything. If the information in our short-term memory isn't acted on (or processed), it will be lost (i.e., forgotten). Information that is processed in some manner such as rehearsal (repeating the information to yourself) will then be transferred to long-term memory, where it can be permanently stored.

Once information is stored in long-term memory the question becomes one of retrieval (remembering). Although the information has been stored, it may decay (decrease in strength) if not utilized. When information is utilized regularly the strength of the memory increases. For example, you would have little trouble rattling off your present phone number or address. However, it would probably take you much longer to call up the address or phone number you had when you were in junior high school. And some information that was once strong may have faded almost entirely (can you recite the quadratic equation?). Retrieval also refers to being able to recall information when needed. It's entirely possible for information to be stored in long-term memory but not to be available on demand. For example, we have all had the experience of trying and failing to recall a name only to suddenly remember it at a later time.

One of the important factors in how easily information can be retrieved is how the information is stored. Short-term memory has a number of "control processes" that are used to process information in a way that makes it easier to remember (Swanson, 1996). These include:

- *Chunking*—grouping information into smaller units. For example changing a series of 10 digits into a phone number, or taking a group of unrelated words and creating a sentence.
- *Clustering*—placing a information into meaningful categories. For example grouping a list of words into animals, colors, or verbs.
- *Mnemonics*—organizing material in a manner that enhances recall. For example ROY G. BIV forms an acronym that helps us to remember the colors of the spectrum in the correct order.

- *Relating information to known material*—using analogies to already existing knowledge. For example, the game of cricket is much easier to understand if you have a working knowledge of baseball.
- *Tagging information*—this involves setting up retrieval paths to help remember information. For example, to remember that "ranid" means frog you might connect the term "ranid" with an image of a frog in the rain.

Another part of short-term memory that is critical for information processing is called working memory. Working memory is where information is temporarily stored when needed to accomplish a specific task. For example, to do a long-division problem you would call up from long-term memory the basic math facts needed to perform each operation along with the knowledge of the steps in the long-division process. Like short-term memory, working memory lasts for only a short while. Once you have used a math fact it will disappear quickly, as it is not needed. Like short-term memory, working memory is also limited. Thus, we couldn't call up all our math facts simultaneously. It would be impossible to maintain that much information in working memory. To return to the computer analogy, if we try to load a file that's too big for the available memory the computer will either freeze up or give an error message. Similarly, if we try to hold too much information in working memory or have to process information in working memory because we can't apply it fluently, our ability to process information suffers and performance begins to decrease.

How Knowledge of Information Processing Helps Strategy Instruction

Knowing how memory operates can help teachers. We need to teach in a manner that will help students process information efficiently and effectively. For example, to help any child get new information into long-term memory you need to teach in ways that encourage him or her to process the information through elaboration or rehearsal techniques. This is especially true for students with LD. There is evidence to suggest that students with LD may have deficiencies in working memory (Swanson, 1999). If working memory is overloaded, then there is insufficient processing space for new information. We see examples of this in the classroom every day. For example, every teacher has experience with children who read a passage painfully sounding out each word. At the end of the passage they can't remember anything they read because all their working memory processing was devoted to decoding. Nothing was left to process information. To be able to read and comprehend, a student needs to be able to use decoding skills fluently so that working memory isn't overloaded. As we will see later, the same analogy is true for strategies.

THE IMPORTANCE OF ATTRIBUTIONS

In Chapter 1, we discussed the problem that many students with LD have with a maladaptive attribution style. Weiner (1979) developed a useful model of causal attribution (see Figure 2.4) that separates attributions into three dimensions:

	Internal		External	
	Stable	Unstable	Stable	Unstable
Controllable	Typical Effort	Immediate Effort	Teacher Bias	Help from Others
Uncontrollable	Ability	Mood	Task Difficulty	Luck

FIGURE 2.4. Weiner's model of causal attribution. Adapted from Weiner, B. (1979). A theory of motivation for some classroom experiences. *Journal of Educational Psychology, 71,* 3–25. Copyright 1979 by the American Psychological Association. Adapted by permission.

1. *Internal versus external.* This dimension refers to whether students see the causes of success or failure as being inside or outside themselves. Examples of internal causes would be ability, effort, aptitude, or mood. External causes could be task difficulty, or actions by another ("She helped me do it").
2. *Controllable versus uncontrollable.* This dimension refers to how strongly students believe that the causes for success or failure are under their direct control or influence. Examples of controllable causes are effort or strategy use. An example of uncontrollable causes is luck.
3. *Stable versus unstable.* This dimension refers to the extent to which the causes of success or failure have remained consistent or unchanging over time. Stable causes are those not likely to change. Unstable causes are those that are due to temporary factors or those that can be changed or modified.

Table 2.1 shows example of possible attributions for each of the three dimensions.

TABLE 2.1. Examples of Attributions Classified by Weiner's Dimensions

Attribution	Type	Comment
"I practiced what the coach told me for 3 weeks and my free-throw shooting got lots better."	Internal, controllable, stable	Success is due to effort and using an effective technique.
"My free-throw shooting sucks. I'm just no good at basketball."	Internal, uncontrollable, stable	Failure is due to a lack of ability that will not change.
"I didn't really study enough for the test because I couldn't get organized."	Internal, controllable, unstable	Failure is due to a circumstance that could be corrected.
"I hurt my leg and couldn't practice for the game."	Internal, uncontrollable, unstable	Failure is due to a chance injury that is not permanent.
"Doctor Graham's tests are so hard I'll never pass them."	External, uncontrollable, stable	Failure is due to an external factor (difficult exam) that is not likely to change.
"I got an A on the test, but it was really easy."	External, uncontrollable, unstable	Success is due to an outside factor that may change.

How Knowledge of Attributions Helps Strategy Instruction

A knowledge of attributions is important for a number of reasons. Research shows that a student's attributional style can directly affect academic performance (Diener & Dweck, 1978; Dweck & Leggett, 1988). Students with maladaptive attributional styles often won't persist in or even try tasks that they perceive as difficult. Unfortunately, teachers tend to react negatively to this "they won't even try" behavior (Weiner, 1992). This in turn makes academic tasks even more threatening and aversive, which makes it more likely that the student will continue to avoid tasks. Students who have maladaptive attributional styles will tend to attribute failures to internal, uncontrollable factors ("I'm dumb") and success to uncontrollable, external factors ("I was lucky"). As a result these students are at risk for developing a negative attitude toward academics and anxiety when faced with academic tasks. They will make more negative statements to themselves ("You'll never get this done") and will develop the belief that they cannot succeed no matter how hard they may try. This in turn results in decreased effort or in simply avoiding tasks that they perceive as difficult. As a result their performance will inevitably decline. This is referred to as the "helpless orientation." In contrast, students who attribute success and failure to internal, controllable factors such as effort will remain positive in the face of a difficult task, and will persist in their efforts much longer. They will not avoid challenging tasks and will actively work to improve their problem-solving skills. This is called the "mastery orientation." The implications for classroom teachers are obvious. We want students to adopt a mastery orientation rather than maintain a helpless orientation.

Research shows that this approach can be effective for students. For example, Dweck (1975) taught students with learned helplessness to attribute failure to insufficient effort. These students showed increased persistence. Other studies have provided students with verbal praise for attributing success and failure to effort (e.g., Andrews & Debus, 1978). These students also increased the time that they would persist at a task. Attribution training also combines well with strategy instruction. For example, Borkowski, Weyhing, and Carr (1988) found that attribution training in combination with strategy instruction resulted in a 50% gain on a reading task. The researchers also suggested that for strategy training to be effective with students who had maladaptive attributions or learned helplessness, it was necessary to teach them a healthy mastery-oriented attributional style.

How do we go about instilling a positive attributional style? Simply put, we need to teach students to attribute success and failure to their own efforts and to the use of an effective strategy. To do this, it's necessary to shift attributions from an ability focus ("You succeed at tasks because you're smart") to a skill and effort focus ("You succeeded because you used an appropriate strategy and you tried hard"). The shift toward the skill and effort focus (or the incremental view of intelligence) is important. From this perspective our intelligence continues to develop as we gain new strategies and skills, *and we can always learn new strategies and skills*. Evidence shows that students who have this incremental perspective are more likely to adopt a mastery orientation.

To make this shift, there are two major tasks for the classroom teacher. First, changing instilled attribution patterns requires the teacher to be aware of why they may occur and how to help students change to a healthier style. For example, one of the primary problems is that students often equate "trying hard" with having less ability. In other words, if you have to try hard to succeed at a task then you must not be very smart. On the other hand, seemingly effortless success signals high ability. Another problem can be seeking help. Many students equate needing help with having low ability. Still another problem is the feedback we give students that may unwittingly reinforce the ability perspective. How many times have you praised a child's success with "You're a genius" or "You're so smart"? Second, teachers must systematically change their classroom behavior to help inculcate a healthy attributional style. This entails systematically working to change students' attributional styles from external and uncontrollable to internal and controllable. It also involves teaching the incremental perspective on intelligence.

Table 2.2 shows a number of suggestions on how teachers can approach this in the classroom. This should be done on an ongoing basis as part of the strategy instruction process. Note that this process will require preparation and planning just as any other instructional activity. For example, Alderman (1999) suggested that teachers might actually write out examples of appropriate feedback or praise statements in advance.

METACOGNITION

What are you doing as you read this book? You almost certainly have a purpose in mind: You want to learn about strategy instruction. You might be underlining or highlighting what you believe are important passages. You may stop and verbally paraphrase a section to yourself or make notes in the margins or a notebook. You might make connections or relate information to your personal experience or other bits of knowledge about instruction. You may be reading some sections more slowly, because the information is unfamiliar or difficult; however, you may breeze through others. While you read, you are probably aware of how well you understand the material. If you realize that you are confused about something you just read, you will probably stop and review the section. You may have actually done some planning before you even began to read, if you allotted time to read the chapter. If you are reading the book for a class, you may have scheduled a time to reread or look at notes. In summary, you are doing much more than simply decoding printed words on a page. You are actively engaged with the learning task at a number of levels.

Students with LD would likely have a much different experience. They may have no particular purpose in mind when they read. Their main goal would be to simply "get through" the task. They would be unlikely to effectively use the activities that would help them retain the information (for example, highlighting or paraphrasing) or be aware of their degree of comprehension, much less use error correction techniques such as rereading. This type of unengaged performance isn't limited to reading. It is typical of how students with LD perform many academic tasks. Often they will make glaring mistakes that seem so obvious that we wonder how they could be unaware of them.

Students with LD are not actively involved in the learning task due in large part to a problem with *metacognition*. Metacognition is defined as one's knowledge concerning

TABLE 2.2. Tips for Changing Attributions

- *Provide students with feedback that stresses effort and/or strategy use.*

  Effort: "Johnny, all that extra spelling practice you did paid off. You got a 96% on your spelling test."

  Strategy: "Helen, you really learned the long-division strategy well! You followed all the steps and you got all the problems correct!"

- *If a student fails at a task, relate the failure to effort or strategy use.*

  Effort: "Well, Emma, your spelling score was only 52%. I noticed that this week you didn't spend as much time practicing your words. I think that you need to spend extra time practicing."

  Strategy: "Hepzibah, I noticed that you missed six problems on your worksheet because you didn't regroup correctly. If you remember the steps in the 4 B's strategy you won't forget to regroup. Would you like go over it again?"

- *Teach children what it means to "really try."*

  Discuss the meaning of effort. Effort means sticking with it, not giving up. Stress that effort is important to success, and that you should always give your best effort. Teach the difference between productive effort and just getting by. For many children just handing in work, regardless of quality, is perceived as effort.

- *Show how effort can affect outcomes.*

  Link effort to success and learning. For example, have students chart the number of spelling practices and their weekly spelling scores. Show how increased practice relates to better spelling scores. Stress the relation between productive work and success. For example, children's social studies grades improve because they worked really hard at getting all their assignments done well.

- *Give students a strategy.*

  Give students a systematic means of completing a task—a strategy. Stress that using the strategy consistently and correctly will lead to success. Treat strategies like "tools"; stress that you can always add another "tool to your tool box."

- *Make "smart" a skill.*

  Stress that what makes you "smart" is the number of skills and strategies you have. You can't change ability, but you can always learn more skills and strategies. You don't learn things because you are "smart"; you learn because of instruction, strategies, and effort, and this makes you "smart."

- *Internalize responsibility for success and failure.*

  Through feedback and modeling stress that the reasons for success and failure are inside us. We succeed because we try hard and use the right strategy. If we fail, we didn't put forth our best effort or use the right strategy. Note that to prevent failure, the teacher must ensure that child has the preskills to do the task and determine whether the child can do the task independently or with assistance.

one's own cognitive processes and the products related to them (Flavel, 1979). Put more simply, metacognition means "thinking about thinking." What is the difference between cognition and metacognition? It is the difference between knowing something and understanding knowledge in terms of awareness and appropriate use (Flavel, 1979). To help understand the distinction we can use an the example of a hammer:

Cognitive	Metacognitive
"That's a hammer."	"A hammer is a tool I'd use to drive a nail. There are different kinds of hammers for different jobs. You need to practice a little before you can use a hammer well. You need to be careful using a hammer or you can hurt yourself."

As you can see, the metacognitive knowledge goes beyond the factual knowledge. It encompasses knowing (1) the purpose a hammer serves, (2) that it's necessary to match the correct hammer to a given task (you wouldn't use a sledge hammer to drive a nail), (3) that there is a skill set needed to use a hammer successfully, and (4) some monitoring is necessary when you use a hammer (if you don't pay attention, you might end up with a very sore thumb!). The hammer example illustrates the importance of metacognition. Students without a metacognitive understanding of a task will obviously not function as well as those who do have such an understanding. This lack of metacognitive knowledge also contributes to a student's frustration. There are three major components of metacognition: metacognitive knowledge, motivational beliefs, and the executive component, or self-regulation (Hacker, 1998).

Metacognitive knowledge refers to a person's (1) acquired knowledge and beliefs about him- or herself as a learner, (2) task demands and how they can be met, and (3) strategies that can or should be used to accomplish a task (Flavell, 1979). Metacognitive knowledge also includes the relation between task and strategy (i.e., what strategies are appropriate to a given task) and a knowledge of how, when, where, and why to use strategy. For example:

Type of knowledge	Example
Self as learner: This may include knowledge of your own capabilities, comparisons with others, and general knowledge of your cognition.	"I'm good at math but my spelling is terrible." "If I don't write something down I'll forget it." "My wife is better at math than I am."
Task demands: This may include knowledge of how different tasks place different demands, and how to approach a task appropriately.	Knowing that you read for detail differently than you would for the main idea.

Type of knowledge	Example
	Knowing that when you read a very dense and complex passage you need to slow down.
Strategy: This may include knowledge of what type of strategy (if any) is appropriate for a task, knowledge of how best to strategically attack a given task, and knowledge that strategies enhance performance.	"A paraphrasing strategy will help my comprehension, but a mnemonic would be better to remember a list." "To write a better story I'll use my Story Grammar strategy." "Using a strategy helps me do better."

Motivational beliefs—which are related to attributions—also play a role in meta-cognition (Borkowski, Estrada, Milstead, & Hale, 1989). Students' beliefs about their competence and control over outcomes can directly affect their choice of strategies and how long they will persist at a task (Bandura, 1993). If students lack confidence in their skills then they may not be able to use their skills effectively. In fact, some studies have shown that students' *belief* in their abilities was a better predictor of positive attitudes toward academic tasks than actual ability (Bandura, 1993). Components of motivational beliefs include:

- *General competency*—How good am I as a learner overall?
- *Competency in specific task*—How good am I at this specific task?
- *Control over outcomes*—Do I have control over how well I do?
- *Causes of failure*—Why did I succeed or fail (internal or external)?
- *Benefits of strategy*—Belief that a strategic approach is effective/superior.

Self-regulation (also referred to as *executive processes*) refers to how learners regulate or manage cognitive and metacognitive processes. Self-regulation is critical for a number of reasons. First, effective learners are self-regulated learners (Butler & Winne, 1995). Students who actively regulate their cognition are more engaged in a task and typically perform better than those who don't. Although self-regulation is complex and there are numerous cognitive and metacognitive activities that can be monitored, there are four commonly recognized self-regulation activities that are important for strategy instruction (e.g., Hacker, 1998). These include:

- *Planning*—adopting a deliberate, organized approach to a task, planning next moves.
- *Monitoring*—checking comprehension and strategy effectiveness, testing, revising, and evaluating strategies, monitoring the effectiveness of attempts.
- *Failure detection*—"Are things going OK?"
- *Failure correction*—"Let's fix it."

Second, there is little use in teaching a strategy that students cannot use independently. For a strategy to be truly useful, students should be able to effectively use and *maintain it* without outside support or guidance. This level of self-regulation is concerned with maintaining effort and appropriate strategy use. It includes functions such as staying on task, blocking out or eliminating negative cognitions ("I can't do this"), and consistently and correctly using a strategy.

How Knowledge of Metacognition Helps Strategy Instruction

For strategy instruction to be effective, students—*especially students with LD*—must have a metacognitive knowledge of how, where, when, and why they are using a strategy, and the underlying reasons behind the components of the strategy (Pressley & Woloshyn, 1995). Students need this metacognitive understanding of a strategy in order to profit fully from strategy instruction (Hacker, 1998). Without this knowledge, there is little chance that a strategy will be maintained or generalized. For strategy instruction, metacognitive knowledge is literally like the mortar in a brick wall. Mortar serves to bind the individual bricks together to make a strong and durable structure. Metacognitive knowledge and self-regulation processes serve a similar function. Strategies are not intended to be performed mindlessly (Harris & Pressley, 1991). Students also need active self-regulation to help both with cognitive processes such as comprehension monitoring and to maintain effort. Developing metacognitive knowledge and self-regulation skills is one of the most critical components of strategy instruction and is an integral part of the SRSD model.

The goal of the SRSD instruction process is to work with students until they have sufficient "ownership" of a strategy to successfully perform academic tasks. To do this, we need to help the child with LD become more like Pressley's "good strategy user" (Pressley, Borkowski, & Schnieder, 1987). Specifically, we work with students until they are able to:

- Know where to use a strategy and why it should be used.
- Monitor the strategy to check whether it is effective.
- Shield themselves from maladaptive thoughts that could impair performance.
- Develop the strong belief that strategy use makes them better thinkers.
- Use a strategy fluently to the point where it becomes automatic.

The background knowledge we discussed relates specifically to these goals. Knowing where and why to use a strategy is an example of metacognitive knowledge. Monitoring the effectiveness of a strategy is also metacognitive—it is self-regulation. Finally, becoming an automatic strategy user depends on being able to process information (i.e., remember and use a strategy) fluently. As you can see, many of the components are interdependent. For example, fluent strategy use is unlikely to develop if a child cannot screen out negative thoughts ("You'll never get this right, so why try?"). Similarly, metacognitive knowledge and self-regulation are also prerequisites for effective and automatic strategy use.

FINAL THOUGHTS

As you can see by now, effective strategy instruction deals with much more than just academic content. For strategy instruction to be effective for students with LD, it's necessary to attend to cognitive processes, motivational aspects, and information processing. In sum, strategy instruction deals with both cognition and emotional/motivational aspects of learning. It also requires teaching that is sensitive to problems students with LD have with information processing. Because effective strategy instruction—especially for students with LD—requires attention to so many aspects of learning, it helps to have a teaching model that will focus attention on these aspects of strategy instruction as well as teaching the actual strategy. And, that's just what the SRSD model was designed to do. It serves as a "template" for teachers to help them attend to all the steps in the strategy instruction process. In the next chapter we discuss the SRSD model in detail.

REFERENCES

Alderman, M. K. (1999). Motivation for achievement: Possibilities for teaching and learning. Mahwah, NJ: Erlbaum.

Alexander, P. A., Graham, S., & Harris, K. R. (1998). A perspective on strategy research: Progress and prospects. *Educational Psychology Review, 10,* 129–154.

Andrews, G. R., & Debus, R. (1978). Persistence and the causal perception of failure: Modifying cognitive attributions. *Journal of Educational Psychology, 70,* 154–166.

Bandura, A. (1993). Perceived self-efficacy in cognitive development and functioning. *Educational Psychologist, 28,* 117–148.

Borkowski, J. G., Estrada, M. T., Milstead, M., & Hale, C. A. (1989). General problem solving skills: Relations between metacognition and strategic processing. *Learning Disability Quarterly, 12,* 57–70.

Borkowski, J. G., Weyhing, R. S., & Carr, M. (1988). Effects of attributional retraining on strategy-based reading comprehension in learning-disabled students. *Journal of Educational Psychology, 80,* 46–53.

Butler, D. L., & Winne, P. H. (1995). Feedback and self-regulated learning: A theoretical synthesis. *Review of Educational Research, 65,* 245–281.

Diener, C. I., & Dweck, C. S. (1978). An analysis of learned helplessness: Continuous changes in performance, strategy, and achievement cognitions following failure. *Journal of Personality and Social Psychology, 36,* 451–462.

Dweck, C. S. (1975). The role of expectations and attributions in the alleviation of learned helplessness. *Journal of Personality and Social Psychology, 31,* 674–685.

Dweck, C. S., & Leggett, E. L. (1988). A social-cognitive approach to motivation and personality. *Psychological Review, 95,* 256–273.

Flavel, J. H. (1979). Metacognition and cognitive monitoring: A new area of cognitive developmental inquiry. *American Psychologist, 34,* 906–911.

Frank, A. R., & Brown, D. (1992). Self-monitoring strategies in arithmetic. *Teaching Exceptional Children, 24*(2), 52–53.

Hacker, D. J. (1998). Definitions and empirical foundations. In D. Hacker, J. Dunlosky, & A.

Graesser (Eds.), *Metacognition in educational theory and practice* (pp. 1–23). Mahwah, NJ: Erlbaum.

Harris, K. R., & Pressley, M. (1991). The nature of cognitive strategy instruction: Interactive strategy instruction. *Exceptional Children, 57,* 392–403.

Lerner, J. (2000). *Learning disabilities: Theories, diagnosis, and teaching strategies* (8th ed.). New York: Houghton Mifflin.

Pressley, M., Borkowski, J. G., & Schnieder, W. (1987). Cognitive strategies: Good strategy users coordinate metacognition and knowledge. In R. Vasta & G. Whitehurst (Eds.), *Annals of child development* (Vol. 5, pp. 89–129). New York: JAI Press.

Pressley, M., & Woloshyn, V. (1995). *Cognitive strategy instruction that really improves children's academic performance.* Cambridge, MA: Brookline Books.

Swanson, H. L. (1996). Information processing: An introduction. In D. K. Reid, W. Hresko, & H. L. Swanson (Eds.), *Cognitive approaches to learning disabilities* (pp. 251–285). Austin, TX: PRO-ED.

Swanson, H. L. (1999). Cognition and learning disabilities. In W. Bender (Ed.), *Professional issues in learning disabilities* (pp. 415–460). Austin, TX: PRO-ED.

Weiner, B. (1979). A theory of motivation for some classroom experiences. *Journal of Educational Psychology, 71,* 3–25.

Weiner, B. (1992). *Human motivation: Metaphors, theories, and research.* Newbury Park, CA: Sage.

CHAPTER 3

The Self-Regulated Strategy
Development Model

In the previous chapters, we presented a rationale for strategy instruction and provided some background knowledge about important characteristics of students with LD that affect strategy instruction. In this chapter we introduce a model for the strategy instruction process. The implementation model is based on Harris and Graham's (1996) Self-Regulated Strategy Development (SRSD) model. We chose this model for four reasons. First, it is based on years of research and, more importantly, has a well-demonstrated 20-year history of effectiveness (Graham & Harris, 2003). Second, the SRSD model is a comprehensive approach to the strategy instruction process that takes into consideration critical cognitive, motivational, and academic characteristics of students with LD. Students with LD have problems that go beyond academics, and these problems can adversely affect academic performance. The SRSD model stresses the need to provide students with essential metacognitive knowledge of the strategies, attends to the problem of maladaptive attributions that are common among students with LD, and stresses instruction that helps students process information more effectively. Third, the SRSD model is intended to be used in conjunction with different self-regulation strategies. This combination is particularly powerful for students with LD. Finally, the SRSD model is practical for the real-world classroom. Teachers won't use models that are unwieldy or impractical. The SRSD model was designed with the needs of students and teachers in mind and has been used effectively by classroom teachers.

We cannot overemphasize how important it is to use an appropriate and effective model for strategy instruction. Following the SRSD model has two major advantages:

1. A good model gives you an instructional road map to follow. You know how to teach the strategy in an *effective, systematic, step-by-step* fashion. This ensures that critical steps in the strategy instruction process are not omitted or short-changed.
2. Second, strategy instruction involves a commitment of time and effort on the part of the teacher. To maximize the chances of a positive outcome (i.e., increased academic performance for students), it is crucial to use approaches that have been well validated.

You may be wondering why we have focused so much on the strategy instruction process and barely mentioned actual strategies. The reason for that is simple. Strategies are the easiest part of the process. In this book we introduce you to many powerful strategies that are effective for students with LD. However it is crucial to understand that *strategies are not magical*. Simply exposing a student with LD to a strategy will not be effective. Strategies are *potentially* powerful, but, unless they are taught correctly, strategies are unlikely to result in improved academic performance. Therefore, for strategy instruction to succeed teachers must adopt a systematic approach such as the SRSD model. The goal of SRSD is to make the use of strategies habitual, flexible, and automatic. Getting to this level will require time, practice, and effort. However, if teachers master the strategy instruction process most students will markedly improve their academic performance.

In this chapter we first discuss the six stages of instruction in the SRSD model. For each step we provide examples of activities and give examples of helpful tools. Second, we discuss evaluation of the SRSD process. Effective ongoing classroom evaluation is important for student growth. Teachers must be able to accurately gauge how well SRSD is working. Students who are taught a strategy that does not work for them will not be enthusiastic about learning a second strategy. Finally, we conclude with general guidelines for strategy instruction.

THE SIX STAGES OF THE SRSD MODEL

The basic stages of the SRSD model are designed to ensure that all necessary aspects of strategy instruction are fully addressed. We present the stages in a commonly used sequence; however, the stages are flexible and may be reordered or combined as deemed appropriate or necessary by the teacher. The model asks teachers to use their own professional judgment when employing it. Further, the SRSD stages are intended to be recursive. Teachers will loop back through stages, and activities will be repeated as necessary. Revisiting stages helps students to rethink and develop metacognitive skills and abilities.

The time required to complete the SRSD process varies depending on the demands of the strategy and the needs of students. Lessons typically last from 20 to 60 minutes (depending on grade level and class schedules) at least three times a week. In practice most strategies can be taught fairly quickly. Harris suggested that in the elementary grades, eight to twelve 30- to 40-minute lessons are usually sufficient for students to complete the stages of the SRSD process (Harris, Graham, & Mason, 2003).

Stage 1: Developing and Activating Background Knowledge

Developing background knowledge sometimes seems so obvious, but in practice it is just this type of obvious task that is often overlooked. It is critical that students master prerequisite skills to effectively use a strategy. For example, trying to teach a long division strategy to a student who had not mastered multiplication or subtraction would be a fruitless endeavor. At this stage there are two essential tasks: (1) define the skills a child needs to perform a strategy, and (2) assess the child's knowledge and/or ability to perform the skills.

Defining Skills

While developing background knowledge, it is necessary to initially define the basic skills needed to perform the strategy. For example, to learn a long division strategy, students need to know basic subtraction, multiplication, and division facts, place value, and even so basic a skill as telling left from right, perhaps. It is also important to make certain that the students understand the components of the strategy. For example, some reading comprehension strategies involve the use of text structures that may not be familiar to students. The best way to identify the basic skills and strategy components necessary is to break down the task in terms of the knowledge needed for success. The task breakdown will help teachers to determine what the students need to know to perform the strategy. The easiest way to break down a task is to make two columns. Label one column "Steps" and the second "Skills." In the first column list the steps the student would need to perform to accomplish the task. In the second list what a child would need to know to perform this step. Tables 3.1 and 3.2 provide examples for a simple math task and a more involved writing task. The easiest way to break down a task is to actually do the task yourself, write down each step, and then ask yourself what you needed to know to perform the step.

Assessing Knowledge

There are many ways that teachers can check students' knowledge. For example, for the long division strategy the teacher could simply use flash cards to assess the student's knowledge of basic multiplication and addition facts. Some commonly used methods include observing student performance, using curriculum-based measures, or simply asking students what they are doing (and how and why). Often, teachers will already be aware of a student's knowledge. Skill deficits should be addressed prior to introducing the new strategy. This means teaching the skill to sufficient mastery for the student to perform the strategy successfully *or* providing a means for the student to compensate for a skill deficit. For example, if a student needed a long division strategy but had difficulty with multiplication facts, the teacher could provide a times table for the student to use. Note that the teacher should still work on building up the student's skill at multiplication in the interim.

TABLE 3.1. Example of Task Breakdown for Two-Digit by Two-Digit Multiplication

Steps	Skills required
Multiply 1's column.	Knowledge of place value Knowledge of multiplication facts
Bring down the 1's digit part of the answer.	Knowledge of place value Where to write answers to vertically written math problems
Carry the 10's digit part of the answer.	Knowledge of place value How to carry numbers
Multiply across, the bottom 1's digit to the top 10's digit.	Knowledge of place value Knowledge of multiplication facts
To that answer add the number that you carried and write that down.	Knowledge of addition facts Where to write answers to vertically written math problems
Under that answer write a 0 in the 1's column.	Knowledge of place value
Multiply the bottom 10's digit to the top 1's digit.	Knowledge of place value Knowledge of multiplication facts
Bring down the 1's digit part of the answer put it in the 10's column.	Knowledge of place value Where to write answers to vertically written math problems
Carry the 10's digit part of the answer.	Knowledge of place value How to carry numbers
Multiply the 10's digit column.	Knowledge of place value Knowledge of multiplication facts
To that answer add the number that you carried and write that down.	Knowledge of addition facts Where to write answers to vertically written math problems
Add your two answers; the number that you get is the *answer*.	Knowledge of addition facts
Write it down.	Where to write answers to vertically written math problems

Stage 2: Discussing the Strategy

Discussion of the strategy is a more involved process than merely going through the steps of a strategy. Remember that one major goal of SRSD is to help students develop into self-regulated learners. In order for this goal to be achieved, students need to be actively involved in and take ownership of the SRSD process. At this stage, teachers will need to "sell" the strategy and get students to "buy in." Students need to believe that the strategy they are learning will help them perform better. This will enable them to be more actively involved, which is the first step in self-regulation. If a student does not want to use a strategy, it is fair to assume that he or she will not use it. Remember

TABLE 3.2. Example of Task Breakdown for Writing a Simple Research Paper

Steps	Skills required
Choose a topic.	Idea generation
Research that topic.	Ability to find source material, use card catalog or other references
Write down important and interesting information on note cards.	Ability to take notes effectively, and to distinguish between relevant and irrelevant information
Sort note cards into categories with similar types of information.	Ability to group information according to similarities

Make an outline including:
   Introduction
   Body—using the two or three categories of note cards that have the most and most interesting information
   Conclusion
	How to write an outline
	   What an introduction should contain
	   What a body should contain
	   What a conclusion should contain

Write a rough draft making sure you have:
   A complete introduction with a complete paragraph or two
   A body that is well supported and written in complete paragraphs, with complete sentences
   A conclusion that summarizes what you said and makes any points that you wanted to make
	Basic knowledge of writing mechanics:
	   Complete sentences
	   Complete paragraphs
	   Organized paragraphs
	   Paper components and how to write them
	     Introduction
	     Body
	     Conclusion

Type out your rough draft using spelling and grammar check to make sure your spelling and grammar are correct, and make any necessary changes.	Typing skills Knowledge of a basic word-processing program
Have a teacher or knowledgeable person proofread your paper and make any changes or give any suggestions that they might have.	Knowing who would be a knowledgeable person to ask for assistance
Rewrite your paper and make any necessary adjustments.	Knowing how to take criticism Knowing how to make corrections with the word-processing program
Look over your paper and make sure it looks good.	Knowledge of what a paper is supposed to look like

that motivational processes have significant effects on learning and effort. Throughout the SRSD process teachers need to be excited, committed, and energized so that students will be too.

It's not hard for teachers to sell a strategy. After all, learning an effective, appropriate strategy will result in improved academic performance. Teachers can provide students with examples of how this strategy or other strategies have improved student performance in the past, and even how strategies have helped them in the past. It is helpful to know what motivates particular students. During this stage it is appropriate for the teachers to explain the benefits of using the strategy, discussing and even providing examples of current performance. For example, teachers can create graphs to show current performance levels. The graphs can also be used to chart progress, which can help motivate students.

The final step of this stage is introducing students to the steps of the strategy. The teacher explains what each step of the strategy is for, how it is used, and where it is useful. This is also where teachers will begin to do some attribution retraining by stressing that good performance is the result of effort and strategy use. During this stage, and those that follow, you will want to be sensitive to student feedback. Teachers must match the strategy to the student. Strategies that are too easy or too difficult are of little use. Teachers should modify a strategy if a student doesn't understand it or is uncomfortable with part of it. Throughout this process you should be closely monitoring students' understanding; ask questions on the steps and probe for comprehension. Remember that strategy instruction is not a one-way street. It is a reciprocal process. Students' aptitudes, deficits, and needs should mold the instruction process.

Stage 3: Modeling the Strategy

Modeling is one of the most crucial components of strategy instruction. Modeling plays a critical role in strategy instruction because modeling is the means to provide students with the metacognitive knowledge of strategy performance. Good modeling allows the student to see an "expert" learner employing the strategy. A critical part of modeling is the "think aloud" process, where teachers or students verbalize their thought processes as they model strategy performance. Modeling increases students' knowledge of the steps of the strategy and improves their cognitive and metacognitive knowledge of the strategy through exposure to the way a skilled learner implements and regulates strategy use. Figure 3.1 shows an example of a think-aloud that was developed for the 4 B's strategy (a subtraction strategy) introduced in Chapter 2. Note that a good "think aloud" goes well beyond merely presenting the process—it provides students with the "why" and the "how" of various strategy steps (i.e., the metacognitive knowledge and self-regulation processes associated with the performance of steps). This is critical. Research clearly shows that without this knowledge students will not fully benefit from the strategy. Note that good modeling serves to teach students that using a strategy requires effort. It also addresses attributions (e.g., "OK, that was easy. I can do this!"), and stresses the value of strategy use—using the strategy results in better performance.

We have found that modeling is one of the more difficult components of the strategy instruction process for teachers. Constructing a good think-aloud is more complex than it may initially seem. The reason for this is twofold. First, there is a tendency for teachers to simply repeat the steps of a strategy or task. We call this "skill stepping." This isn't a bad practice, but it's not sufficient, especially for students with LD, because skill stepping doesn't provide students with the metacognitive knowledge they need. Figure 3.2 shows an example of skill stepping, along with how the same task might be modeled using a think-aloud. The second reason teachers have problems with modeling is that for skilled learners, modeling involves making covert automatic processes overt. That is to say, when you model, you have to think about things you don't nor-

46
−28

All right, what do I need to do here? Well, I know this is a two-digit by two-digit sub-traction problem, because each number has two digits, and I see the "minus" sign. So, what will I need to remember to do this problem? I will need to remember my basic subtraction facts, place value, and the steps for completing a two-digit by two-digit subtraction problem. Hmm . . . sometimes I have problems remembering the steps in a two-digit by two-digit sub-traction problem, especially if there's regrouping. I know that getting the steps in the right order is important, because if I don't get them in the right order I might get the wrong answer. How will I remember the steps? Oh, I know. Ms. Chaffin taught us a strategy the other day to help us remember the steps. It was the 4 B's strategy; Begin, Bigger, Borrow, and Basic facts. OK, I can do this, all I need to do is follow my strategy and try my hardest. Let's see, the first *B* stood for "Begin in the 1's column." That's simple. I know where the 1's col-umn is. The 1's column is the one farthest to the right. That's right, with math problems we start in the right column; if I don't I might not get the values right. Great, what's next? Oh yeah, the next step is "Bigger? Which number is bigger, the bottom or the top?" I know that 8 is bigger than 6, because I know my number values. OK, 8 is bigger and it's on the bottom. Now what? The next step in my 4 B's strategy is "Borrow? If the bottom number is bigger I must borrow." Well, since the bottom number is bigger I will need to borrow. Borrow?!? How do I do that? Well, I know if I don't have enough money to buy something that I want I can just borrow some money from my sister, but I need to make sure I keep track of how much I borrow so I can pay her back. Borrowing in subtraction is kind of like that. If the number in my 1's column isn't big enough I can just borrow from the 10's column, and I will need to keep track of what I borrow so I don't change the value of the original number. OK, so that means I borrow a 10 from the 10's column, and move it over to the 1's column to make it bigger; that makes 16, but since I borrowed a 10 from the 10's column I am taking 1 of my 4 10's, so I only have 3 left. I need to make sure I change that. OK, so now what do I need to do? Well, the last step in my strategy is "Basic Facts. I need to remember to use my math facts!" Wow, I'm up to the last step; now all I need to do is subtract. I'll start with my 1's col-umn (16 − 8 = 8). I need to put that answer in my 1's answer column because I just sub-tracted the 1's column. Now, I need to go to the 10's column, I know to do that because I know my place value, and the 10's column is right next to the 1's column. OK, I have the 4 crossed out, and I wrote 3 above that. I need to remember to use the 3 because I changed that value when I borrowed to subtract the 1's column. All right, so 3 − 2 = 1; I need to put 1 in my 10's answer column. So that gives me an answer of 18. Yeah!!! I did it! My strategy really helped me remember all the steps in a two-digit by two-digit subtraction problem.

FIGURE 3.1. Example of a think-aloud.

mally think about. For example, in the Figure 3.2 example most of us would not even be conscious that we checked the sign to determine what operation we would use, and starting at the right is done automatically. Learning to be aware of and verbalize these automatic, unconscious processes may be difficult at first for some teachers.

There are several ways to make the process of creating good think-alouds easier. One of the tools teachers can use is a "metacognitive task breakdown." This is a straightforward process. For each step in the task, identify metacognitive knowledge or self-regulation processes by asking yourself "why," "how," and "what for" questions.

1. *Why* am I doing this step in the task?
2. *How* did I know to do it?
3. *What* are the important actions, cues, or questions?
4. *What* knowledge do I need?

Jot down your answers to the questions as you go through the task. Sometimes you may need to go over your answers and apply the same process. Try this process with simple tasks like math problems or simple everyday tasks (e.g., making a peanut butter and jelly sandwich). With practice the metacognitive knowledge implicit in academic tasks will be identified readily, and it will be much easier to produce good think-alouds. Another way to get metacognitive information is to ask students who are effective at a task to talk themselves through the how and why of the steps in the task.

Skill steps for two-digit addition	Think-aloud
First I'll add the 1's column. Now I'll write the 5 and carry the 1. Now I'll add the numbers in the 10's column. Finally, I'll write the answer.	What is it I have to do? OK, this is a 2-digit addition problem; I know it's addition because of the "+" sign. That tells me to add. I know how to do this! I need to remember to follow the steps in my strategy and remember my basic facts.
	First I need to start in the 1's column and add those. If I don't start at the 1's column I'll get the wrong answer! The 1's are on the right-hand side. I'll make a little mark to help me remember.
	OK, I'm ready to add the first two numbers. Did I get a two-digit number? Because if I do I need to carry the 10's digit to the next column, to the 10's column. Yep, 15 has two digits. I need to remember to write the numbers down correctly too. I only write one digit down under the line. The one I write down is the 5 'cause that's the digit in the 1's column. I need to be careful to write the 5 down under the 1's column. If I don't I can get my numbers messed up and get the wrong answer. Now what do I do with the 1? Oh, yes, I have to carry that number. I'll write it down above the 10's column of the problem. That way I'll remember that I've carried.
	Now, what do I do next? I know, I need to add all the 10's digits that I have, the two in the original problem, and the one that I carried. I'm almost done, now all I need to do is write down the answer. I need to remember to keep my numbers lined up. I'll write them carefully. I knew I could do it. I took my time, used my strategy, and tried hard, and I got the right answer.

FIGURE 3.2. Skill steps and modeling for adding 26 + 19.

Stage 4: Memorizing the Strategy

In this stage, students commit to memory the steps that constitute the strategy. This is probably the quickest and easiest of the six steps. The goal is for students to quickly and easily remember the steps of the strategy and use them automatically. As students have told us, "You can't use it if you can't remember it." Students must be able to focus their energy and attention on the task at hand—not on struggling to remember the strategy steps per se. Remember that students with LD often have problems with working memory. Struggling to remember what to do next will likely impede performance. Note that this step may even be omitted for very simple strategies (e.g., the math strategy example used in Chapter 2) if students have no trouble remembering the steps. To help students memorize the strategy many teachers make a game of practicing the steps by using round-robin activities or ball-toss games. For example, a teacher says the first step of the strategy and then tosses the ball to a student who relates the second step and so on. Students can go to the next stage in the process before they have reached automaticity if they are provided with prompts or other types of supports (e.g., a card listing the steps in order). However, before completing all stages students must memorize the strategy steps. Note that memorizing a strategy goes well beyond parroting the steps of the strategy. Students need to *know and understand* what is involved with each step in the process. This understanding is crucial if students are to use the strategy successfully.

Stage 5: Supporting the Strategy

Supporting the strategy is another critical step in the SRSD process. In this stage, the teacher and student(s) work together collaboratively and practice using the strategy until the student is able to perform the strategy effectively and independently. During this stage, teachers and students repeatedly model strategy use and discuss how, when, and why to use the strategy. One key aspect of supporting the strategy is the "scaffolding" or "scaffolded instruction" process. The process of scaffolding is analogous to teaching a child to ride a bike. No one would put a child on his first bike, give him a push, and expect him to ride well. Instead, we normally use a process where we start with extensive supports (literally!), which are progressively removed. For example, we would typically start with training wheels and let the child practice with them. Then, we might move the training wheels up, for less support and more practice balancing and riding a little bit more independently. Next, we could take the training wheels off and run behind the child holding the seat. Finally, we would completely let go and let the child ride independently without any support, just our supervision.

Scaffolding instruction works in much the same manner. Initially, teachers perform all or most of a task while modeling and soliciting student input. Over time, the teacher will increasingly shift responsibility for performance to the student. As students gain experience with and confidence in the use of the strategy, teacher support is gradually withdrawn until the student uses the strategy independently. Note that the transfer of strategy performance from teacher to student is *gradual*. It's not realistic to expect students to master a strategy the first time they try it. It's critically important for students to be given *adequate time and support* to master the strategy. Collaborative practice also gives the teacher an opportunity to check for student understanding, provide corrective feedback, and develop any necessary knowledge the student may be lacking. It's also useful in assessment. For example, teachers may discover though interacting with the student that the strategy should be modified, or that earlier SRSD stages need to be revisited. It also gives the teacher another opportunity to make sure that students possess the skills necessary to complete the task successfully.

Exactly how the teacher goes about supporting strategy development through scaffolding and collaborative practice will depend upon the strategies and the needs of the students. The following are some commonly used activities and supports used in the scaffolding process (Dickson, Collins, Simmons, & Kame'enui, 1998).

Content Scaffolding

There are three types of content scaffolding techniques.

1. Initially, teachers can use content material that is at an easy level. For example, for a reading comprehension strategy teachers might use text that was one grade below the students' current level.
2. Use content that the students are familiar with or interested in. Thus, content that featured cars or sports might be highly appropriate for adolescent males.
3. Teach the easier steps of the strategy first, followed by the more difficult steps. Thus, during the initial practice sessions, the student would perform the easy steps while the teacher modeled how to perform the more difficult steps. The student gradually is given responsibility for the more difficult steps.

Task Scaffolding

Ownership of the strategy is gradually transferred by allowing the student to do more and more of the strategy during collaborative practice. For example, (1) the teacher asks the student to name the strategy step that should be performed, then the teacher describes the step and models its use; (2) the teacher asks the student to name the step and describe the step, then the teacher models it; (3) the student names, describes, and models the step.

Material Scaffolding

This type of scaffolding uses prompts and cues to help the student use a strategy. This may take the form of posters or help sheets that list strategy steps. Students can use these as a reference or if they get confused. Typically these prompts and aids are faded over time.

Teachers can also use cooperative groups or peers to help scaffold instruction. For example, a teacher might create heterogeneous groups and have each group go through the steps of a strategy. The group as a whole would be responsible for completing the strategy and for making sure that all group members understood each step of the strategy.

The goal of this stage is for the students to be able to use the strategy effectively and independently. The time it takes for students to reach this level of skill may vary widely. This stage will probably be the longest of the six. That's normal and expectable. In practice, when SRSD procedures are used with appropriate strategies, most students can master a strategy after two to four collaborative, scaffolded experiences. Once again, this is a critical stage of the SRSD process. Skimping at this stage will likely mean that students will not fully master the strategy or may not reach mastery at all. This in turn means that both the teacher's and student's efforts have been for naught.

Stage 6: Independent Performance

At this stage, a student should be ready to use the strategy independently. Your main task will be to monitor the student's performance and to check on proper and consistent strategy use. Monitoring academic performance is critical. Remember that the goal of strategy instruction is increased academic performance. The student's work should show a marked improvement, and it should also remain at a consistent level. There are a number of ways to monitor performance, which we will elaborate on in the next section. Monitoring strategy use is also very important because students sometimes distort the strategy or skip steps when using them independently. However, teachers should always keep in mind that improved academic performance is the goal. If a student modifies a strategy, but performance remains high, there is no cause for concern. Many students will adapt the strategy to meet their needs. This is acceptable as long as the student is still successful in completing the task. Alternatively, if a student is performing the strategy correctly and consistently but a high level of performance is not attained (or maintained), then reteaching the strategy or considering a different strategy is probably in order.

EVALUATING SRSD

With the advent of No Child Left Behind, accountability is receiving ever-increasing attention in schools. Evaluation is an important component of strategy instruction. Unless you systematically assess the outcomes you will have no way of gauging the effect of strategy instruction. SRSD facilitates meaningful assessment: The interactive, collaborative nature of the process allows teachers to easily assess changes in students' cognition, affect, and performance. Harris and Graham (1996) offered basic principles for evaluating the methods and procedures used in strategy instruction. The list is not exhaustive, but provides a working knowledge of how to accomplish effective strategy evaluation.

Including Students as Coevaluators

Students should be encouraged to become partners in the strategy evaluation process. This increases their sense of ownership in the strategy, reinforces progress, and provides a practical way to reduce a teacher's load. Students can help in many ways, such as learning to evaluate their final products or deciding if the necessary criteria for each step of a strategy have been met. Helping students ask appropriate self-questions (e.g., "Am I ready to move on to the next step?") is another effective way to help students evaluate their own progress. Students can also graph or chart their progress.

Considering the Level of Evaluation Needed

Exactly how much time and effort should be expended on evaluation depends on a number of factors. At a minimum, teachers should know if students are actually using the strategy, the effect of the strategy on task performance, and whether students see the strategy as being valuable and easily used. Teachers may also find that evaluating their instruction may be useful. The type of strategy used and previous experience with a strategy are important factors in evaluation. For example, strategies, methods, and procedures that have been previously used and have demonstrated their effectiveness will need less scrutiny than a first-time strategy. As a general rule, the amount of time and effort you need to expend on evaluating the usefulness of a strategy depends on its established validity and your experience with it. However, even well-validated, frequently used strategies still require some evaluation.

Assessing Changes in Performance, Attitudes, and Cognition

Recall that motivation and emotion are important factors that are considered in SRSD. Changing a student's attitude toward a task and success is a critical component of strategy instruction. As a result, the benefits of strategy instruction can go beyond improving academic performance; students' attitudes and cognition may also be affected. For example, after teaching a math strategy, a teacher might observe whether students' attitudes toward math and confidence in their abilities improve. The teacher might also check to see if a student performs the task outside the classroom. For example, after teaching a writing strategy check the amount of writing the student does outside of school. Spontaneous statements are also pertinent. For example, one student we worked with on a math strategy who had struggled previously suddenly stopped in the middle of a problem and stated, "You know, this stuff is really easy!" The use of open-ended questions such as "What is good writing?" or "What do you most like to say to yourself while you do history study questions?" also can help you determine if a strategy has changed students' perceptions of a task. It is important to remember that some changes (such as attitude improvements) take more time than others to obtain. It takes time to overcome years of previous frustration.

Assessing While Instruction Is in Progress

Most assessment occurs after instruction has occurred. However strategy instruction depends upon frequent and ongoing assessment. Assessment procedures for strategy instruction should reflect the developmental and ongoing process of learning to use a strategy. This means that teachers must evaluate success at learning the strategy. Establishing realistic performance criteria for each step of instruction is one way to facilitate this process. For example, if a student can tell you when and where it would be appropriate to use a strategy then one of the goals of Stage 2 has been accomplished. When the student can list and explain steps of the strategy then Stage 3 objectives have been met. By clearly defining what is expected at each stage of strategy instruction, both teachers and students know what needs to be accomplished and what standards will be used to measure progress.

Assessing How Students Actually Use the Strategy

Students will often modify their use of a strategy over time. Sometimes this is a natural and positive effect of becoming fluent with the strategy. Use of steps may become automatic and not readily observable (Alexander, Graham, & Harris, 1998). However, students may also change things for the worse. Therefore, do not automatically assume that students are using a strategy as intended. Some modifications allow the strategy to meet a student's unique needs, but others, such as eliminating a necessary step, may be detrimental. The best way for teachers to monitor strategy usage is to directly observe what students do as they use the strategy. Ask the student to work through a strategy. While the student does this, ask questions and discuss how things are working. Looking for evidence of strategy use in students' work is often useful. Often, students will leave "tracks" that indicate they are using a strategy. For example, students will often write out mnemonics they use to remember a strategy.

Assessing Students' Use of the Strategy over Time and in New Situations

Teachers should not assume that students will continue to use a particular strategy or successfully adapt it to new situations. One of the common problems experienced by students with LD is that they do not automatically generalize skills or strategies to new situations. Karen Harris tells the story of the student who had learned a comprehension strategy and effectively used it in one class. When asked about using it in other classes the child responded, "Was I supposed to?" If you wish for the strategy use to be maintained and generalized you will need to program it. Therefore, it is beneficial to actively promote maintenance and generalization of strategy usage from the inception of strategy instruction. For example, to promote maintenance, teachers could periodically have students explain the purpose of a strategy or have them share ways they have used the strategy. Students also can keep a record of each time they use a strategy or how they modify it for other tasks. It's also useful to chart performance (which hopefully has improved), review it at regular intervals, and relate improvements to the use of the strategy. Generalization may be tougher. It will often be necessary to involve other teachers who were not involved in the strategy instruction process. The teachers will need to be acquainted with the strategy and any procedures involved with its use (e.g., graphic organizers or prompt sheets) and will at a minimum need to remind the student to use the strategy and encourage its use.

Remember that one major goal of strategy instruction is generalization. Thus, it is necessary to determine if students need additional support to consistently apply the strategy in all appropriate situations. Note that if other teachers are involved these teachers should also be involved in evaluating strategy use and promoting its generalization

Utilizing Portfolio Assessment Procedures

Portfolio assessment is an excellent way to implement many of the recommendations we have presented for evaluation of strategy instruction. This type of assessment requires teachers to establish the credibility of, and become intimately involved in the maintenance and evaluation of, student portfolios. Portfolios offer many practical advantages. At a very basic level, portfolios can often help to graphically demonstrate progress. For example, collecting samples of writing over time can make improvements highly visible. They can also help to improve motivation and demonstrate the benefits of strategy use. For example, one junior high teacher kept pre- and poststrategy instruction examples of students' stories. Prestrategy stories were typically around one-half page long. Poststrategy stories averaged over three pages! Students were extremely proud of their obvious progress. Note that these examples can also be effective when trying to get future students to "buy into" using a strategy. Portfolios can also help students engage in reflective self-evaluation, understand that development is as important as achievement, and take greater responsibility for their own learning. Teachers will also gain new insights and understanding about assessment, teaching, and their students' development and learning. As an aside, it important to note that *teachers* will also receive some reinforcement since they can see that their instruction resulted in meaningful change.

PRACTICAL CONSIDERATIONS AND TIPS

As we noted, strategy instruction is one of the most effective method for students with LD. The SRSD model is powerful and effective, but it only works if you do it correctly. There are some common pitfalls. In this section we will present practical tips for teachers.

Take Your Time

Strategy instruction must be closely tailored to the needs of students. Individual students or groups must proceed at their own pace. For example, it is not possible to schedule one day for mastery of the strategy and three days for collaborative practice. With practice, a teacher may be able to closely estimate the time, but—though there are some exceptions—it is critical for students to attain mastery at each stage before proceeding. The SRSD model is scaffolded throughout. It assumes that responsibility for the use of the strategy will be transferred gradually, with increasing responsibility given for strategy performance as competence and confidence are gained. There is sometimes a tendency to overestimate progress. Remember that "One swallow doesn't make a summer," and using a strategy well one time does not mean the student has mastered the strategy. Students need to use the strategy correctly and consistently and develop the metacognitive knowledge of "why" and "how" before they have truly mastered the strategy.

Note also that the SRSD model assumes that teachers will "loop back" through some stages. In fact it is common for lessons to include activities from different stages. For example, teachers should discuss how the strategy can be used during the Support It stage. Practice with mastering the steps of the strategy should also be repeated frequently. For strategy instruction to succeed, a teacher must commit to working with students for whatever amount of time is necessary for them to attain independent performance. Note also that instruction doesn't stop once independent performance is attained. Teachers should continually remind students of opportunities to use a strategy, expose them to modeling and examples of how the strategy can be used, prompt strategy generalization, and encourage verbalization and sharing of strategy use. Remember, the goal of transforming students with LD into active learners is not reached overnight.

Small Is Golden

Because strategy instruction is so powerful and practical there's a natural tendency to want to use it as much as possible. If one strategy is good, two would be even better. At this point you might remember the old saying that you can have "too much of a good thing." The same is true of strategy instruction. We recommend using the "small is golden" principle advocated by Pressley (Pressley & Woloshyn, 1995). Teachers should focus on a small number of strategies and support their use over a sufficient period of time. There's no best number of strategies to teach during a school year; this decision depends on students' needs and abilities. There's also no set time limit for working on a strategy, although in general the more time spent the better the result. It's much better to spend the time focusing in depth on one or two strategies than to teach half a dozen to a much lower level of mastery. Focusing on a limited number of strategies will result in students developing a deeper understanding of the strategy and a realization of how strategy use can improve performance.

Generalization

It's worth repeating that generalization must be programmed—it won't occur on its own. Many students who can benefit the most from strategy instruction will not spontaneously generalize a strategy across settings. Teachers in other settings or grades must know what strategies students have learned and how to encourage their continued development. Note that getting another teacher to support the use of a strategy in his or her class may also involve a "buy in" process. This will likely be new to the teacher and there will be an education process. In practice, one of the best ways to motivate other teachers to help in the generalization process is to show them (by using evaluation materials such as portfolios) how much the strategy has improved performance.

Pick Your Battles

Deciding which strategies to use and which students to use them with is an important decision. There are two things to consider here. First, when starting out with strategy instruction, it is tempting to try it in the curriculum areas that cause the greatest difficulty or with students who are experiencing the most severe problems. This would be a mistake for teachers new to strategy instruction. If strategy instruction is relatively new to both you and your students, it is not fair to anyone to take on too much too fast. The worst thing that a teacher could do is to attempt an ambitious program only to see it fail because of lack of experience. A better approach would be for teachers to begin with a relatively simple strategy in an area where they are comfortable and can reasonably anticipate success. This allows teachers to become more acquainted with the instructional process and hone their skills. It also helps to build confidence. Remember that teachers need to develop mastery just as students do. Second, be sensitive to what students already know and don't try to reinvent the wheel. Some students have developed strategies that are partially effective. It's better to build on what they already know and are accustomed to than to start from scratch. Additionally, because existing strategies look simple many teachers think that it's easy to develop your own. This is decidedly not the case. Most effective strategies are the result of years of development. Rather than attempting to create an effective strategy from scratch we would suggest that you find (or modify) an appropriate strategy that has already been developed and validated.

FINAL THOUGHTS

In this chapter we have presented the SRSD model for strategy instruction and provided examples of activities teachers could perform at each stage. We've also talked about evaluation and practical tips in implementing strategy instruction. In closing we want to stress two things. First, strategy instruction should be seen as a *process*. It is the process that is powerful. Strategies themselves are useless unless the teacher utilizes an effective strategy instruction process that attends to instilling the metacognitive knowledge students need and helps to change maladaptive motivational processes. Second, the strategy instruction process depends on *collaboration*. The teacher and students should work together to develop and evaluate new strategies. Remember that strategies are not "off the rack"; rather, they are custom made. Third, teachers should collaborate with other teachers, as well as their students, during the strategy instruction process. Professional cooperation allows teachers to share their personal triumphs and challenges and serves to facilitate supportive feedback and problem solving. Teachers who use strategy instruction gather powerful new knowledge about what works for students. Although this can be a demanding process, it is an exciting one that we hope you will try.

REFERENCES

Alexander, P. A., Graham, S., & Harris, K. R. (1998). A perspective on strategy research: Progress and prospects. *Educational Psychology Review, 10*, 129–154.

Dickson, S. V., Collins, V. L., Simmons, D. C., & Kame'enui, E. J. (1998). Metacognitive strategies: Instruction and curricular basics and implications. In D. Simmons & E. Kame'enui (Eds.), *What reading research tells us about children with diverse learning needs* (pp. 361–380). Mahwah, NJ: Erlbaum.

Graham, S., & Harris, K. R. (2003). Students with learning disabilities and the process of writing: A meta-analysis of SRSD studies. In H. L. Swanson, K. R. Harris, & S. Graham (Eds.), *Handbook of learning disabilities* (pp. 323–334). New York: Guilford Press.

Harris, K. R., & Graham, S. (1996). *Making the writing process work: Strategies for composition and selfregulation.* Cambridge, MA: Brookline Books.

Harris, K. R., Graham, S., & Mason, L. (2003). Self-regulated strategy development in the classroom: Part of a balanced approach to writing instruction for students with disabilities. *Focus on Exceptional Children, 35*(7), 1–16.

Pressley, M., & Woloshyn, V. (1995). *Cognitive strategy instruction that really improves children's academic performance.* Cambridge, MA: Brookline Books.

CHAPTER 4

How to Implement the SRSD Model

In Chapter 3, we introduced and explained the SRSD model. In this chapter we demonstrate how that instructional template can be used to help teachers implement strategies. We provide two sample implementation plans: (1) the textbook reading comprehension strategy SCROL (Grant, 1993), and (2) the basic story comprehension strategy Story Grammar (Short & Ryan, 1984). These implementation plans present examples of activities for each of the six stages.

There are many different types of strategies. One of the most important differences among strategies lies in whether the strategy is structured or unstructured. We chose these two strategies to illustrate the difference between structured and unstructured strategies. Structured strategies are those strategies that provide an implicit sequence that allow the user (i.e., the student) to use the strategy in a step-by-step fashion. The structure provided also permits teachers to create an implementation plan that is easily sequenced. The SCROL strategy is a structured strategy.

In contrast, unstructured strategies do not provide an implicit guide to strategy performance. This kind of strategy requires the teacher to create a structure to guide students' use of the strategy. This can actually allow for more flexibility. However, additional planning is necessary to create a set of steps to guide students and to design an implementation plan. The Story Grammar strategy is an example of an unstructured strategy. In our example we show how teachers can add structure to a strategy.

STRUCTURED STRATEGY EXAMPLE

SCROL is a reading comprehension strategy designed for students in middle and upper grades to help them to read and understand textbooks and a variety of source books. The strategy encourages students to use text headings to aid their comprehension and help them find and remember important information. The SCROL strategy is composed of five steps. First, the students are instructed to *Survey* chapter headings. This provides students with an idea of what the chapter will be about and prompts them to think about what they already know about the subject, thus activating their prior knowledge of the subject. It also allows them to predict information that the writer may present. Next, students ask themselves how the headings relate to one another and write down any keywords from the headings that might provide *Connections* between them. Third, students *Read* the text and look for words and phrases that express important information about the headings, mark the text, stop to make sure that they understand the major ideas and supporting details, and reread if necessary. Fourth, students *Outline* the text using indentations to reflect text structure. Students are asked to write the heading and then try to outline each heading segment without looking back at the text. This encourages students to use their knowledge of the text to fill in the outline. Finally, students are prompted to *Look back* at the text and check the accuracy of the major ideas and details they wrote down, correct any inaccurate information in their outline, and use the text that they marked to help verify the accuracy of the outline.

Stage 1: Developing and Activating Background Knowledge

Prior to teaching the strategy, it is necessary to evaluate the students' background knowledge. Formal or informal assessments can be used to determine what knowledge and skills the students possess and what skills they lack; doing a task breakdown will provide the information for identifying the knowledge and skills necessary to successfully complete the strategy. Note that it is also important to assess students' motivational beliefs, goals, and metacognitive knowledge. Table 4.1 provides an example of a task breakdown for the SCROL strategy. Chapter 3 provided a task breakdown example that was divided into two parts. Here the task breakdown is divided down into three parts: (1) strategy, (2) skill/knowledge, and (3) assessment. Combining the assessment aspect with the skill and strategy is just another example of the flexibility of the SRSD model. Either method is acceptable.

The strategy section of the task analysis identifies what the students are asked to do as part of the SCROL strategy. The SCROL strategy is broken down into five steps; however, teachers need to be sensitive to skills that are prerequisites for strategy use. For example, SCROL requires that students possess basic literacy skills. It is critical that all necessary skills are identified prior to implementation of the strategy. The skills section details the skills that are necessary for the student to successfully complete each aspect of the strategy. Each skill is listed alongside its corresponding strategy step. Oftentimes the same skill is necessary at various steps in the strategy; however it is not necessary to list them every time.

TABLE 4.1. Example of Task Breakdown for the SCROL Strategy

Strategy	Skills	Assessment
Basic reading skills	Ability to read content material with sufficient fluency	Informal reading assessment
Survey the headings	Knowledge of and ability to identify headings and subheadings	Students will be provided with a text and asked to identify the headings and subheadings.
	Knowledge of topics and how they are sometimes presented in texts	Given a short text, students will be asked to identify and explain the major topics in the text and how they knew what those topics were.
	Ability to generalize information and make predictions or inferences	Students will be given a short text and asked to verbally summarize what they have read, and make any predictions or inferences that they can from the given text.
Connections	Ability to identify connecting words	Students will be given a list of words and asked to identify words that are often connecting words.
Read the text	Ability to identify key words or phrases as they relate to the topic	Given a passage, the student will be asked to underline key words or phrases related to the given topic.
	Ability to check for understanding	Students will be given a short passage to read aloud and periodically stopped and asked to explain what the passage is about.
Outline	Knowledge of outlines	Given a simple text, students will be asked to outline that text using standard outline form.
Look back	Ability to proofread	Students will be given a passage with spelling and grammatical errors and asked to find and correct those errors.
	Ability to compare original text with the outline for accuracy of information	Students will be asked to compare the outline that they produced earlier to the text for accuracy of information.

The assessment section explains how the students will be assessed to determine whether or not they possess the prerequisite skills. If students do not possess the necessary skills, the skills will need to be taught or accommodations made. Accommodations for the SCROL strategy could be texts at the students' independent reading level or premarked text, texts that have the headings, subheadings, and important points highlighted. Accommodations should help the students to use the strategy independently; however, accommodations should be gradually faded as students reach mastery. Assessments of prerequisite skills can be done for each of the skills individually, or students can be given an overall assessment of skills. An example of this would be an informal student survey. Figure 4.1 provides an example of an informal survey for the SCROL strategy. An

Name: _____ Date: _____

1 = Strongly agree   2 = Agree   3 = Not sure   4 = Disagree   5 = Strongly disagree

1. I am able to read and understand my textbooks.
         1   2   3   4   5

2. I can pick out headings and subheadings in my textbooks.
         1   2   3   4   5

3. I can pick out the topic or main idea in the passages of my textbooks.
         1   2   3   4   5

4. When I am done reading I can paraphrase information from my textbooks.
         1   2   3   4   5

5. I am able to identify key words or phrases as they relate to the topic.
         1   2   3   4   5

6. I know if I understand what I have read or not.
         1   2   3   4   5

7. I am able to recall information that I have read.
         1   2   3   4   5

8. I am able to put my thoughts about text that I read into writing.
         1   2   3   4   5

9. I am able to create an outline.
         1   2   3   4   5

10. I am able to compare original text material with my outline to make sure it is right.
         1   2   3   4   5

11. I am able to proofread my own work.
         1   2   3   4   5

FIGURE 4.1. Sample survey for SCROL.

informal s▒ ▒▒▒▒portunity to evaluate their own mastery of necessary skills ▒▒▒▒ survey can be an effective way to gather informa-
tio▒ ▒▒▒ provide valuable insight into how students view
▒ ▒▒▒ hould *not* be the sole means of evaluation. It
▒▒▒ tudents' performance; this data can also
▒▒▒ e strategy. An example of data a teacher
▒▒▒ k that involved responding to questions
▒▒▒ n the next stage to establish a need for the
▒▒▒ vations, and any other information collect-
▒▒▒ cits, instruction should be given to ensure

ACCEL

MAP IT

Stage ▒▒▒▒

This is ▒▒▒▒ the strategy. As discussed in Chapter 3, this stage
requires m▒▒ ▒▒ m▒▒ ▒▒ g through the steps in the strategy. Students need to
take ownership of the strategy. They need to recognize the value of the strategy and
want to use it. The teacher must "sell" the strategy and get the students to "buy in." If
students do not want to use the strategy they are not likely to use it. Teachers must be
excited, committed, and energetic throughout the whole process.

In practice, it is not difficult to sell a strategy to most students. The strategy should
sell itself with the payoff of improved academic performance. However, that may not
be enough for some students. It is often necessary to find out what motivates the students. When do they see reading a text, understanding, and remembering it as important? It may be beneficial to brainstorm with students on situations where reading texts
accurately are important. Teachers may want to come up with a "pitch" to the sell the
students, providing examples of current performance, or examples of students who
have been successful with the strategy in the past. Finding out when students view
comprehending text as important is a good place to start. The teacher may pose a question such as "When would it be important for you to read a text accurately?" The
teacher should have in mind a few responses, in case the students are reluctant to share
or do not mention important times.

Here are some examples:

- For a test
- For an assignment
- Making an informed decision
- Learning more about something of interest to you
- Assembling something
- Operating equipment

As a last resort the teacher may draw up a behavioral contract, where the student tries
the strategy and gets reinforcement.

It is important for students to understand the purpose of a strategy. When discussing the purpose of the strategy, it is necessary to point out situations where the students

would need to understand and remember information that they read in a variety of source books. This helps students understand when, where, and why to use the strategy. This type of knowledge is very important for students with LD. It is also necessary to point out the obvious problems that could arise if they were not accurate in reading certain texts. For example, if students did not read a text accurately they would do poorly on a test. Another practical example would be following directions to put something together. If students did not read accurately, it is not likely that they would be very successful.

During the discussion stage, it is also necessary to discuss students' current performance. One way to do this is to chart performance on completed tasks. Using charts and graphs can also help with motivation because students can see progress. Using the SCROL strategy will help students read their textbooks, take notes, and remember what they have read. The strategy will also help them later. If they have a good grasp of the material being read the first time they go through it, they will have to spend less time studying later. The outline and notes can serve as a quick review of the information. The outline highlights all important information in the text, and the notes explain that information, providing a nice overview of the information.

As we noted in the previous chapter, one important task in the discussion stage (Stage 2) is to get students to buy into using the strategy. For this reason, it is often useful for the teacher to prepare for selling the strategy. Here's an example of a teacher "selling" the SCROL strategy:

> "We just came up with a list of situations when it would be important to read a text accurately [brainstorming]. There are several times that we decided this was important. Someone mentioned when learning and remembering information for a test. Let's take a look at some of our recent test scores [providing graphic representation of test scores would be a way for students to quickly examine their current performance]. It is obvious that we are doing some things well, but there is definitely room for improvement. I have a trick that we can use to boost those test scores and help us remember texts that we have read. It is a strategy called SCROL. The SCROL strategy can help us to remember what we should do when we are reading text for information. . . . "

It is important to remember that students should make the commitment to learn and use the strategy. In practice, this isn't usually hard. Students want to do well. But remember also that there is often a history of failure that must be overcome.

The final step in this stage is introducing the strategy steps. Students are encouraged to take notes and express any ideas they have regarding the strategy. Note that teachers should be sensitive to student input. Students can offer many helpful insights. Remember that strategy instruction is a *dialogue*, not a monologue (Harris & Pressley, 1991). While explaining the strategy, it is important to begin any necessary attribution training, and to stress that improved performance is due to increased effort and strategy use. The strategy is just a tool to use to improve academic performance. The steps of the strategy are illustrated in Figure 4.2. These steps can be placed on a wall chart to help students with the initial usage of the strategy.

SCROL

Survey the headings
- In the assigned text selection, read each heading and subheading.
- For each heading and subheading, try to answer the following questions:
  - ➢ *What do I already know about this topic?*
  - ➢ *What information might the writer present?*

Connect
- Ask yourself, how do the headings relate to one another?
- Write down the key words from the headings that might provide connections between them.

Read the text
- As you read, look for words and phrases that express important information about the headings.
- Mark the text to point out important ideas and details.
- Stop to make sure that you understand the major ideas and supporting details.
- If you do not understand, reread.

Outline
- Using indentions to reflect structure, outline the major ideas and supporting details in the heading segment.
- Write the heading and then try to outline each heading segment without looking back at the text.

Look back
- Now, look back at the text and check the accuracy of the major ideas and details you wrote.
- Correct any inaccurate information in your outline.
- If you marked the text as you read, use this information to help you verify the accuracy of your outline.

FIGURE 4.2. Example of a wall chart for SCROL.

Stage 3: Modeling the Strategy

Modeling the strategy is one of the most critical stages of strategy instruction. This is where the student is exposed to the thought processes of an expert learner. Through repeated exposure and practice, students gain metacognitive knowledge of the strategy, which allows them to profit maximally from using it. In our example, we use a wall chart (see Figure 4.2) to serve as a visual aid and help guide the modeling process. Cue cards or handouts matching the wall chart can also provide students with their own personal reminder of the strategy steps. During the modeling process the teacher uses a "think-aloud" to demonstrate the use of the strategy and expose students to the thought processes of a skilled learner. The purpose of this is to instill metacognitive knowledge of the strategy. A think-aloud can be done using an outline of important points. Think-alouds are not easy for some teachers who are just beginning to use strategy instruction. Many teachers may find it helpful to make a detailed outline, or even write out their complete think-aloud at first. Writing out a think-aloud can help teachers organize their ideas, and can also help them to remember the think-aloud. Here is an example of a think-aloud for the SCROL strategy using a science text about ears and how our ears work.

"OK. What is it I have to do? I need to read this article about 'How You Hear.' To be a more effective reader I can use the SCROL strategy. Just to make sure I remember all the steps I will use the wall chart or my cue card to help me. First is S. That stands for 'Survey the headings and subheadings.' That is simple enough; I can do that. Let's see. . . . How do I identify the headings? Well, headings are usually in bold and at the beginning of a section. I knew that because most of our textbooks are broken up that way. OK, while I am looking at the headings and subheadings I need to ask myself a couple of questions: 'What do I already know about this topic?' and 'What information might the writer present?'

"OK, the first heading is 'The Outer Ear.' I just watched a show on *Discovery* about the way our ears work . . . cool. I bet that is what this is about. I know that there are a couple different parts of the ear. How do I know that? I know that because that's what the show explained. The outer ear is one of those parts. OK, the subheading under that is 'The Middle Ear.' Yeah, that's right—outer ear, middle ear . . . what is the other one? I can't remember, but I do remember that the middle ear has some bones in it; they have funny names. I bet the next heading will tell me what the other part of the ear is. Let's see, 'The Inner Ear.' . . . Yep, that's it. I remember the inner ear helps us with balance. The last heading is . . . 'Keeping Your Balance.' Look at that, I was right. Cool, I already know a lot about this. If I keep using the strategy this will be a piece of cake.

"What is the next step? S . . . C. C stands for 'Connect.' I need to ask myself how these headings relate to one another and write down the key words from the headings that might provide connections between them. All right, well, they are all about the ear. I think I should probably write down the title first since that's what the whole article is about . . . 'How do you Hear?' Then I think probably, 'Outer,' 'Middle,' 'Inner,' and 'Balance,' since those are the other major headings, and they all have to do with the ear, and how we hear. All right, what is next? *S* . . . *C* . . . *R*. *R* is for 'Read the text.' This is the part that I used to start with. OK, as I read I need to remember to look for words and phrases that express important information about the headings. The strategy says to mark the text—usually in my textbook I can't, but my teacher said I could this time because this is just a photocopy and it's mine to keep.

"Let see. I also need to stop every once in a while to make sure that I understand the major ideas and supporting details. If I don't understand then I need to reread. First paragraph—[Reads the paragraph.]—I will mark that ears are organs, I think that is important, and ears collect sound waves and change them into signals that our brain can understand. I would mark that the ear is made up of three different parts, but I already know that. I already have it written down. Second paragraph—[Reads the paragraph.]—I will mark 'ear flap,' 'ear canal,' 'ear drum,' and 'membrane' because they seem to be important terms. I know that because they are defined and explained. This whole paragraph is important.

[Teacher repeats the process with remaining paragraphs.]

"OK. Where am I now? Step 4 is *O*, which stands for 'Outline.' I know how to outline; we went over this. If I need to I can use the wall chart as an example. My outline needs to include headings, major ideas, and supporting details. When I am writing my headings I should try and outline them without looking back at the text. If I can remember it now I will have a much better chance at remembering it later. Let see, my first heading is the title—'How do you hear?'—I remember that the ear is an organ made up of three different parts, listed below. The ear converts sound vibrations to signals that the brain can understand. Outer—the outer ear has an ear flap and ear canal. Middle—the eardrum is made up of a sheet of skin, and three bones: the hammer, anvil, and stirrup. The stirrup vibrates the oval membrane. Inner—the cochlea looks like a snail and has fluid and tiny hairs that vibrate when the oval window vibrates and that sends signals to the brain; then there is the vestibule and semicircular canals. Balance—the semicircular canals are filled with fluid and hairs that move with the movements of the head and send messages to our brain and help us balance. The vestibule has two sacs filled with fluid and chalky stuff that is pulled down by gravity and lets our brain know what position our body is in. The last step—I am almost finished!—*L*. *L* stands for 'Look back.' Now I need to check my memory, and look back to see if what I outlined was accurate. If I did write down something wrong, now is the time to change it. Since I marked my text this should be easy. Let's see. . . . Wow, I really remembered well. I worded some things differently, but I have the same information. YIPPEE!!!!"

Stage 4: Memorizing the Strategy

In this stage students begin committing the steps of the strategy to memory. Memorization can continue into Stage 5. Memorizing the strategy steps is crucial. The idea is to reduce the demands on working memory. Teachers need to plan and prepare activities and monitor their effectiveness. For example, planning for the class to make their own cue cards would be a way to get students actively engaged with the strategy steps. Note that in this case the "SCROL" is a mnemonic that can help memorization.

Memorization Activities

Reciting the SCROL Steps with a Partner. Students will be paired up and recite the stages with a partner, explaining what needs to be done at each stage. Students use the mnemonic chart to check answers. A student who struggles will be matched with a peer who can help with memorization of the strategy.

Making Cue Cards. Students will make their own cue cards with the strategy steps on them. The cue card will have the mnemonic SCROL on it, and the major parts of the strategy, as well as the prompting questions. Students will be able to use these to ensure that all steps of the strategy are completed. They will also be able to use the cards for classes in various content areas to assist them with their reading comprehension.

Memory Circle. Students will be asked to form a circle around one person. The person in the middle calls out letters in the mnemonic, SCROL, and points to someone. That person has 5 seconds to accurately state what the letter stands for. If the student chosen doesn't get done within the 5 seconds then he or she goes to the middle.

Besides the various structured activities, students will be prompted during various times of the day to recite different steps in the SCROL strategy. Students need to understand the significance of memorizing the strategy and should be exposed to it as much as possible.

Stage 5: Supporting the Strategy

In this stage, the teacher and students work together and practice using the strategy until the students are able to perform the strategy fluently and independently. This is a critical part of the strategy instruction process; students need to be given adequate time and support to master the strategy. Just as a scaffolding around a building is gradually removed when the building is strong enough to stand on its own, the teacher gradually transfers strategy performance to student. There are two major pitfall for teachers at this stage. First, teachers may confuse memorization of the strategy steps (from Stage 4) with facility in the use of a strategy. This is analogous to expecting someone who can name the parts of an airplane to be able to fly one. Second, teachers may be under pressure to "cover ground" and get through the curriculum. Thus, they may be tempted to end this stage as soon as students begin to demonstrate some success. This is a mistake, because students need extensive practice before they *master* the use of a strategy. Unless the strategy is taught to mastery, students are unlikely to maintain its use. We provide examples of how a strategy can be supported through content, task, and material scaffolding.

Content Scaffolding

Students will be given short passages to practice the strategy. The texts will be relevant to the curriculum being introduced. The teacher and students will then go over the passage using the SCROL strategy. The teacher will direct the process, and the students will provide answers to teacher-directed questions (e.g., "What are some headings and subheadings?" "What do you think they are talking about here?" "Are there any keywords that provide connections between them?").

Material Scaffolding

Students will be provided with mnemonic prompt cards to be taken to various content-area classes with them. Initially, they will list the steps of the strategy and describe what to do at each step. Over time these cards will provide less direction, first fading the descriptions, and eventually fading the mnemonic and steps altogether. At this point students should have reached mastery of the strategy and be able to work independently.

Task Scaffolding

During collaborative practice the teacher will prompt students to name the step that should be performed, and then the teacher will describe the step and model its use. In subsequent lessons the teacher will ask the student to name all the steps in the SCROL strategy and describe the step to be performed, and then the teacher will model the step. Finally, the student will name, describe, and model the steps of the SCROL strategy.

The students will set individual goals with the teacher for reaching mastery of the strategy. These goals will help guide them to independent performance. If students are having difficulty reaching their goal, it may be necessary to reassess the situation. Reteaching the strategy or clarifying uncertainties may be necessary. In other cases, readjusting the goal may be in order for the student to be successful.

Students need to show mastery of the strategy steps, as well as the ability to use the strategy with text. Each student needs to be able to demonstrate the use of the strategy by doing his or her own think-aloud. When students have successfully demonstrated their use of the strategy they are ready to move on to independent practice.

Stage 6: Independent Performance

During this final stage, students will be given a variety of texts along with their content-specific textbooks. They will be required to use the strategy and turn in their notes for teacher review. The teacher's role has now changed; the main focus of the teacher is to monitor whether the students are using the strategy correctly and consistently, and to evaluate their performance. The teacher will intervene only when students need clarification or reteaching if their performance is declining. Remember that evaluation of students' performance is crucial. The goal of strategy instruction is that students' academic performance should improve. Evaluations do not need be complicated; they can be as simple as grades. The important thing is to be clear that academic performance is improving. More involved forms of evaluation, such as portfolios, may provide more diagnostic information as well as academic improvement. Portfolios are a good way to see trends in students' performance, and determine any areas of deficit.

Students may modify or personalize the strategy for their own use. This is fine as long as they are still successful. Students may also use the strategy more automatically, making it appear as if they skipped steps or altered the strategy. Remember that at this point what matters is that the students can be successful at reading the given text, taking accurate notes, and recalling important information. If modifications to the strategy make the strategy less useful, or inappropriate, then reteaching of the strategy is in order. Additionally, even when students are initially successful, it will be helpful to give booster sessions over time.

UNSTRUCTURED STRATEGY EXAMPLE

The Story Grammar strategy is an example of an unstructured strategy. The Story Grammar strategy is a beginning reading comprehension strategy that provides students with a plan for identifying important story information by asking themselves the five *w* and *h* questions (*who, what, when, where,* and *how*). The Story Grammar strategy is unstructured because procedural information is left out (i.e., exactly what steps the students will perform to use the strategy). This sample implementation plan provides an example of how teachers can create a structure for a strategy. This example will focus primarily on creating a structure.

Stage 1: Developing and Activating Background Knowledge

The process for doing this is identical to the previous example. An example of a task breakdown is provided in Table 4.2. Assessment of skills can either be formal or informal, depending on the skills and the students. This is left up to the teacher's discretion. An example of an informal survey for the Story Grammar strategy is provided in Figure 4.3.

Stage 2: Discussing the Strategy

To explain the steps of the strategy, teachers will have to develop procedures prior to this stage. There are no hard and fast rules for creating a structure for a strategy. The most straightforward way to do this is to practice using the strategy yourself. In this

TABLE 4.2. Example of Task Breakdown for the Story Grammar Strategy

Strategy	Skills
Basic reading skills	Ability to read content material with sufficient fluency
	Knowledge of and ability to identify story components
	Ability to check for understanding
	Ability to recall information that has been read
Who is the main character?	Knowledge of story characters and how they are sometimes presented in texts
Where and when did the story take place?	Knowledge of story setting
What did the main character do?	Knowledge of story actions
How did the main character feel?	Knowledge of emotions and how they are presented in text
How did the story end?	Knowledge of story endings/resolutions

example use the strategy with a simple narrative text. While using the strategy keep in mind how students will keep track of the story information. Identify any useful cues or prompts. Then create a series of steps to help guide the use of the strategy. Remember to keep things *as simple and practical* as possible. Strategies that are cumbersome are unlikely to be accepted by students. Teachers also will need to determine how they want the students to use the strategy. For example, the Story Grammar strategy requires students to answer questions while they read text. This can be distracting for some students and interfere with comprehension. If students are asked to stop while reading text and write down answers this may be enough of a distraction to prevent them from maintaining comprehension. We have chosen to structure the Story Grammar strategy to avoid this. Five steps have been developed to structure the strategy (Figure 4.4). This process is further illustrated during modeling of the strategy.

Stage 3: Modeling the Strategy

Two wall charts will serve as guides during the modeling process (Figure 4.4 and 4.5). Cue cards that mirror the wall charts will also be provided so that each student will have his or her own personal reminder of the strategy prompts. Students will also be given graphic organizers to answer the questions once they are done reading the story (Figure 4.6). A sample script follows:

> "OK. What is it I have to do? I need to read this book, *Arthur Meets the President*. To be a more effective reader I can use my Story Grammar strategy. Just to make sure I remember all of the story part questions I will use the wall chart

Name: _____ Date: _____

1 = Strongly agree   2 = Agree   3 = Not sure   4 = Disagree   5 = Strongly disagree .

1. I understand and am able to answer "wh" questions.

        1   2   3   4   5

2. I am able to read and understand narrative texts.

        1   2   3   4   5

3. I can pick out characters and identify the main character in stories.

        1   2   3   4   5

4. I can describe/pick out settings (time and place) of stories.

        1   2   3   4   5

5. I understand where a story ends and how it is finalized.

        1   2   3   4   5

6. I can understand and describe character emotions/feelings from text that I read.

        1   2   3   4   5

7. I can understand and describe the main characters' actions.

        1   2   3   4   5

8. I am able to identify key words or phrases as they relate to the topic.

        1   2   3   4   5

9. I know if I understand what I have read or not.

        1   2   3   4   5

10. I am able to recall information that I have read.

        1   2   3   4   5

11. I am able to put my thoughts about text that I read into writing.

        1   2   3   4   5

FIGURE 4.3. Sample survey for Story Grammar.

Step 1: *Read your Story Grammar questions*
- This reminds you what information you are looking for.

Step 2: *Read the story* and *mark information with the color-coded sticky tabs.*
- Mark the text that answers the Story Grammar questions.
- Use your cue card or wall chart for the color codes (Figure 4.5).
- Remember you may have more than one answer for some of the questions.
- Mark everything that you think is appropriate.

Step 3: *Look back at the tabs and decide if what you have marked answers the Story Grammar question.*

Step 4: *Fill in your Story Grammar graphic organizer (Figure 4.6)*
- Use the information that you have marked.
- The colors of the sticky tabs match the colors of the graphic organizer.

Step 5: *Read over the Story Grammar graphic organizer and decide if it accurately describes the story.*

FIGURE 4.4. Story Grammar steps.

or my cue card to help me. Let's see, Step 1 was to first review the questions. That will help me remember. Who is the main character? Where and when did the story take place? What did the main character do? How did the story end? How did the main character feel? OK, I can do this!

"Step 2 is to read the text and mark it with my sticky tabs. I will start reading and keep referring back to my prompt card to make sure I am on track. [Reads page 1] Hmm . . . a few characters were mentioned, but from what I already know about reading other books like this one, and by reading the title, I think Arthur is the main character. I will put a blue sticky tab by his name because I want to remind myself that he is the main character and on my cue card the main character question is in blue. I'm sure Arthur is the main character, he always is. OK, that was easy, I can do this!

"What are the next questions? When and where did the story take place? What did the main character do? Well, from what I know now the story takes

Who is the main character?

Where and when did the story take place?

What did the main character do?

How did the story end?

How did the main character feel?

FIGURE 4.5. Story Grammar questions.

Name _____ Date _____

Title _____

Author _____

Who is the main character?

↓

When and where did the story take place?

←————————→

What did the main character do?

↓

How did the main character feel?

↓

How did the story end?

FIGURE 4.6. Story Grammar Organizer.

place at Arthur's school, in his classroom. I'm not sure if this is the main set-ting in the book, but I will put a red sticky tab by that and come back to it after I have read some more. I put a red sticky tab there because my wall chart shows the where and when question in red. I'm not sure what he did. I better read on to find out. [Reads page 2] Hmm . . . . . . I was right, right now the story is taking place in Arthur's classroom, but I'm still not sure if that is the main setting of the story, and it really doesn't say when it took place. I do know that it is during the school year, but I don't know exactly what day it is, or what time of the day it is. This isn't very specific, but I know it is a time and that answers the 'when' question. There really isn't a place for me to put my sticky note, so I will just jot that down on my story grammar organizer right here where it says 'when.'

"OK, the other question that I wasn't sure about was the 'what.' I now know that Arthur is writing a paper about 'How I Can Help Make America Great.' I'm going to put a pink sticky note by that because that's the color of my 'what' question. I better keep reading.

"[Reads pages 3 and 4.] Wow, this is getting exciting! The story is still tak-ing place at school. I want to keep reading. [Reads pages 5 and 6.] Wow, Arthur won! His class is going to Washington, DC, to the White House. That's it; that is the setting, which really makes sense, since the title of the book is *Arthur Meets the President*, and I know that the president lives in the White House, which is in Washington, DC. I am going to mark that with a red sticky tab because that is a place and that fits my 'Where' question.

"This is easy, I just need to read on, keeping in mind the last two ques-tions, and make sure I was right about the action and setting. What are the last two questions again, Hmm . . . I know, How did the story end? How did the main character feel? OK, I should keep reading. [Reads pages 7 and 8.] Hmm . . . here is another action. Arthur needs to memorize the paper that he wrote so that he can recite it in front of the President. I think there is more than one action. Really, there is a kind of a chain of actions and reactions. I will mark them with pink sticky tabs. Let's see, first Arthur wrote a paper on how to make the world a better place, I already marked that, then he won the writing contest, I will mark that, then he had to memorize his paper to recite it for the President, I will mark that also. Ugh, this is getting long, I have used a lot of sticky tabs. But I know this will help me later when I need to answer my com-prehension questions.

"I should keep reading, to see what else happens. [Reads pages 9, 10, and 11.] Another thing—Arthur was nervous and worried, really, that is how he felt. I think I should mark that with a green sticky tab. I know this is a feeling that Arthur had because it says that he was too worried to sleep.

"I better keep reading and see what happens next. [Reads pages 12 through 20.] There was some more action. Arthur, his class, and his family flew to Washington, Arthur practiced reciting his paper, and the class toured Washington, DC. I will mark all of those with pink sticky tabs. There was also more in there about how he felt. It said that he was very nervous about reciting his paper. That's the same feelings he had before. I will mark that again with a green sticky tab.

[Teacher repeats the process.]

"Oh, I am already to the last page, this is how the story ends. Arthur then recited his paper and felt really good, because his whole paper was about helping others. D. W. helped him, and he was happy because of it. I will mark that with a purple sticky tab because the story-ending question on my Story Grammar strategy chart is in purple.

"Wow, I'm all done reading; that was easy! OK, I finished Step 2, now on to Step 3. Hmm . . . what is Step 3? Oh yeah, I need to decide if what I have marked answers the Story Grammar questions. Let's see . . . yes, I think it does!

"OK, what's next? Step 4, what was Step 4? I need to fill in my graphic organizer. I can go back and fill in all of my questions on my Story Grammar organizer by looking at what I marked with my sticky tabs. They should be easy to find.

"I will start with 'who' I know those are the blue tabs . . . Then I will go to the red ones because I know those are the 'where' and 'when' or setting ones. . . . Next I will do the pink ones, which are the action ones, or the 'what' question. . . . Then I will go to my purple tab and write down how it ended. . . . Last, I will look at my green tabs and write down how he felt.

"OK, Step 5: I need to read what I have written down, and see if I've answered all the questions correctly. . . . Yes, I think I did answer all the questions right. Yippee, I'm done! That really did help. I was able to answer all of my Story Grammar questions."

Stage 4: Memorizing the Strategy

Memorization activities for an unstructured strategy are similar to those for a structured strategy. The activities for the Story Grammar strategy could be the same as those for the SCROL strategy. Students will simply follow the structure or steps that the teacher has established. Following our example, students would need to state the color of sticky tab that they would use to mark their text.

Stage 5: Supporting the Strategy

Scaffolding procedures in this stage are similar to those described in the SCROL implementation plan. For the Story Grammar strategy we have added a new type of activity. We have included a graph for students to monitor their progress (Figure 4.7). Students will be given a sheet of Story Grammar Rockets and instructed to color in a square on one rocket for every box in the Story Grammar Organizer that they have filled in correctly. This graph serves two purposes. First, it serves to help motivate students. Students can see their progress by how many parts of the rocket they have colored in.

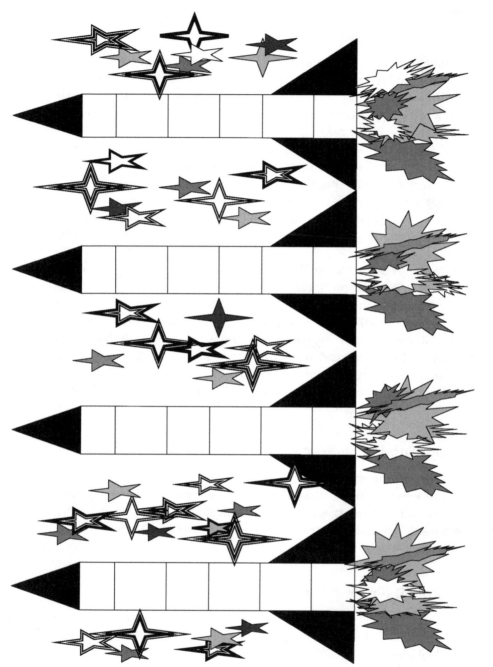

FIGURE 4.7. Story Grammar Rockets.

Additionally, students are allowed to "bust out" their rocket if they have more than one correct answer for each question.

The second function is self-regulation. The rockets help students monitor how many of the Story Grammar questions they have answered. Initially, the teacher needs to make the determination whether or not the Story Grammar Organizer is filled in correctly and tell students how many squares in the rocket they can color in. After students have shown that they can use the Rockets independently, they will be allowed to work with a partner or a small group assigned by the teacher to check their answers. After students have shown the ability to work effectively with their peers on performance assessment they can be allowed to work independently. The eventual goal is that students will be able to check the accuracy of their performance independently. Note that as with any other activity, the use of the Rockets needs to be modeled.

> "OK, I have my Story Grammar Organizer all filled out and the teacher has put stars by the boxes that I have filled in correctly. Now I can use these cool rockets to graph my progress. Let's see . . . 'Who is the main character?' Right, that's Arthur. I know that because I got a star. I get to color in the bottom box of the rocket. I also got a star by the second question, 'When and where did the story take place?' because I got that one right too. I can color in another box on my rocket. Right here, I will color in this one, above the last one I colored. It looks like I also got 'What did the main character do?' right, because there is a star by that one too. I will color in another box. My rocket is half filled in; this is cool! Uh-oh, it looks like I missed something on 'How did the main character feel?' because there is no star by that box. I will need to go back and look at the story again to find the right answer. That way I know what to do next time to have a full rocket. I'm up to the last question, 'How did the story end?' I know I got that one right, because I see another star next to my box. I get to fill in another box. Wow, look at that—I almost have a full rocket. That is so cool! I need to be really careful when I answer my questions so I can have a full colored-in rocket. Kids who have full colored-in rockets get to put them up on the wall. I want to get mine put up too!"

Initially teachers will need to monitor students' use of the self-regulation component. This is to ensure that students are consistent in their use of the rockets, and to make sure they do not have any difficulty filling them in. If this is the case, prompting, modeling, or reteaching may be necessary. When the students demonstrate fluent and independent use of the strategy multiple times they are ready to move on to independent practice.

Stage 6: Independent Performance

Teaching for this stage can follow procedures similar to those for the SCROL strategy. Variations on strategy use should be noted. Evaluation should focus on how well the student can answer questions pertaining to story components (e.g., "Who were three characters in the story?").

FINAL THOUGHTS

Once teachers have an SRSD plan completed, it can be used many times, allowing improvements and tailoring to the needs of individual students. Moreover, after teachers have done one strategy, it is much easier to do a different strategy because they have gained experience in the process. In closing we would stress:

- When teachers design SRSD instructional plans, their job is to fit the instruction to the student, rather than vice versa. Strategy instruction is tailored to the student, not "off the rack."
- Don't rush the modeling or support stages. It's far better to overteach a strategy than to underteach. This is especially true for students with LD. Students need to develop *facility* with the strategy, and understand where, how, and why it should be used. If teachers don't spend enough time at this stage, then all their work may go for nothing.
- If one goal of strategy instruction is for students to generalize strategy use across academic areas (e.g., the student might use the SCROL strategy for science and history), then collaboration between teachers is necessary. Students with LD typically need support to generalize strategy use. Teachers must actively program for generalization with students and all other teachers. Prompts or reminders to help the student remember to use the strategy will often be necessary.

REFERENCES

Grant, R. (1993). Strategic training for using text headings to improve students' processing of content. *Journal of Reading, 36*, 482–488.

Harris, K. R. & Pressley, M. (1991). The nature of cognitive strategy instruction: Interactive strategy construction. *Exceptional Children, 57*, 392–403.

Short, E. J., & Ryan, E. B. (1984). Metacognitive differences between skilled and less skilled readers: Remediating deficits through story grammar and attribution training. *Journal of Educational Psychology, 76*, 225–235.

CHAPTER 5

Self-Regulation Strategies

Self-regulation has long been important in research and intervention in LD (Graham, Harris, & Reid, 1992). Self-regulation strategies are important for struggling learners because there is good reason to believe that the academic difficulties of these students is due, at least in part, to problems in self-regulation of organized, strategic behaviors (Graham et al., 1992). Recall that in previous chapters we stressed that often problems of students with LD were due to lack of effective strategies as opposed to deficits in specific abilities. The same perspective holds for the area of self-regulation. There are a number of self-regulation strategies that can be effectively taught to students. Four of the major ones are self-monitoring (also called self-assessment or self-recording), self-instruction, goal setting, and self-reinforcement. All of these aspects of self-regulation have been thoroughly researched and classroom tested and have demonstrated efficacy for students with LD (Mace, Belfiore, & Hutchinson, 2001; Reid, 1996, 1999). Though we discuss each separately, we stress that these self-regulation procedures are commonly and effectively combined in practice. The strategies we introduce can be extremely useful as stand-alone interventions. However, self-regulation strategies become even more powerful when used in conjunction with effective strategies. Recall that the "SR" in SRSD stands for self-regulated. One of the major goals of the SRSD model is *to develop self-regulated learners*. To do this, *effective strategies should be combined with appropriate self-regulation strategies*.

We discuss the four major self-regulation techniques listed above. We focus primarily on self-monitoring and self-instruction, because they are both powerful and are the ones most commonly used. For each strategy, we provide background information, discuss its uses, and provide a step-by-step guide to implementing it.

71

SELF-MONITORING

Self-monitoring is one of the most thoroughly researched self-regulation strategies (Reid, 1996). It was originally developed as an assessment procedure designed to allow psychologists to gather information from patients in order to evaluate effectiveness of interventions (Kanfer, 1977). However, much to their surprise the psychologists discovered the act of self-monitoring a behavior caused changes in the behavior. This led to the use of self-monitoring as an intervention. Self-monitoring occurs when an individual self-assesses whether or not a target behavior has occurred and then self-records the occurrence, frequency, and duration of the target behavior (Nelson & Hayes, 1981). For example, in one of the earliest self-monitoring studies, researchers taught a student to periodically ask herself whether or not she was working or paying attention in class and to then self-record the results (Broden, Hall, & Mitts, 1971). In contrast to behavioral approaches, self-monitoring usually does not involve the use of external reinforcers; however, in some cases, self-monitoring has been effectively combined with external reinforcers (e.g., Barkley, Copeland, & Sivage, 1980).

Self-monitoring can be used with a broad variety of behaviors. For our purposes, we focus on areas that most directly concern strategy instruction: on-task behavior and academic responding. There are two major types of self-monitoring interventions: self-monitoring of attention (SMA) and self-monitoring of performance (SMP). In SMA, students self-assess whether or not they are paying attention when cued (typically, cuing is performed through the use of randomly presented taped tones) and self-record the results. In SMP, students self-assess some aspect of academic performance (e.g., number of correct practices) and self-record the results (Reid, 1993; Reid & Harris, 1989). There are many types of SMP. For example, students may self-assess their productivity (e.g., the number of math problems they attempted), accuracy (e.g., the number of math problems completed correctly), or strategy use (e.g., whether or not steps in a strategy were performed). Self-assessments may occur during a work session (sometimes using taped tones as cues) or after a work session (without cueing). SMP also typically involves the use of charting or graphing.

Teaching a student to use self-monitoring is straightforward. Reid (1993) outlined the following steps:

Step 1: Selecting a Target Variable

The teacher must first determine what behavior will be self-monitored. Though the behavior targeted for change and the behavior that is self-monitored are often the same, they are not necessarily *always* the same. Thus a student might, for example, self-monitor the amount of on-task behavior, even though the teacher was actually concerned with increasing the amount of seatwork that was completed. A good target behavior is Specific, Observable, Appropriate, and a Personal Match.

Specific

The teacher must be able to *exactly* define the target behavior. Because the self-monitoring process begins with self-assessment, students must be able to easily and accurately determine whether or not a target behavior has occurred. Target behaviors such as "better reading" or "being good" are not appropriate; instead, use behaviors such as "number of math problems correct" or "listening to the teacher," which are easily understandable and readily assessed by the student. Note that a number of behaviors can be targeted (e.g., being in my seat, having my work,) so long as they are all well specified.

Observable

Students must be *aware* of the occurrence of a target behavior. Students who engage in a behavior impulsively and/or unconsciously may be unaware of the occurrence of the behavior and thus be unable to self-assess the behavior. For example, students who impulsively talk out of turn may be unaware of the behavior. The lack of awareness would preclude effective self-monitoring. In the case of students who talked out of turn the teacher might ask them to self-monitor the number of times they raised their hand to speak as this might be more observable for the student.

Appropriate

When selecting a target behavior, teachers should consider two factors: setting and task. It is important to be sensitive to the environment where self-monitoring will take place. Although self-monitoring has been used effectively in whole-class, small-group, and individualized settings (Reid, 1996), it is advisable to try to visualize possible problems that could arise. Avoid procedures that could cause a student to be embarrassed or that could disturb other students. For example if SMA, which typically uses taped tones to cue students to self-assess, were used in a group setting and resulted in a student feeling as though she or he were singled out, it would be inappropriate. The fit between self-monitoring procedures and academic tasks should also be closely examined. In some cases, self-monitoring procedures can be intrusive and can detract from successful performance (Reid, 1996). For example, using SMA procedures that require students to self-assess and self-record frequently would probably be inappropriate during a small-group reading lesson. There are no established guidelines to help select the most appropriate target behavior for any given combination of environment and task. One practical method might be to simply expose students to a variety of target behaviors and allow them to choose the behavior they felt was most appropriate or effective for them to self-monitor. Research has shown (Maag, Reid, & DiGangi, 1993) that students are capable of selecting the most effective target behavior when given a choice between several alternatives.

Personal Match

Self-monitoring may not appropriate for students who are very young or are immature because students must be able to understand the connection between self-monitoring procedures and the target behavior (Graham et al., 1992). If this connection is not made in the mind of the student, reactivity will not occur. For example, imagine a student who self-monitored the number of arithmetic problems completed and graphed the results. For self-monitoring to be effective the student must be able to relate the graph to the work completed (i.e., be able to comprehend that the graph represented the amount of work completed). Unless the student can meaningfully connect the work done with the graphic portrayal of results, reactivity (in the form of increased number of problems worked) will probably not occur. Teachers should also be sensitive to developmental factors. Students' developmental level may affect the perceived value or salience of target behaviors. Although developmental effects on self-monitoring are only beginning to be addressed, there is evidence of differential effectiveness of target variables across age levels (Maag et al., 1993).

Step 2: Collecting Baseline Data

At this stage, baseline data should be gathered and recorded. This should not be a strenuous or time-consuming procedure. The teacher should first define when and where the self-monitoring intervention will take place. Next he or she should determine how to collect data. For example, if the intervention was to be directed at out-of-seat behavior the teacher would simply count the number of times the student was out of his or her seat during the period of time when the intervention occurred. In the case of interventions directed to academic accuracy or productivity, baseline data collection could be as simple as collecting work samples. Collecting baseline data is important for two reasons. First, it provides an objective benchmark to evaluate the success of the intervention. Second, collecting objective data on the extent of the problem may obviate the need for an intervention! Practitioners sometimes find that the problem was not nearly as serious as they believed. Or they may discover that they have targeted the wrong behavior.

Step 3: Obtaining Willing Cooperation

The "self" is the active ingredient in self-monitoring. This means that the teacher will need active and willing cooperation on the part of the student. Teachers should schedule a conference with the student and address problem areas frankly. Discuss the benefits to the student (e.g., staying in your seat means you don't lose recess; doing all your arithmetic problems means you'll do better on the test). Don't promise the moon; students are unlikely to respond to inflated or exaggerated claims (Reid & Harris, 1989). Be optimistic, but realistic; describe self-monitoring as "something that helped a lot of students like you with the same kind problem." If students are unsure, try using a contingency contract. This means that if students commit to trying self-monitoring for a specified period of time they will receive a reinforcer. Typically the improvements will sell themselves very quickly. After you have enlisted cooperation, establish when and where self-monitoring will be used.

Step 4: Instruction in Self-Monitoring Procedures

During this stage teachers are not only teaching skills, they are also "selling" the self-monitoring. It is important to go through each step in succession; however, the time spent at any one step may vary widely depending on the student and the choice of target variables. Students should master each step in turn before proceeding to the next step. Note that while there are a number of steps, students typically can learn to self-monitor quickly and easily with total training time typically well under one hour.

Defining the Target Behavior

Explain to the student exactly what constitutes the target behavior. For most types of self-monitoring this is quite simple. For example in SMP defining the target variable may involve little more than telling the student to count correct answers. For other types of self-monitoring, defining the target variable may be more complex. For example in SMA interventions the student must understand what it means to "pay attention." Here the teacher must teach the student a list of specific behaviors that constitute "paying attention," such as: looking at the teacher or your work, writing answers, listening to the teacher, or asking a question. Remember that students must understand the target behavior before proceeding.

Discrimination of Target Behavior

The student should be able to discriminate between the target behavior and other behaviors. One simple way to teach discrimination is for the teacher to model examples and nonexamples of the target behavior and ask the student to determine if they are or are not examples of the target behavior. This whole process may take only a few minutes, but it provides reinforcement of the knowledge of the target variable gained in the previous stage and also provides evaluative feedback for the teacher. Note that for some types of self-monitoring this would not be necessary (e.g., self-monitoring the number of practice items completed).

Explanation of Self-Monitoring Procedures

In this stage the teacher explains where and when self-monitoring will be used and teaches the actual procedures used in self-monitoring. First, the teacher directly explains the procedures involved in self-assessing and self-recording. Next, the teacher models proper performance while verbalizing the steps. The student is then asked to verbalize the steps as the teacher performs them. Following this, the student is asked to model and verbalize the procedures. It is extremely important that the student attain a high degree of mastery (Mace & Kratochwill, 1988). Self-monitoring procedures should be minimally distracting for the student; thus a high degree of automaticity is necessary for effectiveness. After the student is able to demonstrate the procedures correctly, provide a brief period of guided practice. This provides structured experience for the student and also allows the teacher to assess mastery. Again, this entire procedure can be done very quickly.

Independent Performance

At this stage, the student is ready to use self-monitoring. Before the student begins self-monitoring for the first time, it is wise to prompt the student to use the procedures and/or to check for knowledge of the target variable. During the first few sessions, make sure that the self-monitoring procedures are used consistently and properly. If any problems are evident, reteach the procedures. Remember that self-monitoring procedures must be used properly and consistently if self-monitoring is to be effective. If a student appears to be having problems there are several options available to the teacher. In some instances, additional training may be indicated. For less serious problems simply providing students with prompts, such as reminders of what constitutes the target behavior or cues to self-assess or self-record, may be all that is required. However, if students consistently experience problems it may be best to rethink whether self-monitoring is appropriate.

Evaluation

After the student has begun to self-monitor independently, the teacher should continue to collect data in order to assess the effectiveness of the intervention. If the intervention is effective, research suggests that improvement should occur rapidly. The teacher should also conduct periodic probes to assess maintenance. In practice, students have been able to maintain increased performance levels for considerable periods of time in the classroom (e.g., Harris, 1986). However, if the student's performance begins to deteriorate, additional "booster sessions" in self-monitoring procedures may be necessary.

Frequently Asked Questions

There are a number of questions that teachers new to self-monitoring regularly ask. In this section we will address some of the FAQs.

How Accurate Is Students' Self-Recording?

Many teachers are concerned about the accuracy of students self-recording. Or, to be more precise, about what to do if students willfully misrepresent their behavior when self-recording (i.e., they cheat). Accuracy of self-recording does not seem to be a critical factor in behavior change (Hallahan & Sapona, 1983). In fact, it is common to see meaningful change when self-recording accuracy was quite low (e.g., Broden et al., 1971; Reid & Harris, 1993). Remember that the goal is improvement of behavior, not accurate self-recording. There is one instance where accuracy is important. This occurs when students are inaccurate because they cannot consistently discriminate the target behavior from other behaviors. If this is a problem retraining is indicated. In this case teachers need to reexplain the target behavior, and provide examples and nonexamples to give the child to practice discriminating the target behavior.

What If Procedures Are Not Followed?

For self-monitoring to be effective, procedures should be used properly and *consistently*. For example, if a teacher was using SMA it would be a good idea to see if the student was self-recording at every cue. Sometimes students need to be reminded to use self-monitoring consistently. One technique that has been used effectively in these situations is to reinforce students for properly and consistently using self-monitoring procedures. For example, Rooney, Hallahan, and Lloyd (1984) reinforced students if their number of self-recorded tallies closely matched the number of taped tones used to cue self-recording (e.g., if there were 18 tones and students had from 16 to 20 tallies they were rewarded). This resulted in students using the procedures more consistently and increased the amount of on-task behavior.

What Are Some Problems with Self-Recording Procedures

Sometimes the procedures used to self-record can pose problems. This is most often the case in SMP interventions, where it is fairly common for some students to exhibit problems accurately counting up work or properly graphing. In situations like this aids such as paper with numbered lines or simplified graphs can be used to overcome problems.

Whom Should I Use Self-Monitoring with?

Remember that self-monitoring does not create new behaviors; it simply alters existing behaviors in terms of frequency, intensity, duration, and so forth. Self-monitoring will not be successful unless students already have the behaviors in question in their repertoire. For example, Reid (1993) noted that if the goal of a self-monitoring intervention was to increase the amount of time a student spent in his or her seat, the student would have to be able to spend at least some time in the seat. Remember that while self-monitoring can be quite effective for academic variables, self-monitoring alone does not produce new learning or academic skills (Reid, 1993). Note also that a student who is totally out of control or is exhibiting severe problems is not a good candidate for self-monitoring.

What Is the "Best" Target Behavior for Self-Monitoring?

At this point in time we can't answer this question. There is no way to predict whether any specific target behavior is the most effective in any given situation. Both SMA and SMP interventions are effective at increasing on-task behavior and academic productivity. There appear to be few if any differences between the two interventions in terms of their effects on on-task behaviors (Lloyd, Bateman, Landrum, & Hallahan, 1989; Reid & Harris, 1993).

How Long Should I Use Self-Monitoring?

Self-monitoring interventions have been used effectively for prolonged periods of time in classroom environments (e.g., Harris, 1986). There does not appear to be an upper limit on the amount of time they can be used effectively. However, for SMA interventions there is an effective procedure to "wean" students from the procedures (Hallahan, Marshall, & Lloyd, 1981). First students are asked to self-assess without self-recording the results. If students' behavior is maintained, the taped cues are eliminated and students are asked to self-assess when they think of it. Self-praise may also be effective during the weaning procedure (Hallahan, Lloyd, Kosiewicz, Kauffman, & Graves, 1979).

SELF-INSTRUCTION

If you've ever watched young children at play you probably noticed that they often talk to themselves. This is termed self-talk or private speech. Private speech is used by students to help self-regulate and guide behavior, and it is a part of the normal developmental process (Harris, 1990). Self-instruction techniques take advantage of the fact that language is often used to self-regulate behavior. Self-instruction interventions involve the use of *induced* self-statements to direct or self-regulate behavior (Graham et al., 1992). Put simply, with self-instructions students quite literally learn to talk themselves through a task or activity. There are two levels of self-instructions: (1) task approach, which is general and appropriate for a wide range of situations, and (2) task specific, which is aimed a particular situation and would not generalize. Both types are useful. Self-instructions can serve many functions. Table 5.1 shows six basic functions of self-instructions identified by Graham et al. (1992).

Self-instruction techniques are both powerful and flexible. They have a well-demonstrated record of effectiveness for students with LD (Swanson, Hoskyn, & Lee,

TABLE 5.1. Examples of Self-Statements Associated with Six Functions of Self-Instruction

Type of self-instruction	Examples
Problem definition—defining the nature and demands of a task	"OK. What do I need to do now?" "What's my next step?"
Focusing attention/planning—attending to task and generating plans	"I need to take my time and concentrate." "What's the best way to do this problem?"
Strategy related—engaging and using a strategy	"I need to remember to use my strategy." "OK, what I need to do is remember my 4 B's strategy."
Self-evaluation—error detection and correction	"I need to check and see how I am doing." "Does this answer make sense?" "Oops, this isn't right. I need to fix it."
Coping—dealing with difficulties/ failures	"I can do this if I keep at it." "This isn't rocket science. I know I can do it." "Take a deep breath and relax."
Self-reinforcement—rewarding oneself	"I did it! Great job!" "I worked hard and I got it right!"

1999). They are also commonly used as a component in strategy-instruction interventions (e.g., Graham & Harris, 1996). Note that self-instructions can also work on motivational processes. Many times teachers will incorporate self-instructions that deal with coping or with continuing a task that is difficult. An example of how this was done in one classroom is included in Figure 5.1, which relates Karen Harris's classic story of "The Little Professor." Error detection and correction are also useful areas for self-instructions.

Teaching students to use self-instructions involves a simple, four-step process (Graham et al., 1992). *Step 1* involves discussing the importance of verbalizations. The teacher explains how what we say to ourselves can help or hurt us. This is very important because students with LD often will exhibit high rates of very negative self-

A puzzle was rigged (it could not be successfully completed) to study the private speech of children with and without learning problems. As expected, the normally achieving children used a number of strategies to try to complete the puzzle, and they produced a sizable amount of relevant, helpful self-speech. The children with learning problems, on the other hand, typically did not approach the task strategically and used irrelevant self-statements, many of which were negative. Examples of children using irrelevant self-statements included one girl who talked at length about what she would do at her Brownies meeting (which wouldn't take place for another 4 days), and a boy who sang a song about taking a trip to Idaho. Negative statements included "I hate puzzles" and "I'm no good at puzzles." Most of the students with LD stopped trying to work the puzzle before ever reaching the rigged piece.

Toward the end of the study, an adorable young man with a crewcut and horn-rimmed glasses, wearing a coat and bow tie, came to work on the puzzle. After explaining the task, the student was asked to complete the puzzle and then went to the other end of the room. Things appeared to be going as they had with the other students with LD. The student seemed to become frustrated quickly. Just when he seemed about to quit, however, he pushed himself back from the table, folded his hands in his lap, took a deep breath, and chanted, "I'm not going to get mad; mad makes me do bad." The "Little Professor" used the same self-instruction many times while working on the puzzle. He was able to fit more pieces and persisted longer than any of the other children with learning problems.

The classroom teacher was not familiar with research or concepts such as self-statements. She simply believed that what we say to ourselves affects what we do. During weekly class meetings the students helped one another identify problem areas and develop self-statements to deal with their problems. The Little Professor had identified getting mad as a problem that had prevented him from doing his best. Together the class had worked out the procedure of pushing back his chair, taking a deep breath, folding his hands, and using the self-statements.

FIGURE 5.1. The Little Professor. From Graham, S., Harris, K. R., & Reid, R. (1992). Developing self-regulated learners. *Focus on Exceptional Children, 24,* 1–16. Copyright 1992 by Love Publishing. Reprinted by permission.

statements (e.g., "I'm stupid; I'll never get this"). The teacher stresses the need to use words to help yourself. In *Step 2* the teacher and student develop meaningful, individualized task-appropriate self-statements together. It's important to remember that self-instruction is not simply parroting back statements provided by the teacher. To reiterate our comment about strategy instruction, self-instruction training is a *dialogue*, not a monologue. If self-instruction is to be successful, then the self-statements must be meaningful to the student. And, the most meaningful statements often are those that the student develops. Note, however, that this does *not* mean that a student should not use an example provided by a teacher. If students like a teacher's example it's perfectly appropriate for them to use it. In *Step 3* the teacher and student model the use of self-statements and discuss how and when they would use them. At this stage it is very useful for the student to see a peer use self-instructions (if possible). Peer examples are extremely powerful motivators. Some teachers actually videotape students who have successfully mastered a self-instruction technique. The videotapes are a motivator for the student and useful as examples when teaching self-instructions to new students. Finally, in *Step 4* the teacher provides opportunities for collaborative practice in the use of self-instructions to perform the task. This would include modeling the self-statements and discussing how and when to use them. The ultimate goal is for students to progress from the use of modeled, overt self-statements (i.e., talking aloud to oneself) to covert, internalized speech (Harris, 1990).

GOAL SETTING

Effective learners are goal-oriented (Winne, 1997), and goal setting is viewed as an important aspect of self-regulation (Bandura, 1986). Goals serve extremely useful functions for learners. Goals serve three major functions (Schunk, 1990):

1. Goals structure effort by providing a target for our efforts (e.g., "I'm going to lose 10 pounds on the diet"). This in turn gives us information on what we need to do to accomplish the goal (e.g., cut down on calories, increase exercise).
2. Goals provide information on progress. To continue the previous example, we could track our weight loss to monitor how close we had come to meeting the goal.
3. Finally, goals serve to motivate performance. Achieving goals serves to reinforce effort. To put it plainly, it feels good to accomplish our goals.

There are three important features of effective goals: specificity, proximity, and difficulty (Bandura, 1988). Specificity refers to how well a goal is defined. Goals that are vague (e.g., "Do your best on the test") are not as effective as those that are well specified (e.g., "Achieve at least 80% correct on the test"). Proximity refers to temporal aspects of goals. Proximal goals can be completed in the near term (e.g., "Copy my spelling words three times by the end of class") and are generally more effective than distal goals, which can only be completed in the far future (e.g., "Learn 100 new spelling words by the end of the year"). Note, however, that it is possible to use a series of proximal goals to accomplish a distal goal. Difficulty refers to how challenging a goal is. Goals that are easily attained do not serve to enhance or maintain effort (Johnson & Graham, 1990). The most effective goals are those that are moderately challenging. That is, those that are neither too easy nor too difficult.

There is also a distinction to make in assessing whether or not a goal is met. Goals may be either absolute (i.e., with a fixed standard such as completing 20 math problems correctly in 6 minutes) or normative (i.e., doing as well as another student on the math problems). There is some evidence that the most appropriate goals for students with LD might be normative, as these types of goals may enhance self-efficacy and motivation (Schunk, 1987). That is, students believe that if Joe Smith can do it then they can do it. However, there are no hard-and-fast rules here. Teachers should pick the standard that best fits the student and the situation. Also remember that monitoring progress is a key to success. Students who see satisfactory progress toward a goal are more likely to sustain effort (Bandura, 1986). Alternatively, a student who does not perceive progress (even though there may indeed be progress) is not likely to sustain effort.

Just as with self-monitoring, goal setting often involves a self-evaluative process that consists of comparing current performance with a goal (Schunk, 2001). This is the source of motivation. Note that for goal setting to affect behavior, goals *must be valued*. If a goal has little or no importance to the student, then it is unlikely to improve performance or maintain motivation or effort. Thus, teachers may need to point out the benefits of accomplishing a goal (e.g., getting homework completed will prevent being grounded and improve social life). Additionally, attributions (the perceived cause of an outcome) must be considered (Schunk, 2001). Students should see that progress toward a goal is the result of their efforts rather than simply luck or factors outside their control (e.g., "The teacher helped me").

Goal setting is a straightforward process. The teacher and student meet and discuss performance in an area (e.g., spelling test results). Together the teacher and student decide on an appropriate goal, determine a timeline for meeting the goal, and establish how progress toward the goal may be monitored. It's best for the teacher to help with setting the goal to ensure that it is realistic and attainable. Many students with LD will set goals that are either much too high or much too easy. As we noted previously goals should be moderately challenging. It is also important for students to be aware of progress toward their goals. This provides them with self-evaluative feedback that increases motivation. Note that students may focus on a distal goal (e.g., "Getting an A in spelling"). This is perfectly understandable. In such cases, the teacher should establish more proximal (and attainable) goals (e.g., "Getting a C on this week's spelling test"). Note also that the teacher needs to establish procedures to help the student attain the goal. For example, to extend the spelling example, the teacher might suggest daily 10-minute spelling practice sessions.

SELF-REINFORCEMENT

Self-reinforcement occurs when an individual identifies a reinforcer and self-awards it when a predetermined criterion is reached or exceeded (e.g., "If I study for 2 hours then

I get to watch *The West Wing*") (Graham et al., 1992). For example, one writer we know will treat himself to a very decadent dessert when he meets his weekly writing goal. This process mirrors the natural developmental process where a child learns that meeting expectations typically results in positive reinforcement (e.g., praise, attention), while the opposite typically results in no response or perhaps a negative response (Mace et al., 2001). As a result of this environmental shaping, students learn to self-reinforce (or self-punish) their own behavior. Implementing self-reinforcement involves a four-step process. First, teachers should determine the standard that must be met for receiving rewards. Standards should be clear and objective. For example, "Getting better at spelling" would not be a good standard; "Getting 80% on my weekly test" would be more appropriate. Second, the teacher should select a reinforcer. If possible, involve the student in this process. This is for strictly pragmatic reasons. Students know what is rewarding to them. Third, determine how students will evaluate their work. For example, the student may self-correct or bring the work to you to check. Finally, if the student met or exceeded the criterion they may award themselves the reinforcer. The reinforcement step does not need to be totally independent. For example, the student could be taught to check with you before self-awarding reinforcement. Self-reinforcement is often combined with other self-regulation techniques. For example, self-reinforcement and goal setting can work very well together since they have so much in common. Self-reinforcement has also been combined with self-monitoring. We should note that the notion that individuals can actually engage in self-reinforcement may be seen by some as counter to a strict behavioral perspective on self-regulation (see Mace et al., 2001, for a detailed critique); regardless, the technique itself is quite effective.

THE CASE FOR SELF-REGULATION

Self-regulation strategies are not only effective but also provide two distinct advantages over other possible choices. First, self-regulation strategies avoid the "hidden curriculum" that is implicit in more behavioral approaches. With self-regulation, students are the agent of change rather than the teacher or another adult figure. The lesson here is one of empowerment—students can independently make changes in their behavior (Graham et al., 1992). For students with learned helplessness and other motivational problems this is an important consideration. Second, and equally important, self-regulation strategies offer a distinct practical advantage over many other approaches. After the initial data collection and instruction the teacher's involvement is minimal, because the child is literally running the intervention. The savings in time can be considerable in contrast to other approaches. For example, self-regulation strategies do not require teachers to take the time to constantly reinforce behaviors or track points earned through token economies; instead teachers are free to perform other instructional duties.

We would stress that although self-regulation strategies are powerful, they are *not a panacea*. No intervention can claim to be 100% effective for every student. Further, as

Reid (1993) noted, it is important for practitioners to realize that to effectively implement self-regulation teachers must follow both the "letter" and the "spirit" of the procedures outlined above. However, with these caveats in mind, we should emphasize that because self-regulation strategies can be easily implemented in the classroom and have a demonstrated track record, educators should strongly consider using self-regulation strategies in their classrooms. Additionally, as we noted earlier, self-regulation strategies are useful in their own right, but they are even more powerful when combined with content-area strategies as a part of the SRSD process.

FINAL THOUGHTS

In closing, we stress that self-regulation does not take place in a vacuum. The environment is a significant factor in self-regulation (e.g., Mace et al., 2001; Schunk, 2001). Changing the environment can enhance or enable self-regulation (e.g., taking a limited amount of cash prevents overspending) (Mace et al., 2001). Students also may self-regulate their environment to help themselves complete tasks (e.g., finding a place to study that is quiet and free of outside distractions). Providing students with a structured environment and predictable, stable routines is an important prerequisite for self-regulation. Additionally, a stable environment can increase the likelihood of effective self-regulation.

Note also that even in the *best possible* environment students with LD will probably have some problem with self-regulation. In an environment that is disordered or chaotic, successful self-regulation is unlikely to occur. Luckily, there are numerous simple, practical, environmental changes that can enhance self-regulation, such as providing students with folders to serve as organizers for assignments, taping prompts to lockers ("Did you remember to bring your book?"), or using prompt cards that list the steps for a task and serve to cue performance. The major point that teachers need to remember is to attend to both self-regulation strategies and to supportive environments.

REFERENCES

Bandura, A. (1986). *Social foundations of thought and action.* Englewood Cliffs, NJ: Prentice Hall.

Bandura, A. (1988). Self-regulation of motivation and action through goal systems. In V. Hamilton, G. H. Browder, & N. H. Frijda (Eds.), *Cognitive perspectives on emotion and motivation* (pp. 37–61). Dordrecht, The Netherlands: Kluwer Academic.

Barkley, R. A. (1998). *Attention-deficit hyperactivity disorder: A handbook for diagnosis and treatment* (2nd ed.). New York: Guilford Press.

Barkley, R. A., Copeland, A. P., & Sivage, C. (1980). A self-control classroom for hyperactive children. *Journal of Autism and Developmental Disorders, 10,* 75–89.

Broden, M., Hall, R. V., & Mitts, B. (1971). The effects of self-recording on the classroom behavior of two eighth-grade students. *Journal of Applied Behavior Analysis, 4,* 191–199.

DuPaul, G. J., & Stoner, G. (2003). *ADHD in the schools: Assessment and intervention strategies* (2nd ed.). New York: Guilford Press.

Graham, S., & Harris, K. R. (1992). *Helping young writers master the craft: Strategy instruction and self-regulation in the writing process*. Cambridge, MA: Brookline Books.

Graham, S., & Harris, K. R. (1996). Self-regulation and strategy instruction for students who find writing and learning challenging. In C. M. Levy & S. Randall (Eds.), *The science of writing: Theories, methods, individual differences, and applications* (pp. 347–360). Mahwah, NJ: Erlbaum.

Graham, S., Harris, K. R., & Reid, R. (1992). Developing self-regulated learners. *Focus on Exceptional Children, 24*, 1–16.

Hallahan, D. P., Lloyd, J. W., Kosiewicz, M. M., Kauffman, J. M., & Graves, A. W. (1979). Self-monitoring of attention as a treatment for a learning disabled boy's off-task behavior. *Learning Disability Quarterly, 2*, 24–32.

Hallahan, D. P., Marshall, K. J., & Lloyd, J. W. (1981). Self-recording during group instruction: Effects on attention to task. *Learning Disability Quarterly, 4*, 407–413.

Hallahan, D. P., & Sapona, R. (1983). Self-monitoring of attention with learning disabled children: Past research and current issues. *Journal of Learning Disabilities, 15*, 616–620.

Harris, K. R. (1986). Self-monitoring of attentional behavior versus self-monitoring of productivity: Effects on on-task behavior and academic response rate among learning disabled children. *Journal of Applied Behavior Analysis, 19*, 417–423.

Harris, K. R. (1990). Developing self-regulated learners: The role of private speech and self-instructions. *Educational Psychologist, 25*, 35–49.

Johnson, L., & Graham, S. (1990). Goal setting and its application with exceptional learners. *Preventing School Failure, 34*, 4–8.

Kanfer, F. H. (1977). The many faces of self-control, or behavior modification changes its focus. In R. B. Stuart (Ed.), *Behavioral self-management* (pp. 1–48). New York: Brunner/Mazel.

Lloyd, J. W., Bateman, D. F., Landrum, T. J., & Hallahan, D. P. (1989). Self-recording of attention versus productivity. *Journal of Applied Behavior Analysis, 22*, 315–323.

Maag, J. W., Reid, R., & DiGangi, S. A. (1993) Differential effects of self-monitoring attention, accuracy, and productivity. *Journal of Applied Behavior Analysis, 26*, 329–344.

Mace, F. C., Belfiore, P. J., & Hutchinson, J. M. (2001). Operant theory and research on self-regulation. In B. Zimmerman & D. Schunk (Eds.), *Self-regulated learning and academic achievement* (pp. 39–65). Mahwah, NJ: Erlbaum.

Mace, F. C., & Kratochwill, T. R. (1988). Self-monitoring. In J. C. Witt, S. N. Eliott, & F. M. Gresham (Eds.), *Handbook of behavior therapy in education* (pp. 489–522). New York: Plenum Press.

Nelson, R. O., & Hayes, S. C. (1981). Theoretical explanations for reactivity in self-monitoring. *Behavior Modification, 5*, 3–14.

Reid, R. (1993). Implementing self-monitoring interventions in the classroom: Lessons from research. *Monograph in Behavior Disorders: Severe Behavior Disorders in Youth, 16*, 43–54.

Reid, R. (1996). Self-monitoring for students with learning disabilities: The present, the prospects, the pitfalls. *Journal of Learning Disabilities, 29*, 317–331.

Reid, R. (1999). Attention deficit hyperactivity disorder: Effective methods for the classroom. *Focus on Exceptional Children, 32*(4), 1–20.

Reid, R., & Harris, K. R. (1989). Self-monitoring of performance. *LD Forum, 15*, 39–42.

Reid, R., & Harris, K. R. (1993). Self-monitoring of attention versus self-monitoring of performance: Effects on attention and academic performance. *Exceptional Children, 60*, 29–40.

Rooney, K. J., Hallahan, D. P., & Lloyd, J. W. (1984). Self-recording of attention by learning disabled students in the regular classroom. *Journal of Learning Disabilities, 17*, 360–364.

Schunk, D. (1987). Peer models and children's behavioral change. *Review of Educational Research, 57*, 149–174.

Schunk, D. (1990). Goal setting and self-efficacy during self-regulated learning. *Educational Psychologist, 25*, 71–86.

Schunk, D. H. (2001). Social cognitive theory and self-regulated learning. In B. Zimmerman & D. H. Schunk (Eds.), *Self-regulated learning and academic achievement* (pp. 125–151). Mahwah, NJ: Erlbaum.

Swanson, H. L., Hoskyn, M., & Lee, C. (1999). *Interventions for students with learning disabilities: A meta-analysis of treatment outcomes.* New York: Guilford Press.

Winne, P. H. (1997). Experimenting to bootstrap self-regulated learning. *Journal of Educational Psychology, 89,* 397–410.

Zimmerman, B. J. (1998). Developing self-fulfilling cycles of academic regulation: An analysis of exemplary instructional models. In D. H. Schunk & B. J. Zimmerman (Eds.), *Self-regulated learning: From teaching to self-reflective practice* (pp. 1–19). New York: Guilford Press.

CHAPTER 6

Implementing
Self-Regulation Strategies

In the previous chapter, we presented the four self-regulation strategies: self-monitoring, self-instruction, goal setting, and self-reinforcement. In this chapter we provide examples of how the four self-regulation strategies can be implemented in practice. We also provide examples of support materials (e.g., self-monitoring graphs, example self-statements) that teachers can use to implement self-regulation strategies. Note that the steps in implementing self-regulation interventions have much in common with the SRSD model. For example, both involve discussing the strategies and enlisting willing cooperation. Note also that although we discuss each strategy separately, they can also be combined (e.g., self-monitoring could be used with goal setting).

IMPLEMENTING SELF-MONITORING

In this section, we present examples of how commonly used self-monitoring strategies can be implemented in the classroom. The focus is on the practical activities involved in implementing self-monitoring interventions in the classroom. We present two examples: self-monitoring of attention (SMA), where students are cued to self-assess and self-record via taped tones, and self-monitoring of performance (SMP), where students self-assess by counting practices and self-record via graphing.

Example 1: Self-Monitoring of Attention

SMA is an excellent way to increase the time a student is on-task, because SMA helps students maintain effort and focus. Increasing time on-task results in increased engagement with a task and improved academic performance. SMA can also serve to inhibit inappropriate behavior. Having to self-assess and self-record can interrupt inappropriate behaviors. For example, if Emma is playing with her pencil, she will need to stop this behavior to self-assess and self-record. In this example we use a hypothetical student, Steve. Steve has a great deal of difficulty staying on task. He daydreams or wanders around the room, sometimes shooting make-believe jump shots. When he stays on task, however, he has no difficulty doing the work. The problem seems to occur frequently during spelling practice. His main problem is that he becomes distracted very easily and engages in impulsive behaviors. Here's an example of how SMA instruction for Steve might go.

Step 1: Defining the Target Behavior

Steve's teacher, Mrs. Barrett, wants to reduce the time Steve is daydreaming or wandering around the room. To do this she will try to increase the time Steve spends in his seat doing his work. The behaviors she will target for self-monitoring are (1) writing spelling words, (2) raising his hand for help, (3) watching the teacher, (4) staying in his seat.

Step 2: Collecting Baseline Data

To collect baseline data Mrs. Barrett will count the number of times that Steve gets up from his seat during spelling practice time over a period of 3 or 4 days. She will make a tally mark on a 3" × 5" card each time the behavior occurs. At the end of the period she will graph the data.

Step 3: Obtaining Willing Cooperation

At this stage Mrs. Barrett meets with Steve to discuss the problem and get him to buy into trying SMA. Here's an example:

> "Steve, I wanted to talk with you today about some problems you've been having. You are really having problems paying attention to your work and this has been going on for a while. Last week you missed recess three times because you didn't get your spelling work done. But I've noticed that when you finish all your practice, your spelling is great. I know a way to help you out with the problem you're having. I've done this with kids just like you and it worked really well. I think it would really help you to pay attention better. That way you won't miss out on playing basketball at recess. Would you like to try it?"

After the buy-in it's time to explain the procedures.

Step 4: Instruction in Self-Monitoring Procedures

At this step Mrs. Barrett (1) defines the behavior Steve student will self-monitor, (2) ensures that he can discriminate the behavior, and (3) explains the self-monitoring procedures.

"OK, Steve, let's talk about paying attention. Why is it important to pay attention?"

Mrs. Barrett discusses the benefits of paying attention (e.g., get work finished, learn more, don't miss recess, get better grades). Next, she discusses the specific behaviors involved in paying attention.

"Now, Steve, can you tell me some things you do when you're paying attention? Let's make a list."

She makes a list of the behaviors, and discusses each one briefly, focusing on the behaviors that she wants Steve to self-monitor (e.g., looking at the teacher, being in his seat, listening to the teacher, doing work, asking for help). Next, she discusses behaviors that happen when Steve is *not* paying attention.

"You did a really good job with what you do when you pay attention. Now let's talk about what you do when you're not paying attention."

As before, she makes a list and discusses the behaviors (e.g., looking out the window, walking around the room, playing with his pencil). Then she asks Steve to demonstrate behaviors that show paying attention and not paying attention, in order to ensure that he can discriminate the behaviors that indicate he is paying attention from those that show he is not paying attention.

Next she introduces the "beep tape" used to cue students to self-assess and the self-recording sheet. Figure 6.1 gives instructions on how to make a tape. Figures 6.2 and 6.3 show examples of self-recording sheets. Note that these sheets can be very simple. However, it's a good idea to include reminders on the sheets (i.e., the specific behaviors that indicate paying attention). Here's how Mrs. Barrett instructs the student in the procedures.

"Now, Steve, I'm going to show you how to help yourself pay attention. In a minute I'm going to start a tape. On the tape, every once in a while, you will hear a beep. When you hear the beep, you should ask yourself, 'Was I paying attention?' What do you do when you hear the beep? [Steve responds.] That's right. You ask yourself was I paying attention. Then you use this sheet [introduces recording sheet] and mark 'yes' if you were paying attention and 'no' if you were not paying attention. Look at the top of the sheet. It has a list of what it means to pay attention. Let's practice a little. I'll pretend to be the student and you tell me what to do."

She starts the tape. When he hears the beep Steve should be able to tell Mrs. Barrett she should ask if she was paying attention and mark the sheet. You may also wish to model paying attention and not paying attention and marking the sheet accordingly.

Steve appears to grasp the procedures, so he is ready to try them himself.

By far the easiest way to implement self-monitoring of attention in the classroom is to use a "beep" tape. A beep tape is simply a tape on which you have recorded some type of auditory cue (e.g., a beep, chime, click, or an oral reminder to self-assess). Research suggests that the cues should be random, with intervals of from 10 to 90 seconds between them (Reid, 1996). It's important for the cues to be *random*. If cues are at regular intervals students will quickly sense the rhythm and will know when they will be asked to self-assess. Making a beep tape is simple:

1. Find a source of random numbers. One good source is your old statistics books (which often have tables of random numbers in the back). Another source that everyone has is simply a phone book. We'll use the phone book example here, but the random numbers table works the same way.

2. Pick a page in the phone book randomly. Then randomly pick a starting point (e.g., halfway down the middle column).

3. Ignore the first three digits in the number. Break the last four digits into pairs of two-digit numbers (e.g., the number 2466 would be broken into 24 and 66). Ignore number pairs that are less that 10 or greater than 90. Write down each number separately.

4. Using a calculator, enter the numbers and sum them. You need to sum the numbers to make sure that the tape will be long enough. For example, to make a 30-minute beep tape, you need to sum to around 1,800.

5. Repeat Steps 3 and 4 until you have sufficient numbers.

6. Find a suitable cue. Anything that will be easily audible will work. Teachers have used buzzers, beeps, chimes (from a toy xylophone), or other sources.

7. Find a quiet room. Lay out your list of numbers where it's easy to see. These numbers are the intervals between beeps (e.g., 44, 19, 84). Use a watch or a clock with sweep second hand to time intervals. Start the tape. Wait the appropriate time (e.g., in the example above, 44 seconds), then record the cue. Repeat until you've made the entire tape. Don't worry if your timing isn't exact. A few seconds either way are not critical.

FIGURE 6.1. Making a "beep" tape.

Was I Paying Attention?

When you hear the beep, ask yourself if you are:

- writing spelling words
- raising my hand
- watching the teacher
- in my seat

If the answer is yes to any of these things, then place a check in the "Yes" column. If the answer is no, than place a check in the "No" column.

	YES	NO
1		
2		
3		
4		
5		
6		
7		
8		
9		
10		

	YES	NO
11		
12		
13		
14		
15		
16		
17		
18		
19		
20		

FIGURE 6.2. Example of a self-recording sheet

Was I Paying Attention?

- Listening to the teacher
- Doing my work
- In my seat

Yes	No

FIGURE 6.3. Example of a self-recording sheet.

> "OK, Steve, now it's your turn to practice. Let's do some spelling practice. Do it just like you normally would. Remember to listen for the beeps. When you hear the beep ask yourself, 'Was I paying attention?' and mark your sheet. Let's try it."

Mrs. Barrett starts the tape and lets Steve use the procedure for two or three minutes to make sure he can do it properly. Finally, she establishes when and where the self-monitoring procedures will be used.

> "Now, Steve, tomorrow when you do your spelling work we will use the beeps to help you pay attention and do your work better. We will do it just like we practiced today."

Step 5: Independent Performance

The next day, she gives Steve the self-monitoring sheet, then gives him a brief reminder.

> "OK, Steve, remember to listen to the beeps. Every time you hear a beep ask yourself, 'Was I paying attention?' and mark your sheet."

Now she starts the tape. The first few times it's a good idea to monitor students unobtrusively to make sure that they are properly following procedures. Most students have no trouble mastering these procedures. Total time to train the student in procedures should be less than half an hour.

Step 6: Evaluation

To evaluate the effects of SMA Mrs. Barrett repeats the procedure used to collect baseline data. She counts the number of times that Steve gets up from his seat and graphs the daily results. Typically there will be a marked improvement in behavior very quickly.

Example 2: Self-Monitoring of Performance

Self-monitoring of performance (SMP) is an excellent intervention for children who need to improve the rate at which they work or have problems finishing work. It is especially useful for drill-and-practice or seatwork situations when building fluency is important. SMP typically uses graphs for self-recording. The graphs provide visual feedback on performance and can be quite motivating. For this example we use another hypothetical student, Karen, to see how self-monitoring of performance could be used with spelling. Karen hates spelling; she'd much rather think about riding her horse. During the time when she is to practice spelling she does very little practicing, which in turn means that her scores on the weekly spelling tests are poor. Her teacher, Mr. Graham, decides to use SMP along with a simple spelling practice strategy (the Fitzgerald method) to help improve her spelling. Note that self-monitoring will *not* in and of itself create new skills or knowledge. However, increasing the amount a child practices *can* help improve fluency or retention. Here's how training would look.

Step 1: Defining the Target Behavior

The target behavior here is the number of spelling practices. Each word written out correctly counts as one practice.

Step 2: Collecting Baseline Data

To collect baseline data, Mr. Graham collects Karen's spelling practice work for three days. Each day Mr. Graham counts up the number of practices and graphs the number.

Step 3: Obtaining Willing Cooperation

Mr. Graham sets up a conference with Karen.

> "Karen, I want to talk to you about your spelling. I know that you don't like spelling and that you've had some problems on your spelling tests. On your last report card your grade was a D and I know you didn't like that. I think that one problem is that you need to practice your words more so that you can remember your words. You know that old saying 'Practice makes perfect.' Well, it's true for spelling. I know a way to help you practice more. I used it with Bobby last year and now he does much better on spelling tests. Plus it helps in your writing class. It's a lot easier to write when you can spell the words. I'd like you to try it for two weeks and see if it helps. How about it?"

After Karen agrees he explains the procedures.

Step 4: Instruction in Self-Monitoring Procedures

Here is how instruction in procedures might look. Note that because the target behavior—spelling practices—is familiar to Karen, Mr. Graham doesn't need to discuss or define it.

> "OK, Karen, we'll use our regular spelling list. You will practice the words for 10 minutes a day. On Friday you'll take the test just like we always do. Now, the first thing we're going to do is to show you a good way to study your words. Here's how we'll do it. First, you look at the word and say the word. Then you cover the word with your finger and practice writing it three times. After you write it, you check to see if you spelled it correctly. That's important because you don't want to practice a wrong spelling. If you got it right, then you can go on to the next word. Now let me show you how you'll do it. [Models and verbalizes the steps.] Your turn. Show me how you'll do your practice. Tell me what you do at each step. [Karen models and verbalizes the

steps correctly.] You'll keep doing this for the whole 10 minutes. If you get to the end of the list, then you can go back and practice any hard words or just start at the beginning of the list.

"We'll set a timer for 10 minutes so you'll know how long to practice. When the timer goes off you need to check to see how many practices you did. To help you see how much you've practiced, we'll use this graph [shown in Figure 6.4]. What you do is count up the number of practices and then put them on this graph. [Lets the student examine the graph briefly.] Now let's practice what you'll do. Here's your spelling list. I'll set the timer for 3 minutes. Remember to look at the word, say the word, cover the word, and copy it three times. Ready? OK, let's go."

He starts the timer. After 3 minutes he cues Karen to count up the number of practices and graph them.

"Good job, Karen. Now tomorrow we'll start doing this for real. Would you like to decorate your graph now? Maybe you could draw a horse and see how high it could jump? The bars on the graph could be like fences that the horse could jump over."

Letting the student personalize the graph helps with ownership and makes the process more enjoyable.

Step 5: Independent Performance

Before starting self-monitoring, it's a good idea to briefly review the procedures. Mr. Graham reminds Karen how to practice and to count up and graph her words at the end of 10 minutes. After Karen graphs her words he checks to see that she is counting and graphing correctly.

Step 6: Evaluation

To evaluate the effects of SMP, Mr. Graham compares the graphs that Karen made to the baseline data. This technique can be very helpful at increasing effective practices and improving weekly spelling test scores. We used it with one class and raised the average score on weekly spelling tests to 100%.

IMPLEMENTING SELF-INSTRUCTION

Self-instruction strategies are powerful and extremely flexible tools for the classroom teacher. Self-instruction strategies have been used successfully with a wide range of children including children with traumatic brain injury, cognitive deficits, behavior disorders, and LD (e.g., Browder & Minarovic, 2000; Hux, Reid, & Luggert, 1994; Smith & Sugai, 2000). The range of application is very broad. Self-instructions can be used to

My Spelling Graph

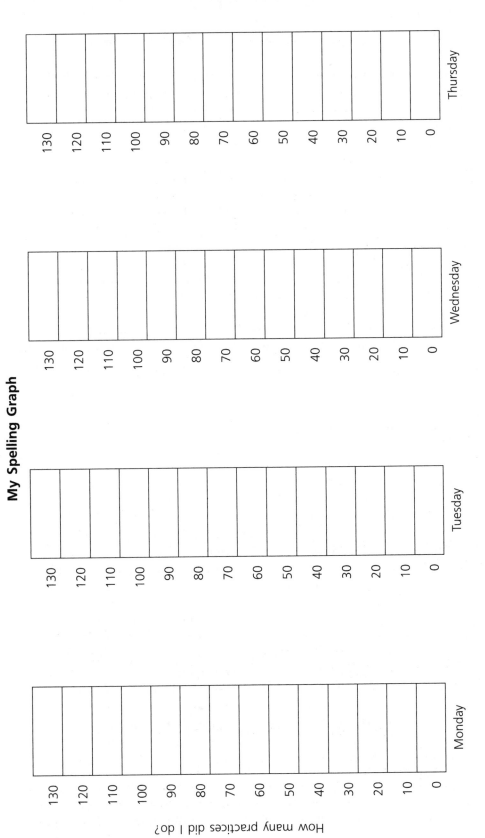

How many practices did I do?

FIGURE 6.4. Example of a self-monitoring graph.

help a child use a strategy, focus on important aspects of a problem, or cope with a situation that provokes anxiety, frustration, anger, or other emotions. In this section we provide examples of how self-instruction strategies can be implemented in the classroom.

Example 1: Self-Instructions for Coping with Anxiety

As we noted earlier, motivational aspects of academic performance are very important for children with LD. This is an important use for strategy instruction. In the previous chapter we gave the example of the "Little Professor" who used self-instructions to help him deal with frustration. Dealing with frustration is particularly relevant for students with LD as they commonly have problems with negative self-statements and thoughts that impede learning (Harris, 1982; Wong, Harris, & Graham, 1991). In fact, self-instructions were designed in part exactly for situations such as this (Meichanbaum, 1977). In this example, we show how two researchers (Kamann & Wong, 1993) helped students with LD reduce their math anxiety. Note that although math is used in this example the same technique could be used for any situation.

Step 1: Discussing Importance of Verbalizations

Here is how a teacher might discuss this with a student.

> "I've noticed that you really had a lot of problems with the math test last week. You also had some problems finishing your homework. Now we've worked together at a lot of the skills you use, like borrowing and math facts, so I don't think that's the problem. I was watching you do some math work the other day and I heard you saying things to yourself like 'I'll never get this right' or 'I'm dumb at math.' I'd like to talk to you about something we can work on that might make it easier for you to do your math work. It might seem silly, but what you say to yourself can make a difference in what you do. Do you remember the old story about the little engine that could? Remember how the little engine had to pull a heavy load up a big hill? The engine told himself over and over again, 'I think I can.' That helped the engine to keep trying and sure enough he was able to make it up the hill. You know I did the same thing when I was in school. I had one course that was really tough. I would say to myself, 'This isn't rocket science. I can do this.' It really helped me. But you know what, if you say negative things it can actually hurt you. If you tell yourself 'I can't do this.' then pretty soon you start believing it and you quit trying."

Discuss other examples. Try to bring out examples of positive self-statements.

Step 2: Developing Self-Statements

Here the teacher and student need to generate statements to help deal with problems encountered during math work. In this stage, they will work together to generate appropriate self-statements. Table 6.1 presents examples of types of self-statements that might be appropriate for the problem. The first type of statement deals with defining the problem. The second deals with approaching math tasks. The third addresses recognizing negative thoughts. The next involves coping/controlling when feeling stressed and the last is about reinforcing. Note that all types of self-statements may not be appropriate. For example, self-statements dealing with error detection and error correction aren't necessary for this situation.

Here's how you might generate self-statements.

"We need to think of some positive things to say to help with math. First we need to think about what to say when we get ready to do math. Let's think about what we can say to ourselves when we start doing math work. Remember that it needs to be positive to help us get through the work. Sometimes I like to start by asking myself what I need to do or remember about doing problems. I might ask myself, 'OK, what's the first thing I need to do?' or I might say, 'Pay attention and remember your math facts.' "

Discuss possible problem definition and approaching task statements. Then go on to coping.

TABLE 6.1. Examples of Self-Statements for Math Problems

Type of statement	Examples
Problem definition	"OK. What do I need to do now?" "What's my next step?"
Approaching task	"I can do this." "I need to pay attention and remember my math facts." "I'll take my time and be careful and I can do it."
Recognition	"OK, now I'm getting scared." "Uh-oh. I'm saying bad things to myself. I need to think positive."
Coping/ controlling	"It's all right. I'm doing OK. Just keep on working." "Be calm and relax." "You can do this. Just keep trying hard."
Reinforcing	"Sweet!!" "I did it!!" "Outstanding!"

"You know it is really important not to let yourself get frustrated or scared. You don't want to start thinking negative thoughts. I remember what I like to tell myself: 'This isn't rocket science.' That really helps me. If I feel myself getting upset I tell myself something positive too. Sometimes I tell myself 'Just settle down.' Here are some examples of things you could say to yourself."

Present a cue card with examples and brainstorm possible statements with the student. Write out a list and lets the child choose which ones she likes. It's fine if she likes one from the list or one that you've modeled. It's best if students generate their own statements. These are typically the most meaningful self-statements. However, it's not absolutely necessary. After this, move to recognizing negative thoughts.

"The first thing to think about is that after we get started we need to be ready if we start thinking negative thoughts. This is like the weather report. We need to look for black clouds that might sneak up on us. That way we'll know when we're saying things that can keep us from doing our best."

Show examples. As before, generate self-statements and discuss them.

"After we know that we're thinking negative thoughts, then we need to be ready to have good things to say to ourselves. These good things are like umbrellas. They keep off the bad thoughts. And they help us keep going. If we tell ourselves we can do it, then lots of the time we really can. We just keep saying we can do it, and then we do it! We talk ourselves through. Here are some things some kids have used."

Again show examples and generate and discuss self-statements for the student. If students bring out specific problems they encounter (e.g., while working on one problem worrying about other math problems, feeling panicky, feeling rushed), then work on statements that address the problems. Finally work on developing a reinforcing statement.

"After we get done with our math and we did our best job then we need to say something nice to ourselves. We kept telling ourselves we could do it and we did, so we deserve to feel good about it. Here are some things you might say."

Again show the cue card. Next give the student a sheet to write down the self-statements (see Figure 6.5). The student can use this to help remember the self-statements and for practice. Exactly how many and what types of self-statements are generated should be decided by the student and teacher (Harris & Graham, 1996). Too many self-statements may be confusing to the student. And, the student should decide what type (e.g., coping) should be used initially.

Before I start I say . . .

When I see rain clouds I say . . .

To help me keep going I say . . .

When I'm done I say . . .

FIGURE 6.5. Example of a self-instruction sheet.

Step 3: Modeling Self-Statements and Discussing When They Would Be Used

During this stage the teacher and the student model the self-statements and discuss when and how they might be used. For example, the teacher might model coping in this manner.

> "Man, this problem is hard. Ohhh. I don't think I can do this. OK. That's a black cloud. OK, I need to stop and take a deep breath. Now, just keep cool. If I keep cool I can do this problem."

Step 4: Collaborative Practice

The final step is to work together collaboratively with the student to practice using the self-instructions. For example, the teacher might model a math task using the previously generated self-statements during the task. The student could prompt the teacher to use the self-instructions. Then the student would model the use of the instructions. Remember that one of the keys to using self-instruction successfully is to make sure that the student understands why the self-statements are useful, and that the self-statements used are developmentally appropriate and meaningful to the student (Graham, Harris, & Reid, 1992).

Example 2: Self-Instructions for Number Writing

In the previous example we saw how self-instructions could help with coping. Self-instructions can also help to guide students through a task. This can be done is several ways. For example, self-instructions can step them through a task (i.e., the students literally talk their way through a task). Or, self-instructions can help students call up and store information in memory to aid them with a task. Here's an example of how self-instructions could be used to help students perform a task. The task is writing numbers correctly. Self-instructions are used for two purposes. The first purpose is to provide a structure for students (i.e., to help step them through the task). The self-instruction actually functions as a simple strategy. The second purpose is to help them remember how to correctly write a number (i.e., call up information from memory to aid them with a task). The strategy is called STAR (Boom & Fine, 1995).

> *S = Stop.* Stop and ask myself what I am expected to do (for example, write the number that the teacher is saying).
> *T = Think.* Think of using a saying to help in forming the number.
> *A = Ask.* Ask myself which saying should be used for this number.
> *R = Recite.* Recite the saying while I write the number.

The letters in STAR are a mnemonic to help students remember self-instructions. The first letter, *S,* serves to orient the student to the task (i.e., writing a number). The last three letters remind students to identify the appropriate self-instructions (see Figure

To make 0: The woman went around in a circle until she got home.

To make 1: The man went straight down, like a stick.

To make 2: The woman went right and around, slid down the hill to the left, then made a line across the ground.

To make 3: The man went right and around, then around again.

To make 4: The woman went down the street, turned to the right, then back to the top for a straight ride down.

To make 5: The man went down the street, around the corner, and his hat blew off.

To make 6: The woman made a curve and then a circle at the bottom

To make 7: The man made a line across the top, then slid down the hill to the left.

To make 8: The woman made a half circle to the left, another to the right, and then she found her way back up to the top again.

To make 9: The man made a small circle and then a straight line down.

FIGURE 6.6. Self-instructions for forming numerals. From Boom, S. E., & Fine, E. (1995). STAR: A number-writing strategy. *Teaching Exceptional Children, 27*(2), 42–45. Copyright 1995 by The Council for Exceptional Children. Reprinted by permission.

6.6) and retrieve information to help them with the task. Here's how it might work in practice.

Step 1: Discussing the Importance of Verbalizations

The teacher would meet with the student and explain exactly how the strategy works (i.e., it helps you remember what to do) and what the student would use it for (helping to write numbers).

Step 2: Developing Self-Statements

In this case there is no need to generate self-statements, because they have already been developed. The teacher would go over the self-instructions in Figure 6.6. During this process, the teacher should be sensitive to the match between the student and the self-statements. If the student does not understand a self-statement, then it would need to be explained or modified.

Step 3: Modeling Self-Statements and Discussing When They Would Be Used

Next the teacher would model the strategy. For example:

"OK, I have to write a seven. I get mad when I write it backwards. I want to do it right. I'm going to use my new STAR strategy. The first thing I have to do is Stop and ask myself what I have to do. OK, I have to write a good seven on this line. Now I have to Think. Let's see, to remember which way the seven goes, I can use one of the sayings. Now I have to Ask myself which saying to use. Which one is it? I know. Seven is the one with the man who made a line at the top. Now I have to Recite the saying while I do it. Here's my pencil. The man made a line across the top, and then he slid down the hill to the left. That's a good seven. I know it's facing the right way. I'll check it with the card to make sure."

Step 4: Collaborative Practice

The teacher should model other numerals, this time stopping after the varying STAR steps to ask the students, "What should I tell myself to do next?"—thus giving the students practice in using the self-statements. Next the student would memorize the steps in STAR, and the self-instructions for each number. Note that teachers would probably work most closely on the numbers that students had difficulty with. Next the teacher would practice using controlled materials. Some good ways to do this would be to practice one number at a time through dictating numbers, doing simple math, or asking questions that require a given number as the question. The teacher should provide immediate feedback on the elements of the strategy that are being done correctly and point out any steps that are done improperly. Again note that if a child changes a self-instruction (e.g., changes the saying for 9 to "a balloon on a stick") this is fine. Self-instruction must be meaningful to the child to be effective.

IMPLEMENTING GOAL SETTING

Goals can be powerful sources of motivation. Goal setting has been successfully implemented in a number of different manners. However, there are some commonalities across studies. We present recommendations suggested by Alderman (1999) and Licht (1993).

Step 1: Establishing the Goals

The first step in the process is to establish the goals. The teacher and student can work together to set the goal or it may be desirable for the student to set goals independently. Whether or not student-created goals are superior to those developed by others (e.g., teachers) isn't yet clear (e.g., Locke & Latham, 1990). What does seem to be important is that students accept the goals, as this seems to be an important element in success (Locke & Latham, 1990). This is understandable. Goals that we accept and want to accomplish are those that most inspire effort. It's possible that jointly set goals (i.e., goals collaboratively developed by the student and teacher) may actually help increase the extent to which students accept goals (Alderman, 1999).

Step 2: Ensuring That Goals Are Appropriate

The second step is to work with the student to ensure that the goals that are set are appropriate. Many students do not know how to set goals that are realistic or measurable. Thus, as with any other skill, this must be taught. Note that this is important whether the student sets the goal independently or jointly with the teacher. Here the teacher will explain how to recognize a good goal (i.e., specific, proximal, and moderately challenging). Alderman (1999) suggested that it is also useful to present student examples of poor goals (e.g., "I will be a good speller") and let students identify problems and correct them to create an appropriate goal (e.g., "I will raise my spelling test score to 80% on weekly tests"). Then ask the students to independently create two or three appropriate goals.

Next you and the student can discuss product goals and process goals (Graham, MacArthur, Schwartz, & Page-Voth, 1992). Product goals refer to an end stage. For example, the previous goal to raise spelling test scores to 80% would be a product goal. Process goals refer to the means to accomplish the end stage. To continue with the spelling example, process goals might include: (1) "I will practice my spelling words 20 minutes a week"; (2) "I will use my spelling strategy"; (3) "I will use my self-monitoring graph to increase my amount of practicing." After realistic goals have been created, you may wish to make the goals public by posting them. There is evidence to suggest that public goals are more effective than private goals (Martin & Pear, 2003). However, teachers should use discretion. Public goals may be threatening to students with a history of failure. A reasonable compromise might be to let the initial goal be private, but after it has been met, make subsequent goals public.

Step 3: Establishing Feedback and Monitoring Procedures

As we noted in the previous chapter, one of the important aspects of goals is that they can provide feedback on progress. Teachers should be sensitive to this during goal setting (or any other intervention, for that matter). The type of feedback teachers provide can directly affect student effort and progress toward meeting goals. Feedback should stress progress or comparison with prior performance, rather than comparison with normative standards or with peers (Bandura, 1993; Licht, 1993). To continue the spelling example, if the child got 70% on a spelling test a good comment might be one such as "Good job on the test. You went from 60% to 70%. You're halfway to your goal!" This feedback emphasized progress and noted specific progress to the goal of 80%. Feedback on specific errors could focus on areas of strength and those that need improvement (e.g., "You got all the *ie* words correct but a few of the *ei* words fooled you. We can work on a trick to help you with those.") The teacher should stress effort and correct use of strategies.

Progress monitoring is an important factor in the success of goals. Remember that one of the characteristics of goals is that they provide information on progress, which is in turn in motivational. Thus, ongoing progress monitoring should be built into the goal-setting process. Progress should be evaluated frequently. Evaluation should be at least weekly, and at best daily (assuming that this is appropriate). This is very easily accomplished. One possibility is to use logs or journals (Alderman, Klein, Seeley, & Sanders, 1993). This entails having the student provide a narrative that details progress toward the goal and reflects on problems and successes. This would likely be more appropriate for middle school or high school students. Another suggestion is to use

---

My Goals This Week

Goal 1: <u>I will practice my spelling words 30 minutes a week</u>
How Did I Do? <u>I did 20 minutes of practice</u>

Goal 2: <u>I will use my spelling strategy</u>
How Did I Do? <u>I did it!</u>

Goal 3: <u>I will use my self-monitoring graph to help me practice more</u>
How Did I Do? <u>I did 16 more practices</u>

Can I Do Anything Better? <u>Next week I will try to do all 30 minutes of practice</u>

FIGURE 6.7. Example of a completed goal card.

goal cards (Smolen, Newman, Walthen, & Lee, 1995). Goal cards list a student's goals for a period of time (e.g., today or this week). At the end of the period the student will write a brief response to show progress toward the goal. This may even include a brief evaluation. Figure 6.7 shows an example of a goal card for the spelling example.

Step 4: Starting Up

At this point the appropriate goals have been established and monitoring and feedback procedures have been established. Now the student should start toward attaining the goals. Teachers should be careful to *monitor progress carefully*. If goals were too difficult or would take too long to reach they should be adjusted. Teachers should provide frequent targeted feedback on progress toward the goals. This can enhance motivation.

IMPLEMENTING SELF-REINFORCEMENT

Self-reinforcement is a powerful intervention that has been demonstrated to be effective in increasing academic productivity. Some studies have suggested that self-reinforcement may even be superior to teacher-awarded reinforcement (Lovitt & Curtis, 1969). The procedure for self-reinforcement is as follows:

Step 1: Setting Explicit Standards for Reinforcement

This may be done by the teacher or by teacher and student. It is probably best to set standards jointly, because allowing students to set standards for reinforcement independently often results in very lenient standards. It is important to set the standards for reinforcement at an appropriate level of difficulty. Harris and Graham (1996) suggest that standards should be stringent because stringent standards produce better results. Note that stringent is a relative term. What is stringent for one student might be lenient for another. If students set overly lenient standards, teachers may prompt them to make the standards more stringent or allow initial lenient standards and then work toward making standards more challenging. In contrast, some students may suggest standards that are much too difficult. This is a problem because if the standards are too high, the student will not receive any reinforcement. The teacher should take pains to set standards that ensure the student will earn at least *some* reinforcement. Otherwise, the intervention will not be effective.

Step 2: Selecting the Reinforcer

One of the best ways to do this is to use a reinforcement menu (Maag, 2004). Note that this will involve determining both the reinforcer itself and the amount of behavior needed to earn it (e.g., for every 10 spelling practices you get 1 minute of free time). It is important that the amount of reinforcement that can be earned *be explicitly defined and stated*.

Step 3: Determining How Students Will Evaluate Their Work

For self-reinforcement to succeed, students must be able to accurately self-evaluate their work. For example, students may self-correct or bring the work to the teacher to check, and then determine the amount of reinforcement earned. It is best if explicit, objective criteria for evaluation are determined in advance. When evaluation criteria are subjective, students may be too hard or too easy on themselves. In cases where explicit, objective criteria may be difficult to define (e.g., overall quality of a writing assignment), teachers and students should collaborate on evaluations.

Lynn's Spelling Rewards

Daily Rewards

Good match	2 minutes of computer time
For every 10 correct practices	1 minute of computer time
100 practices in one session	10 extra minutes of computer time

Weekly Reward

Spelling test score of	70–75	1 sticker
	76–79	2 stickers
	80–90	A soft drink
	91 or more	Lunch with Mr. Fuchs!

FIGURE 6.8. Example of a reinforcement menu for self-reinforcement.

Step 4: Self-Award Reinforcement

If the student met the criterion she or he may be awarded the reinforcer. In theory (Bandura, 1997) the student should control access to the reinforcer and administer it. In practice, teachers may be uncomfortable with this. A good middle ground is for students to show the teacher the work and the amount of reinforcement they believe they should self-award. One good way to involve the teacher is to award students extra reinforcement for accurately determining how much they have earned. For example if a student accurately counted up the number of practices and determined the correct amount of reinforcement he or she would receive a bonus. Note that self-reinforcement *does not mean* that the teacher should refrain from or reduce other forms of reinforcement. Teachers should continue to provide social reinforcement (e.g., a wink, a "Good job," a pat on the back, etc.). Over time, teachers should encourage children to move from tangible or activity reinforcers to self-praise (Harris & Graham, 1996).

Here is how you might teach a student to use self-reinforcement.

"Hi, Lynn, I wanted to talk with you today about your spelling. I know you don't like spelling much and that you don't really like to practice it. On the last report card your average was only 64% and your mom was really upset. Well, guess what! We're going to treat spelling just like a real job! When you do a real job you get paid, don't you? Of course they don't pay you for nothing, do they? Right, you have to work for your pay and do a good job. Well, from now on we are going to pay you for doing your spelling. Let's figure out how we could pay you. We'll make a list of some rewards you could earn."

At this point the teacher and student confer about the possible rewards.

"OK, Lynn, you seem to like extra computer time so let's make that the everyday award. Now let's decide how many practices you should do to earn extra computer time."

Now the teacher and student negotiate the number of practices necessary to earn rewards. Note that it's a good idea to track the amount of the behavior that the student would normally produce (i.e., in this case how many practices the student normally would do daily). You can use this as a baseline for setting reinforcement levels. Also note that reinforcement levels can and should change when performance improves.

"Well, Lynn, I think we decided what you can earn. Let's write it down so we can remember it, then later I will make a card for you. You'll keep the card in your spelling folder. It will help you remember what you can earn. Now let me show you how your job will work. Every day you will have 10 minutes to practice your spelling. You can use the spelling strategy we always use to help you. When 10 minutes are up, I want you to count the number of practices you did and write the number on the top of the sheet. Then, I want you decide how much computer time you earned and write it on the top of the sheet.

After you've done that, come to me. I'll check it. If you counted correctly and figured out what you earned right, I will give you a bonus! You'll get two extra minutes of computer time. Now, on Friday you take your spelling test. We'll do pretty much the same thing. You'll check your test just like always. Put your percent correct at the top. Then figure out the reward and write it at the top. I'll check it just like we do every day. Now let's go over how we do this."

Walk the student through the steps once and model the process. Then ask Lynn to tell you in her own words how she will do it.

COMBINING STRATEGIES

In the previous sections, we treated each self-regulation strategy separately. However, self-regulation strategies can be very effectively *combined*. For example, in the goal-setting example, we really combined goal setting with self-monitoring because the student actually self-monitored progress. This is a natural and very powerful combination. In fact, it's not unusual for students to spontaneously engage in goal setting when using self-monitoring of performance if graphing is involved. For example, a child might do 35 practices on Monday. After counting the practices and coloring in the bar graph he or she might look at the next day and draw a line at 50. If this occurs the teacher should briefly discuss what happened with the student and explain how setting goals is a very positive thing. Then the next day they can note whether the student met the goal and set a new goal for the next day. Another example of how self-regulation strategies could be combined would be to use self-instruction with self-reinforcement. In the previous number-writing example, students could self-reinforce themselves for the number of correctly formed letters. Note that it is not necessary or even desirable to combine *all* the self-regulation strategies. This could easily result in procedures that are cumbersome, confusing, or even aversive.

FINAL THOUGHTS

In this chapter we provided examples of how self-monitoring, self-instruction, goal-setting, and self-reinforcement might be implemented. We would stress that these examples should be considered as guidelines. So long as the implementation process is followed, the materials or the exact language teachers might use to explain steps or model processes can vary considerably (e.g., teachers would approach the process much differently for a kindergartner than for a high school student). We should also stress that these strategies can be used on a stand-alone basis. Self-regulation strategies do not have to be combined with content-area strategies. For example, self-monitoring is quite effective at increasing time on task or the amount of seatwork. And, self-instructions can help students cope with stressful situations or talk their way through tasks. Finally we would note that self-regulation strategies can be easily and fruitfully combined. In closing, we would caution that self-regulation strategies are not appropriate for some tasks. For example, overt self-instruction may interfere with behaviors that require speedy, reflexive performance or that require complex processing (Harris, 1982).

REFERENCES

Alderman, M. K. (1999). *Motivation for achievement: Possibilities for teaching and learning.* Mahwah, NJ: Erlbaum.

Alderman, M. K., Klein, R., Seeley, S., & Sanders, M. (1993). Preservice teachers as learners in formation: Metacognitive self-portraits. *Reading Research and Instruction, 32,* 38–54.

Bandura, S. (1993). Perceived self-efficacy in cognitive development and functioning. *Educational Psychologist, 28,* 117–148.

Bandura, S. (1997). *Self-efficacy: The exercise of control.* New York: Freeman.

Boom, S. E., & Fine, E. (1995). STAR: A number-writing strategy. *Teaching Exceptional Children* 27(2), 42–45.

Browder, D. M., & Minarovic, T. J. (2000). Utilizing sight words in self-instruction training for employees with moderate mental retardation in competitive jobs. *Education and Training in Mental Retardation and Developmental Disabilities, 35,* 78–89.

Graham, S., Harris, K. R., & Reid, R. (1992). Developing self-regulated learners. *Focus on Exceptional Children, 24,* 1–116.

Graham, S., MacArthur, C., Schwartz, S., & Page-Voth, T. (1992). Improving the compositions of students with learning disabilities using a strategy involving product and process goal setting. *Exceptional Children, 58,* 322–344.

Harris, K. R. (1982). Cognitive behavior modification: Application with exceptional students. *Focus on Exceptional Children, 15*(2), 1–16.

Harris, K. R., & Graham, S. (1996). *Making the writing process work.* Cambridge, MA: Brookline Books.

Hux, K., Reid, R., & Luggert, M. (1994). Self-instruction training following neurological injury. *Applied Cognitive Psychology, 8,* 259–271.

Kamann, M. P., & Wong, B. Y. L. (1993). Inducing adaptive coping self-statements in children with learning disabilities through self-instruction training. *Journal of Learning Disabilities, 26,* 630–639.

Licht, B. G. (1993). Achievement-related beliefs in children with learning disabilities: Impact on motivation and strategic learning. In L. Meltzer (Ed.), *Strategy assessment and instruction for students with learning disabilities* (pp. 195–220). Austin, TX: PRO-ED.

Locke, E. A., & Latham, G. P. (1990). *A theory of goal setting and task performance.* Englewood Cliffs, NJ: Prentice Hall.

Lovitt, T. C., & Curtis, K. A. (1969). Academic response rate as a function of teacher- and self-imposed contingencies. *Journal of Applied Behavior Analysis, 2,* 49–53.

Maag, J. W. (2004). *Behavior management: From theoretical implications to practical applications.* Belmont, CA: Wadsworth.

Martin, G., & Pear, J. (2003). *Behavior modification: What it is and how to do it* (7th ed.). Upper Saddle River, NJ: Prentice Hall.

Meichanbaum, D. (1977). *Cognitive-behavior modification: An integrative approach.* New York: Plenum Press.

Reid, R. (1996). Self-monitoring for students with learning disabilities: The present, the prospects, the pitfalls. *Journal of Learning Disabilities, 29*, 317–331.

Smith, B. W., & Sugai, G. (2000). A self-management functional assessment-based behavior support plan for a middle school student with EBD. *Journal of Positive Behavior Interventions, 2*, 208–217.

Smolen, L., Newman, C., Walthen, T., & Lee, D. (1995). Developing student self-assessment strategies. *TESOL Journal, 5*, 22–26.

Wong, B. Y. L., Harris, K. R., & Graham, S. (1991). Academic applications of cognitive-behavioral programs with learning disabled students. In P. C. Kendall (Ed.), *Child and adolescent therapy: Cognitive-behavioral procedures* (pp. 245–275). New York: Guilford Press.

CHAPTER 7

Integrating Strategies and Self-Regulation

One of the major strengths of the SRSD model is the stress placed on creating independent learners. A strategy that can only be used with a teacher's help, that requires constant prompting to use, or that won't be maintained is not desirable. As we noted earlier, students with LD commonly have problems remembering to use strategies, using strategies successfully, and generalizing their use. Problems of this sort are at the heart of the academic difficulties of students with LD. Thus, for these students, self-regulation is crucial. As shown in the last chapter, self-regulation strategies can be very useful alone or in combination. However, they can be even more powerful when combined with strategy instruction. Self-regulation strategies can be used in conjunction with content-area strategies in many beneficial ways. They can (1) cue the student to use the content strategy, (2) help students remember the steps of a content strategy, (3) ensure that the content strategy steps are used correctly, (4) guide content strategy use, and (5) help the student screen out outside distractions, improve motivation, and maintain effort.

Until now we have treated content strategies and self-regulation strategies separately. In our experience, teachers sometimes have problems combining content strategies and self-regulation strategies. This is due in part to the fact that teachers often perceive content strategies and self-regulation strategies as separate. There is a tendency to see self-regulation as directed toward problem behavior and content strategies as academic activities. As a result, some teachers may treat them separately when planning for strategy implementation. This, in turn, can lead to problems with integrating self-regulation strategies and strategy instruction. It's important to remember that self-regulation strategies should be an integral part of the strategy instruction process. As we noted in our discussion of the SRSD model, strategies are explicitly taught, memorized, modeled, and practiced. The same principle applies to self-regulation.

Just as students need scaffolding when learning a new strategy, teachers who wish to master the SRSD model often need examples of how content strategies and self-regulation strategies can be combined. As we noted above, there are many functions that self-regulation strategies can serve. There are also many ways in which content strategies and self-regulation strategies can be integrated. In this chapter, we present examples of how they can be combined. These examples are drawn from research and practice in real-world classrooms. In these examples we do not provide full-blown instructional plans for either the content strategies or self-regulation strategies. Most of this information has already been provided elsewhere. Instead we focus on how self-regulation strategies have been used and combined with content strategies.

SELF-MONITORING, GOAL SETTING, AND A SPELLING STRATEGY

Problems with spelling are common among students with LD. They can have negative effects on both written language and reading (Graham & Harris, 2000). Some educators place an emphasis on acquired spelling skills, whereby a student learns to spell through reading and written-language activities (e.g., writing stories or compositions) (Graham, 2000). Unfortunately this poses problems for students with LD, and most teachers believe that explicit instruction in spelling is necessary (Graham, 2000). One important factor in learning new spelling words is the decidedly old-fashioned practice of simply writing the word down on paper. Elaborating on information (i.e., writing a word) helps to store it in long-term memory. However, practicing spelling words in this manner may be difficult for some students because of the need to maintain focus and effort on a highly repetitive task.

We recently worked with a team of teachers in a sixth-grade class who had problems with poor spelling performance. Students were given weekly spelling lists on Monday and were told to practice the words at home in preparation for the test on Friday. Unfortunately, many of the students did little or no practice, and spelling performance overall was not at the level the teachers had hoped for. Based on the situation, we decided that two related actions were needed: (1) students needed to use an effective spelling practice strategy, and (2) students needed to increase the amount of spelling practice. To address the first problem we used a well-validated spelling strategy (Harris, Graham, & Freeman, 1988). The strategy consisted of the following steps: (1) look a the word, (2) say the word, (3) cover the word, (4) write the word three times, and (5) check to see if the word is correct. If it's not, repeat Steps 1–5; if it is, go on to another word. Teaching the strategy was quite simple. First we told the students that we were going to show them something that would help them do better on their weekly spelling test. We wrote the steps of the strategy on the board and went over them with the class. Then we modeled the steps before the entire class. Next, we asked selected students to model the steps in the process aloud for the class. We then told the class that they would be practicing spelling for 10 minutes a day from Monday through Thursday. The spelling test would be on Friday, as usual.

After the spelling practice session was done, we introduced the self-monitoring strategy. Using self-monitoring of performance (SMP), we had students count and graph the number of daily practices. This was a simple, non-intrusive method intended to increase the number of practices in the daily session. To introduce the self-monitoring, we passed out Spelling Rockets graphs. These were simple bar graphs in the shape of rockets. Each page had four separate bars (one for each practice day). We then told the class that we would like them to count up the number of practices they did and fill in their graph for Monday. During this time, we circulated through the class to check whether students could correctly fill out their graphs. After the students had filled in their graphs, we explained that the reason for the graphs was to help them keep track of the number of practices they did every day. Next, we asked the students why it was important to practice and brought out the fact that the more they practiced the better they would remember their spelling words and the better they would do on the weekly test. Finally, we asked the students to set a goal for the number of practices that they would do for the next day by marking a line across the bar for Tuesday.

The total time needed to teach this strategy was around half an hour. The results were immediately evident. The number of practices increased dramatically over the course of the week. Most students doubled or tripled their number of practices. The effects on spelling were also dramatic. For most weeks, the class spelling average was 100%. The teachers were pleased with the intervention. It improved the spelling performance of the class and did not require any additional time commitment on their part. In fact, because the students worked independently during the spelling practice sessions the teachers actually had 10 minutes to use for other purposes. This is an example of how self-regulation can help students improve performance through maintaining effort.

SELF-MONITORING AND A MATH STRATEGY

Many students with LD have difficulties with math. Although the types of difficulties vary, one aspect of math that frequently causes students with LD difficulties is following the procedures needed to solve problems involving multiple steps such as long division or subtraction with regrouping. These types of problems pose difficulties because the child must be able to correctly recall the steps involved and understand what is involved in each step, all the while maintaining and utilizing the necessary basic math facts in working memory. One group of researchers (Dunlap & Dunlap, 1989) used a simple and straightforward self-monitoring checklist (which served as a strategy) to help students solve subtraction problems with regrouping.

None of the students had problems with basic math facts, which would obviously be a critical pre-skill. However, the students all had problems with subtraction that involved regrouping. The first step in the intervention was to develop an individualized strategy for each student. To do this, the researchers analyzed the types of errors each student committed. This involved looking at each student's past work and compiling a list of each type of error the student made. The next step was to compile an individualized checklist for each student. This checklist was based on the errors the student typically made. Figure 7.1 shows an example of a math checklist. The checklist provided the steps in the strategy. Each checklist used "I" statements that served as specific reminders (Harris, 1986) for operations that the student had problems with (e.g., copying the problem correctly, crossing out and changing regrouped numbers).

Students were given the checklists and told that they were to use the checklists while they worked their math problems. After they worked each problem, students were told to go through each item on their checklist. If they had performed the item, they were to put a plus sign by the item. If not, they were to put a minus sign by the item. The minus served to emphasize that the student had omitted a step. If students recorded a minus they were to rework the problem and attend to the step they omitted. When the students completed their worksheet, the teacher and student had a brief conference to discuss the results. The teacher awarded points (redeemable for reinforcers) for each correct answer and an additional point for problems in which the student self-monitored all the steps on his or her checklist. Any errors were also discussed and the teacher provided corrective feedback. After each child had demonstrated improvement and performance had stabilized, the checklists were removed to assess whether the improvements would be maintained. The results of the study were dramatic. The use of the check sheets increased accuracy levels from 30 to 50% across the class. More important, the high levels of performance were maintained after the checklists were removed. This suggested that the students were able to independently perform the strategy.

There are several instructive aspects to this study. First, the strategy was constructed individually for each student. This was possible in large part because math is a highly procedural subject. It's easy to identify and isolate the specific problems of each student. Though we would not recommend that teachers attempt to develop their own strategies as a general rule, in some areas (such as math), it may be possible and desirable for teachers to create strategies that are individualized for their students. In this case, a simple task breakdown was used to identify the steps that the student had difficulty performing correctly. Second, the researchers *directly linked* the strategy and the self-regulation technique. That is, they used self-monitoring to ensure that the student performed the steps of the strategy consistently. Recall that the strategy steps were the operations (in the form of a checklist) that the students tended to forget. The self-monitoring ensured that crucial steps in the subtraction procedure would not be omitted. Thus, it is not surprising that the students' accuracy improved. Finally, this study utilized reinforcement in addition to the strategy and self-regulation technique. It's not absolutely necessary to combine strategy instruction with outside reinforcement. In many cases, simple verbal praise and awareness of improved performance will be sufficient reinforcement. However, it's also not forbidden to use external reinforcement in the SRSD model. Teachers should use their best judgment. It's quite possible that judicious use of reinforcers would be appropriate in many cases. If you choose to use reinforcement, however, it is important that the students be aware that the reinforcement was due to improved performance because of effort and the use of the strategy.

Subtraction Example

1. I copied the problem correctly.

2. I underlined all the top numbers that were smaller than the bottom.

3. I put a 1 next to each underlined number.

4. I borrowed correctly (number crossed out is one bigger).

5. I subtracted all the numbers.

6. I subtracted correctly.

Multiplication Example

1. I started in the 1's column.

2. If the product was more than 9, I remembered to regroup.

3. I wrote the regrouped number above the next column.

4. I remembered to check my multiplication facts.

FIGURE 7.1. Example of a self-monitoring checklist for math.

SELF-INSTRUCTION AND A WRITING STRATEGY

The writing process poses many challenges for students with LD. Many students lack a knowledge of basic text structures (e.g., the parts of a story or the methods of organizing expository text). They must deal with mechanics (e.g., transcription skills, spelling, sentence structure), planning, organization, and revising. Dealing with these processes, often simultaneously, can be both cognitively demanding and emotionally stressful. One very effective strategy to help students learn to write narrative text (i.e., stories) is the WWW, What = 2, How = 2 strategy. Table 7.1 shows the strategy. This strategy is unusual in that it was designed to integrate self-instructions and a content strategy. Thus the self-regulation component is literally built into the strategy. In this case, the self-instructions are designed to ensure that the student focuses on

TABLE 7.1. Self-Instruction Strategy for WWW, What = 2, How = 2

Step 1. Think of a story to share with others.

Step 2. Let your mind be free.

Step 3. Write down the story part reminder: WWW, What = 2 How = 2
  - *Who* is the main character? *Who* else is in the story?
  - *When* does the story take place?
  - *Where* does the story take place?
  - *What* does the main character do?
  - *What* happens when they try to do it?
  - *How* does the story end?
  - *How* does the main character feel?

Step 4. Write down story part ideas for each part.

Step 5. Write your story. Use good parts and make sense."

Note. Based on Graham, S., Harris, K. R., & Sawyer, R. (1987). Composition instruction with learning disabled students: Self-instructional strategy training. *Focus on Exceptional Children, 20*(4), 1–11.

important tasks in the writing process and deploys and uses the content strategy. Each step of the strategy is a self-instruction directed toward an important aspect in the writing process. The self-instructions serve to focus the student on important aspects of the task, to cope with possible anxiety, to deploy a content strategy (i.e., the story parts), to use the content strategy, and to self-monitor the quality of the story that is written.

When teaching strategies such as WWW, What = 2, How = 2 that have both content and self-regulation strategies, it's important to explicitly teach and model both the content and self-regulation strategies. Figure 7.2 shows how a teacher might model the strategy. Note that the design of this strategy is intended to let students "talk themselves through" the story-writing process. Students quite literally tell themselves what to do at each step in the process.

There is another important aspect of self-instructions that teachers should understand. Self-instructions can be used effectively to help students with motivational problems. As a part of the strategy process, students can be taught specific self-statements designed to help them cope with negative thoughts or feelings that may occur. Students may also be taught to self-reinforce. Note that self-reinforcement does not have to be tangible. Positive self-statements can be quite effective. The following are some examples of self-statements that can be used for self-reinforcement:

"Awesome!"	"Sweet!"
"Nice job!"	"Outstanding!"
"That was my best!"	"Score!"
"I can do this!"	"Super!"
"I did it!"	"Excellent!"

"What am I being asked to do? Mrs. Parde said I am going to use the WWW, What = 2, How = 2 strategy to write a story. I need to remember the parts that go into a story and this strategy will help me.

Now STEP 1 of WWW, What = 2, How = 2 says to Think of a Story. Mrs. Parde showed us a picture of this bird flying into a deli shop window and a man feeding the bird. I think I will use this for my story. OK, STEP 1 is done. This picture will be fun to write a story about.

On to STEP 2, "Let your mind be free." Well, I know it always helps me if I clear all the distractions from my workspace. I better put these books away and clear those papers off my desk. OK, now take some deep breaths and begin my work. It is important to do this so I'm not distracted and can focus on my writing. My mind is free. I'm ready and excited to start writing.

Now STEP 3. This is a big step, but very important. I see lots of questions. Hey, I bet this is where the WWW, What = 2, How = 2 mnemonic helps me remember all the questions I must answer to write my story. Why are these so important? Oh yeah, they help me to make sure I have all the important parts of my story. OK, so I think I should write the mnemonic on my paper so I'll commit this to my memory. I know I have Mrs. Parde's sheet here to help me, but just so I can become better at this strategy I better try writing the questions out on my own.

Now how will I remember the exact questions that must go with all these W's? And why is it important that I do? Well it's important I remember all these "W" questions so I do the strategy correctly. We always ask who, what, when, why, and where when we read and write other stories, I think that will help me remember these. So we need to know "*Who* is the main character?" and along with that "*Who* else is in the story?" I have characters, now I need a setting and time, so a when and where. So "*When* does the story take place?" and "*Where* does the story take place?" I now have a "who," "when," and "where." There's two "what"s. I remember stories must have a plot or a problem. So maybe one question is "*What* does the main character do?" and "*What* happens when they try to do it?" The "what"s are now answered, now on to the "how"s. I bet the how's have to do with "*How* the story ends" and how everything is tied up and ended. I also know it's important to know "*How* the main character feels." OK, so now I've determined all the questions, now I must answer them. I know I have them all correct as I look back on the sheet Mrs. Parde gave me to remember the strategy.

Now I need to look at the picture again and begin answering the questions. The picture shows a man and bird. I think my main character will be the man, and I think I'll name him Fred. Other characters will be the bird and other customers at the deli. *When* does

(cont.)

FIGURE 7.2. Example of a think-aloud for WWW, What = 2, How = 2. This think-aloud was developed by Aimee Parde and is used by permission.

the story take place? Well, it looks like the middle of the afternoon on a beautiful Sunday afternoon. *Where* does it take place? At Freddy's, because I think Fred, the main character, owns the deli. *What* does the main character do? Well Fred looks to have made friends with a beautiful blue bird, and it looks like the bird has stopped by Freddy's for the Sunday afternoon special. *What* happens when Fred tries to feed the bird? I think the bird is a regular and Fred often feeds the friendly bird. The story ends with this event happening several times and the deli earns a new name of the "bird café." How does the main character feel? I think Fred feels very happy and looks forward to seeing the bird every day. OK, so now I've answered all the WWW, What = 2, How = 2 questions, now on to STEP 4.

STEP 4. "Write down the story part ideas for each part." Well, I've already done that as I was trying to think of the answers to the question to help create my story. Yeah, that was really easy to work into STEP 3, so I can move on to STEP 5.

STEP 5. "Write your story. Use good parts and make sense. "Well, what do I do to write a story? Well, we've been writing lots of stories. There must be a beginning, this is where you "set the stage." I like this part because you can create the setting and let the reader see exactly where the story is taking place. The beginning must be catchy too so the reader stays interested and wants to read more. I know my mom would really like to read a story I wrote and probably Mrs. Parde too. Since she assigned us to write a story, she'll want to read it too. I know she likes humor and excitement, I think that will be easy because the picture is funny. The middle is where the story builds to a climax with the plot or the problem developing. And the end ties it all together, solving the problem. So now I can begin writing my story. I remember Mrs. Parde always says to skip lines when you write, but why? Oh yeah, that's so when I go back and reread my story and proofread and revise I can make changes. Just so I remember that I better put a little dash along the side of my paper on every other line, or I could get some of Mrs. Parde's colored paper with every other line grayed out. That would be good to do. It's important to remember to use paragraphs when writing. Paragraphs are good for helping to organize ideas and to keep like topics together. OK, here I go . . .

FIGURE 7.2. *(cont.)*

GOAL SETTING AND A READING COMPREHENSION STRATEGY

Students with LD often experience problems remembering what they read. In some cases this is due to problems with decoding. For these students, getting through the words is so demanding that the meaning of text is lost along the way. However, there are also instances where students with LD fail to remember what they read because they do not know what elements of text are important. Johnson and Graham (1997) used a combination of a reading comprehension strategy and goal setting to help improve students' recall of stories. The first step in the process was to teach the students the important parts of a story, based on the Story Grammar strategy of Short and Ryan (1984). Table 7.2 shows the story parts used. The students were also provided

TABLE 7.2. Story parts and Graphic Symbols

Story part	Symbol
Characters	Stick figure
When the story took place	Clock
Where the story occurred	Picture of a room
The story problem	Question mark
Characters' goals	An arrow
How the characters achieved the goals	The numbers 1, 2, 3 for sequence of events to accomplish goals
The ending	Checkered flag
How the characters felt	A heart

Note. Based on Johnson, L., & Graham, S. G. (1997). The effects of goal setting and self-instruction on learning a reading comprehension strategy: A study of students with learning disabilities. *Journal of Learning Disabilities, 30,* 80–91.

with a graphic reminder for each story part. These visual cues were used on a prompt card and could also be used by the student as a part of the strategy. The reading comprehension strategy was a four-step process:

1. *Write and say the story parts* (this prompts students to write down the story parts, which focuses attention on the story parts and activates prior knowledge before reading the story).
2. *Read and think* (this step prompts the students to look for story elements while reading).
3. *Remember and write* (this reminds students to write notes about each story part).
4. *Look back and check* (this prompts students to go back through the story and check their work, and they may also add information).

These steps were designed to focus students' attention on the important elements of a story and to prompt them to locate and write down story elements.

Goal setting was used to help improve motivation and increase the likelihood that the students would use the strategy correctly and consistently. Students were taught to make two types of goals. The first type of goal was a performance goal. This goal referred to overall improvement in remembering the elements of a story. A performance goal is analogous to a product goal. The second type of goal was a process goal. This goal involved the identification of the steps the student would use to meet the performance goal. For example, the students' process goals might be to use the strategy, try hard, concentrate, and so forth. The students were also taught specific procedures to determine the progress they had made toward their performance goals. In this case progress was monitored by counting the number of story elements students could recall when asked to retell a story they had read, and by assessing the extent to which they had followed their process goals. Steps for goal setting and monitoring were practiced and committed to memory. Note that this is an important aspect of training. Just as the steps for a strategy must be committed to memory, so must self-regulation strategies.

SELF-MONITORING AND A MAIN IDEA COMPREHENSION STRATEGY

As we noted in the previous example, many students with LD have difficulty identifying the important details in text. Another common problem experienced by students with LD is difficulty finding the main idea of a passage. The ability to locate the main idea is an essential skill. It affects students' ability to study effectively, draw inferences, and read critically (Williams, 1988). There is good evidence that strategy instruction can improve students' ability to locate the main idea in text (e.g., Carnine, Silbert, Kame'enui, & Tarver, 2004; Malone & Mastropieri, 1992). However, it's also important to remember that students with LD may need help to activate and correctly use a strategy that would help them identify the main idea.

With this in mind, Jitendra and colleagues (Jitendra, Hoppes, & Xin, 2000) developed a main idea comprehension strategy that used self-monitoring to help self-regulate the correct use of the strategy. An eight-step instruction process was used:

1. Students were taught the rule "Name the person and tell the main thing the person did in all the sentences."
2. Students were taught to generate a group name and tell the main things the group did.
3. Next students were given practice in discriminating main ideas by selecting a sentence that best described a sample passage.
4. At this stage distracter sentences (i.e., sentences not related to the main idea) were introduced. Students were taught to find the distracter and then to create a main idea sentence that reflected most of the sentences in a passage.
5–8. The remainder of the lessons focused on creating main idea sentences for passages that described where, when, why, or how something looked or was done. For each lesson, students were provided with a prompt sheet (see Figure 7.3) that helped to cue them to activate the strategy.

To help cue students to use the strategy, the researchers used self-monitoring. Students were provided with a card to help them check to see if they had used each step of the strategy. As they performed the strategy, students were to place a check mark by each of four steps as they performed them:

- "I read the paragraph."
- "I used the prompt card to recall the strategy steps."
- "I applied the strategy to identify the main idea and construct a main idea sentence."
- "I wrote out the main idea sentence."

This self-monitoring procedure was used throughout the instruction process and was modeled and discussed as teachers would with any other SRSD component. Figure 7.4 shows an excerpt from a sample script used. This example is similar to the math strategy (Dunlap & Dunlap, 1989) discussed earlier. Once again the students are self-monitoring the use of the strategy in order to ensure that the strategy is used correctly

---

Finding the Main Idea

Does the paragraph tell:

What or who the:
  Subject is?   Action is?
  (single or group) (category)

Why something happened?

Where something happened?

When something happened?

How something looks or is done?

Note: Some paragraphs may contain a sentence or two that don't tell about the main idea!

FIGURE 7.3. Main idea prompt sheet. From Jitendra, A. K., Hoppes, M. K., & Xin, Y. P. (2000). Enhancing main idea comprehension for students with learning problems: The role of a summarization strategy and self-monitoring instruction. *Journal of Special Education, 34,* 127–139. Copyright 2000 by PRO-ED, Inc. Reprinted by permission.

Now let's use the four steps on this card [the card with the self-monitoring steps] to help us identify the main idea. The first step says to read the paragraph [teacher reads passage aloud]: "Ann went to the park. She swung on the swings. She slid down the slide. She climbed on the bars." I read the paragraph, so I will put a check by "read the paragraph" [teacher makes a check mark]. The second step tells me to use the prompt card to help me find the main idea of this passage. The prompt reminds me to name the subject (i.e., who the passage is mainly about) and categorize the action (i.e., the main thing the subject did in all the sentences). I used the prompt card to remind me of the rule or strategy, so I will put a check by "used the prompt card" [teacher checks card]. The third step tells me to use the strategy to generate the main idea. The rule tells me to name the subject and categorize the action. In this passage, the subject is Ann. Because all the sentences tell that Ann played in the park, the action category is played. Now I will put a check by "used the strategy" [teacher checks]. Next I will write the main idea (i.e., Ann played in the park) and put a check by the fourth step, "wrote the main idea" [teacher checks].

FIGURE 7.4. Excerpt from a sample script for self-monitoring and reading comprehension. From Jitendra, A. K., Hoppes, M. K., & Xin, Y. P. (2000). Enhancing main idea comprehension for students with learning problems: The role of a summarization strategy and self-monitoring instruction. *Journal of Special Education, 34,* 127–139. Copyright 2000 by PRO-ED, Inc. Reprinted by permission.

and consistently. This is an important consideration, because as we noted earlier, students with LD will often skip steps or forget to use a strategy. Self-monitoring helps to focus attention on the steps of the strategy. Note also that the skills involved in the strategy are at a higher cognitive level than those required for the math strategy.

INTEGRATING STRATEGIES TO SOLVE MATH WORD PROBLEMS

Research has consistently shown that students with LD have difficulty solving arithmetic word problems (Case, Harris, & Graham, 1992; Parmar, Cawley, & Miller, 1994). One of the difficulties encountered by students with LD is translating written problems into math sentences. Apart from any problem caused by reading difficulties, word problems pose special problems because students must (1) understand what question is being asked, (2) locate the relevant information within the problem, (3) set up the problem correctly, and (4) determine what arithmetic operations will be used to solve the problem.

Cassel and Reid (1996) developed the FAST DRAW strategy to help students with LD successfully solve word problems. FAST DRAW combines a content strategy with a self-instruction strategy, self-monitoring, and self-reinforcement. The strategy is designed to help students find the important information in word problems, set up the problem properly (i.e., use the correct operations), and solve the problem. The steps of the FAST DRAW strategy are shown in Table 7.3.

After the strategy has been discussed, the teacher can discuss the importance of self-speech and how what we say can affect what we do and how we feel. The student and teacher then work together to generate statements he or she could say to help use the strategy and record the self-statements on a strategy check-off sheet. Some examples of these statements are: (1) to find the question, look for the sentence ending with a question mark; (2) when setting up the problem, remember to write the larger number on top; (3) to tie down the sign, ask, "Am I putting together, so my answer will be larger than the other numbers?" (if yes, use addition), or "Am I taking apart, so my answer will be smaller than the largest number?" (if yes, use subtraction).

TABLE 7.3. FAST DRAW Strategy

- Find and highlight the question, then write the label.
- Ask "what are the parts of the problem?" then circle the numbers needed.
- Set up the problem by writing and labeling the numbers.
- Tie down the sign (i.e., decide whether to use addition or subtraction).
- Discover the sign (recheck the previous step).
- Read the number problem.
- Answer the number problem.
- Write the answer and check to see if the answer makes sense.

Note. Based on Cassel, A. J., & Reid, R. (1996). Use of a self-regulated strategy intervention to improve word problem solving skills of students with mild disabilities. *Journal of Behavioral Education, 6*, 153–172.

The instructor models the use of the strategy using the following self-instructions:

- Problem definition—"What is it I have to do?"
- Planning—"How can I solve this problem?"
- Strategy use—"FAST DRAW will help me organize my problem solving and remember all the things I need to do in order to successfully complete a word problem."
- Self-monitor—"To help me remember what I have done, I can check off the steps of the strategy as they are completed."
- Self-evaluation—"How am I doing? Does what I am doing make sense? Did I complete all the steps?"
- Self-reinforcement—"Great, I'm halfway through the strategy. Oops, I made a mistake, but that's OK because I can correct it. Fantastic!"

Following the modeling, the teacher and student discuss how self-statements helped the teacher use the strategy. Next, the student generates and records on his or her strategy check-off sheet examples of statements for each of the six categories. The teacher and student discuss how self-instructions do not always have to be spoken aloud, but can be whispered or thought to oneself. The instructor and student review the assessment and recording process for self-monitoring strategy use (i.e., using the check-off sheet to record strategy steps and self-instructions. during the support stage, the instructor uses collaborative practice to support the student as he or she moves toward independently solving word problems while using the strategy and self-instructions. The instructor prompts and facilitates the student's strategy use. Corrective feedback and positive reinforcement are initially provided by the instructor to facilitate correct use of the strategy and self-instructions.

FINAL THOUGHTS

In this chapter we presented examples of how self-regulation procedures (i.e., self-monitoring, self-instruction, self-reinforcement, and goal setting) can be combined with strategy instruction. The combination of self-regulation and strategies is a powerful instructional tool. To reemphasize some of the points made in the chapter: First, it is important that teachers *integrate* the strategy and the self-regulation procedures. This entails making the self-regulation mesh with the strategy. Self-regulation procedures should enhance the students' ability to use strategies consistently and correctly. It should not interfere with strategy use (i.e., they should not be cumbersome, time consuming, or aversive to the student). Some strategies (e.g., WWW, What = 2, How = 2) have already integrated self-regulation with a powerful strategy. However, this tends to be the exception. In most cases, teachers will need to develop appropriate self-regulation procedures and integrate them. Note that research suggests that sometimes simply teaching a strategy can enhance self-regulation (e.g., Reid & Harris, 1993). Second, self-regulation strategy procedures must be included in the instructional process. The self-regulation procedure must be discussed, modeled, committed to memory, and practiced collaboratively, just as you would a content-area strategy. Teachers cannot assume that students will simply "pick up" the self-regulation strategy.

Third, there is no "best" way to self-regulate. Teachers frequently ask, "What is the best self-regulation strategy?" They need to consider the match between the student, the strategy, the task, and the environment. For example, we have worked with some students who had a great deal of difficulty with self-monitoring. However, they could use self-instructions quite easily and effectively. Sometimes there may be a mismatch between the task and the self-regulation method. For example, self-monitoring attention may interrupt students while they are performing a task. Some students dislike this, and prefer self-monitoring performance because they don't need to stop to self-record at frequent intervals. Alternatively, some students dislike self-monitoring performance because it requires counting up practices.

Finally, several examples used multiple self-regulation strategies. This can lead to the impression that if using one self-regulation strategy is good, using two must be even better, and so on. That would be wonderful if true, but in practice you can overload students with self-regulation strategies. Resist the temptation to load up every self-regulation procedure you can fit. It can literally be too much of a good thing. When procedures become time consuming and unwieldy, students resist using them. This defeats the purpose of strategy instruction. The idea is to use just as much self-regulation as necessary and no more. Remember that the purpose of self-regulation is to make students effective, independent strategy users.

REFERENCES

Carnine, D., Silbert, J., Kame'enui, E. J., & Tarver, S. (2004). *Direct instruction reading* (4th ed.). Upper Saddle River, NJ: Prentice Hall.

Case, L. P., Harris, K. R., & Graham, S. (1992). Improving the mathematical problem-solving skills of students with learning disabilities: Self-regulated strategy development. *Journal of Special Education, 26,* 1–19.

Cassel, A. J., & Reid, R. (1996). Use of a self-regulated strategy intervention to improve word problem solving skills of students with mild disabilities. *Journal of Behavioral Education, 6,* 153–172.

Dunlap, L. K., & Dunlap, G. (1989). A self-monitoring package for teaching subtraction with regrouping to students with learning disabilities. *Journal of Applied Behavior Analysis, 22,* 309–314.

Graham, S. (2000). Should the natural learning approach replace the traditional spelling instruction? *Journal of Educational Psychology, 92,* 235–247.

Graham, S., & Harris, K. R. (2000). The role of self-regulation and transcription skills in writing and writing development. *Educational Psychologist, 35,* 3–12.

Graham, S., & Harris, K. R., & Sawyer, R. (1987). Composition instruction with learning disabled students: Self-instructional strategy training. *Focus on Exceptional Children, 20*(4), 4–11.

Harris, K. R. (1986). The effects of cognitive-behavior modification on private speech and task performance during problem solving among learning-disabled and normally achieving children. *Journal of Abnormal Child Psychology, 14,* 63–76.

Harris, K. R., Graham, S., & Freeman, S. (1988). Effects of strategy training on metamemory among learning disabled students. *Exceptional Children, 54,* 332–338.

Jitendra, A. K., Hoppes, M. K., & Xin, Y. P. (2000). Enhancing main idea comprehension for students with learning problems: The role of summarization strategy and self-monitoring instruction. *Journal of Special Education, 34,* 127–139.

Johnson, L., & Graham, S. G. (1997). The effects of goal setting and self-instruction on learning a reading comprehension strategy: A study of students with learning disabilities. *Journal of Learning Disabilities, 30,* 80–91.

Malone, L. D., & Mastropieri, M. (1992). Reading comprehension instruction: Summarization and self-monitoring training for students with learning disabilities. *Exceptional Children, 58,* 270–279.

Parmar, R., Cawley, J., & Miller, J. (1994). Differences in mathematics performance between students with learning disabilities and students with mild retardation. *Exceptional Children, 60,* 549–563.

Reid, R., & Harris, K. R. (1993). Self-monitoring of attention versus self-monitoring of performance: Effects on attention and academic performance. *Exceptional Children, 60,* 29–40.

Short, E., & Ryan, E. (1984). Metacognitive differences between skilled and less skilled readers: Remediating deficits through story grammar and attribution training. *Journal of Educational Psychology, 76,* 225–235.

Williams, J. P. (1988). Identifying main ideas: A basic aspect of reading comprehension. *Topics in Language Disorders, 8,* 1–13.

CHAPTER 8

Strategies in Written Language

Writing is a difficult and demanding task requiring attention to multiple processes. Not only do students need to learn to attend to the mechanics of writing, they also need to develop effective and efficient composition skills (Graham & Harris, 2003). Writing involves three fundamental processes: (1) planning what to write and how to organize the composition, (2) translating that into written language, and (3) revising what is written to make improvements. All of these processes are essential in proficient writing. Moreover, writing requires constant self-regulation and attention control. Skilled writers use strategies to plan, write, and revise their compositions, as well as strategies to self-regulate performance. The ability to regulate and monitor one's own composing process is an important part of writing (Graham & Harris, 2003).

Because of the complexity of the writing process many students experience difficulty. National and state writing assessments provide evidence that a majority of American students need to improve their writing skills (De La Paz, 1999). Negotiating and coordinating basic skills, knowledge, strategies, and conventions of written language can be difficult for even skilled writers. Often students are not equipped with appropriate strategies to overcome obstacles presented with composing. Five areas that present particular difficulties are (1) content generation, (2) creating and organizing structure for compositions, (3) formulation of goals and higher-level plans, (4) quick and efficient execution of the mechanical aspects of writing, and (5) revising text and reformulating goals (Graham & Harris, 2003).

PROBLEMS FOR STUDENTS WITH LEARNING DISABILITIES

Students with LD often experience greater difficulties with writing than their nondisabled peers. It is well documented that the writing of students with LD is less polished, coherent, expansive, and effective (Englert & Raphael, 1988; Graham, 1990; Graham & Harris, 1989; Montague, Graves, & Leavell, 1991; Newcomer & Barenbaum, 1991; Wong, Wong, & Blenkinsop, 1989). Although students with LD represent a heterogeneous population there are some commonalties that can be noted. Wong (2000) identified five areas in which students with LD differ significantly from their nondisabled peers.

1. Students with LD have difficulty expressing their ideas in writing.
2. Students with LD tend to have a warped conception of good writing. They focus on the mechanics of writing (spelling, punctuation, etc.) versus clarification and organization.
3. Students with LD use unproductive strategies to make up for their limited vocabularies. When they are unable to find or spell the appropriate word to express their thoughts they tend to substitute another, simpler word that does not fully communicate what is intended.
4. Students with LD make quantitatively more mechanical errors.
5. Students with LD require more practice to achieve mastery of a writing strategy.

Students with LD typically do not see writing as purposeful or a way to communicate and control the world around them, and even if they do, they are often not equipped with appropriate strategies to facilitate written communication. They tend to have a warped conception of good writing, and focus on mechanics versus clarification and organization. Writing instruction should help students develop a more sophisticated approach to composing (Graham & Harris, 2003). Students with LD must learn that writing is a process involving mastery of critical recursive elements. There are three critical elements in writing: (1) planning, (2) writing, and (3) revising, as well as attention to mechanical aspects of composition (Wong, 2000).

Planning

For students with LD, planning for writing is, at best, minimal. Students with LD often choose a single composition approach: the solitary act of generating written content (Graham & Harris, 2003). They tend to jump right into writing before doing any sort of planning; Scardamalia and Bereiter (1987) termed this behavior "knowledge telling." Any information relevant to the topic is written down without regard to organization, goals, or audience; there is minimal metacognitive control (Graham & Harris, 1997). Little attention is directed toward the goal of the composition, which is to express an idea or thought through written communication. A main objective of writing strategy instruction for students with LD is to enable them to become more planful. Students must be taught to integrate some of the same types of planning strategies, or schemas, that skilled writers utilize. One of the most effective ways to do this is through direct instruction of planning strategies such as brainstorming or semantic webbing. The strategy STOP & LIST can be used as an advanced planning strategy. This strategy prompts students to be more planful. The acronym STOP & LIST (Stop, Think Of Purpose, & List Ideas, Sequence Them) is used to facilitate the use of essential planning components. It encourages students to identify the purpose of their paper, brainstorm ideas, and organize those ideas (Troia & Graham, 2002). The use of such a strategy prior to writing can lead to more planful, organized compositions.

Organizing

Englert and Mariage (1991) noted two kinds of organizational knowledge that influence skilled writers' performance:

1. *Understanding of recurring patterns or text structures.* A writer's ability to recognize and appreciate that text has structures and to use cues related to those structures is crucial to successful composition and comprehension of texts. One of the first text structures that students are exposed to is narrative text structure. Students often understand and recognize narrative or story structure first.

Unfortunately, students with LD are often unaware of patterns or structures in text. They do not analyze text or recognize recurring patterns in text that they read or are exposed to. Therefore, they do not utilize these patterns while generating their own compositions. When given a topic, they simply start writing what they know about the topic, letting each thought prompt the next; minimal effort is made to assess what is written, or to regard the constraints of the topic, audience needs, or text organization (Graham & Harris, 2003). Instruction for students with LD must address these issues.

2. *Employing strategies specific to the writing domain.* Organization of written compositions is largely strategic. Instructing students to utilize appropriate organizational strategies will help them to be understood by others, as well as improve their ability to interpret and negotiate the meaning of text (Englert & Mariage, 1991). While composing, students with LD often fail to employ effective or efficient writing strategies to guide composition generation; as a result written work is often difficult and discouraging for both students with LD and their teachers. Directly teaching organizational patterns and strategies to guide composition has proven to be highly effective in improving academic performance of students with LD (Harris & Graham, 1992). Enabling students to utilize appropriate organizational strategies will help them in interpreting and negotiating the meaning of their texts, as well as making themselves understood by others (Englert & Mariage, 1991).

Revision and Mechanics

Revision skills for students with LD often emphasize the mechanics of writing including handwriting, spelling, grammar, punctuation, and format, rather than revising for clarity of meaning. This is understandable considering that the writing of students with LD is often laden with mechanical errors, including malformed letters, misspelled words, and errors in punctuation and capitalization (Graham & Harris, 2003). These errors inevitably affect students' written compositions, as well as their execution of the writing process. Having to attend to obstacles such as how to spell a word or write a letter can interfere with students' writing flow, leading them to forget writing plans or ideas being held in their working memory. Students who have difficulty with handwriting can likewise lose ideas or plans because their handwriting is not fast enough to keep up with their thought process (Graham & Harris, 2003).

Students with LD tend to focus their revision efforts on these mechanical errors. They employ a "thesaurus" approach, focusing on word substitutions when trying to enrich their compositions, as well as attempting to "clean up" spelling, grammar, punctuation, format, and other mechanical errors. They are focused on the overall appearance of the composition. These changes are only slightly effective; the quality of the composition or clarity of meaning generally remains unchanged (Graham & Harris, 2003).

PREREQUISITE SKILLS

It is essential to consider the prerequisite skills necessary for a student to be a successful writer, not the least of those being transcription skills. Transcription skills are basic skills, including handwriting and spelling. Proficient writing requires mastery of these basic transcription skills in order for attentional resources to be focused on the greater task at hand, writing a composition for meaning. If students have not yet mastered the mechanics of writing and need to concentrate on putting their language onto paper, they are unable to attend to higher-level skills, such as planning and organizing. For young writers these basic transcription skills can be so demanding it may be necessary to minimize writing tasks (Graham & Harris, 2000).

Graham and Harris (2003, p. 325) cited three sources of information supporting the effect of mechanical difficulties on writing output.

1. Handwriting fluency and spelling account for 66% and 41% of the variability in writing output of primary and intermediate grade students, respectively (Graham, Berninger, & Abbott, 1997).
2. Removal of mechanical demands through dictation usually results in a corresponding increase in written output (De La Paz & Graham, 1995). For instance, the length of stories produced by fifth- and sixth-grade students with LD tripled when they were asked to dictate rather than write or type their compositions (MacArthur & Graham, 1987).
3. Providing extra handwriting instruction for poor writers has a positive impact on their writing output (Berninger et al., 1997, 1998).

It may be necessary to adjust demands on students' transcription skills in order to promote effective and efficient composition skills.

INSTRUCTION IN THE WRITING PROCESS

The process of writing requires frequent reexamination and reworking of text, as well as multiple opportunities for practice. Research suggests that effective writing instruction involves scaffolded writing activities, which teach students common structures of composition, as well as actively involving them in the writing process. In the sections that follow, we provide example strategies for teaching narrative and expository text structures, as well as strategies for editing and revising.

Narrative Text Structure Strategies

Narrative text structure is one of the first structures that students are exposed to; not surprisingly it is also one of the earliest composition structures acquired by students. Stories follow a pattern that is easily understood by students: setting, episode, and conclusion. Often narrative texts are structured around a main character, a conflict presented to the main character, the action or goal of the main character for solving the problem, outcomes of their actions, and the story conclusion (Englert & Mariage, 1991). Utilizing students' knowledge of story structure to teach them composition skills is highly beneficial. Students who are aware of the basic parts of a narrative text are often more successful at writing stories, as well as understanding stories that they have read.

WWW, What = 2, How = 2

Narrative compositions require students to possess a basic understanding of story structure. Story structure may be familiar to students; however, they still may be unclear about how to use story structure to compose a complete story. Graham and Harris (1989) utilized Story Grammar elements, prompting students, through a series of questions, to generate narrative prose. These questions encourage students to include all necessary components of a complete narrative composition. The strategy consists of five steps.

The mnemonic WWW, What = 2, How = 2 was developed to help students remember these critical questions (see Table 7.1 in Chapter 7). A series of five steps is used to assist students in the composition process. Students are initially prompted, in Step 1, to *think of a story that they would like to share with others.* Considering their audience and what their audience's needs and wants are is important. Most of the time, this sets the tone for the composition. Students are then reminded, in Step 2, *to let their mind be free.* This is intended to increase students' focus on the task of composing by having them free their minds of distractions and focus on their story. The third step of the strategy is prompting the students to *write down the story part reminder:* WWW, What = 2, How = 2. This step helps students start to plan and organize their stories, keeping in mind the essential components of a story. Having students write down the questions before they start writing down their ideas ensures that they will attend to each of the essential components, not just start writing without consideration of these crucial elements. In the fourth step students are asked to *write down story part ideas for each story part.* This is where the students get to put in their ideas. Answering the story part questions will help students with the initial generation of content for their stories. In the final step, students put together all of their ideas into a complete story. Students are reminded to *use good parts, and make sense.* After all of the steps are completed students should have a narrative composition that is interesting to their audience and easy to follow, and possesses all the essential components of a good story.

Story Map

Knowledge of text structure can provide a map for students to produce well-developed compositions. A graphic organizer (Figure 8.1) such as the one created by Englert et al. (1985) can provide a template for student composition. Such an organizer can prompt students to consider what ideas to include, how to organize these ideas, and when the composition is complete (Englert & Mariage, 1991). This organizer can be used for both composition generation and reading comprehension.

Expository Text Structure Strategies

The concept of using a schema, or plan, such as WWW, What = 2, How = 2, or a story map, to produce narrative prose, can also be utilized with various expository compositions. The use of strategies or schemas for composing single-genre essays is a good place to start with emergent writers. Teaching students one form of writing enables them to concentrate on basic structural concepts. We started with narrative compositions because of the familiarity of that form of text to young writers. However, various expository text structures can be similarly taught.

Understanding and utilizing text structure is essential to composition. Different text structures can be used for planning, organizing, and drafting various types of expository text. It is important to understand that each type of expository text structure answers different text structure questions, such as: What is alike? What is different? How are they the same? What is being explained? The answers to these questions are indicated by a range of meaning and sentence structure systems. Certain keyword indicators can be found in either topic sentences or concluding sentences. For example, "Fresh water and salt water fish are similar in many ways, yet they are very different in others." The structure of this topic sentence and the keywords (similar, yet different) are indicators of a compare/contrast composition (Englert & Mariage, 1991). Students with LD often have difficulty picking up on these cues in text. They may understand that a text is explaining what is similar or different about two entities; however they are often unaware of how the piece is structured. Explicit instruction about various text structures is necessary.

TREE

The TREE strategy (Graham, Harris, & Sawyer, 1987) can be used to guide students' composition of opinion essays. The TREE strategy is composed of four self-directional prompts used to guide the fundamental form of an opinion essay. To most effectively

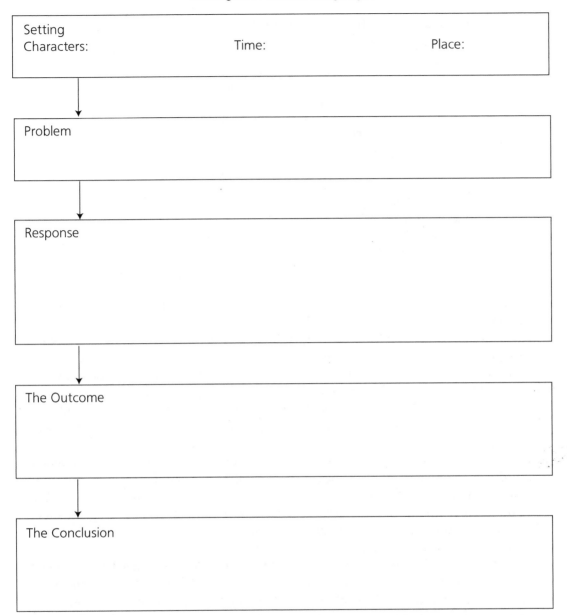

FIGURE 8.1. Story Grammar map/narrative planning guide. From Englert, C. S., Raphael, T. E., & Anderson, L. (1985). *Teaching cognitive strategies to the mildly handicapped: A classroom intervention study.* The Cognitive Strategy Instruction in Writing Project. Project funded by the U.S. Department of Education Office of Special Education Programs. East Lansing: Michigan State University.

TABLE 8.1. The POW + TREE Strategy

P	Pick my idea.	
O	Organize my notes using TREE.	
	Topic Sentence	Tell what you believe.
	Reasons	Three or more.
	Examples	Why do I believe this?
		Will my readers believe this?
	Ending	Wrap it up right!
W	Write and say more.	

Note. Based on Graham, S., Harris, K. R., & Mason, L. (2005). Improving the writing performance, knowledge, and self-efficacy of struggling young writers: The effects of self-regulated strategy development. *Contemporary Educational Psychology, 30,* 207–241.

use the TREE strategy students are taught to use TREE within a general three-step planning strategy: POW (Table 8.1). The POW strategy is used to frame the writing process; TREE is used to organize the written prose. First, students are asked to pick an idea. Picking an idea helps students narrow their focus and begin to conceptualize what they will be writing about. Then, students are prompted to organize their notes using TREE. Students organize their thoughts and ideas in the fashion of a typical opinion essay, starting with a topic sentence, which is the first step in TREE. Students are taught that a topic sentence tells what you believe clearly and concisely. The topic sentence makes the author's opinion clear.

Students are then asked to provide three or more reasons to support their opinion (TREE). These reasons are then to be supported with examples. Students are prompted to ask themselves, "Why do I believe this?" and "Will my readers believe this?" This not only helps the student elaborate and support their opinion, it also prompts them to consider the audience's thoughts on their rationale. The final step in the TREE strategy is the ending. Students need to write a concluding statement, a statement that will wrap it up right! The final or ending statement should let the reader know that the essay is complete. This statement finishes off the paper and usually reiterates the opinion. The final step (POW) is to write and say more. Students are prompted to check over their compositions for completeness. If any areas are found that need further development students should work on them until the composition is complete and fully expresses their opinion.

POWER

Englert and colleagues (1985, 1988) developed an organizational writing strategy called POWER, which organizes all the steps in the writing process and teaches students different organizational structures for composition. The POWER strategy can be used with various text structures and is used in combination with pattern guides for writing. These pattern guides include compare/contrast structure (Figure 8.2), explanation

What is being
  compared/contrasted?

On what?

Alike?

Different?

On what?

Alike?

Different?

On what?

Alike?

Different?

FIGURE 8.2. POWER planning guide: Comparison/contrast organization form. From Englert, C. S., Raphael, T. E., & Anderson, L. (1985). *Teaching cognitive strategies to the mildly handicapped: A classroom intervention study.* The Cognitive Strategy Instruction in Writing Project. Project funded by the U.S. Department of Education Office of Special Education Programs. East Lansing: Michigan State University.

structure (Figure 8.3), and narrative or story structure (Figure 8.1). The example provided in Figure 8.1 can be use for the narrative or story structure pattern guide. The first step in the POWER strategy is planning. Students are encouraged to focus on three things; (1) the audience for the paper, (2) the purpose of the paper, and (3) the background knowledge that is necessary to write the paper. This provides students with a solid foundation to build their composition. The second step is organizing. Students complete a pattern guide to help them organize their papers; this is an organizing think sheet, and represents the text structure being studied.

Students follow this pattern guide to ensure essential components are included in their written compositions. The third step is writing. This step involves the student taking the information from the planning guide and generating a first draft. Students must understand that this is a first draft, and that the process of writing is recursive. The next step is editing. This step teaches students to critique their own writing and to identify areas in which they need clarification or assistance, an important self evaluation skill. The editing process is a two-step process involving student self-evaluation and peer editing. During the self-evaluation students reread and evaluate their draft, starring sections of the paper they like best and putting question marks in the margins by passages they think may be unclear. Then, they think of two questions to ask their peer editors. During peer editing students read their papers to a peer editor. Peer editors then summarize the paper. Next, the editor evaluates the paper, giving an analysis of salient features of the writing that might guide a revision or lead to improvement. For example, the peer editor might suggest that the writer add keywords or reorganize the paper for clarity. These suggestions are shared with the writer. Then the peer editor and the writer brainstorm ways to improve the paper.

The final step is revising. During the revising step students decide on changes to be made using their self-evaluation sheet and peer feedback. Teacher modeling on how to insert new text or change the order of information is suggested. Another part of the revision process is a teacher–student conference. The teacher and the student have a conference, where changes in writing mechanics are suggested. This way if a student is still having difficulty with clarity or errors have gone undetected through the other two evaluations, the teacher will be able to make suggestions. A final draft is then composed on a clean sheet of paper. Students can use the checklist in Figure 8.4 to ensure all steps in the process are followed.

Editing and Revising Strategies

In the writing process, revising tends to receive the least amount of time and effort; revisions are generally limited to proofreading for errors. Students with LD have greater difficulty than their nondisabled peers monitoring the content of their writing, and traditionally are not encouraged to. Emphasis in instruction is often placed on the mechanics of writing—handwriting, grammar, and spelling—rather than on developing meaning. However, research indicates that effective teaching involves problem-solving activities that encourage students to focus their attention on strategies for gathering, analyzing, and structuring information (Reynolds, Hill, Swassing, & Ward, 1988).

What is being explained?	

	Materials/things you need?

	Setting?

	First,
	Next,
	Third,
	Then,
	Last,

What are the steps?

FIGURE 8.3. POWER planning guide: Explanation organization form. From Englert, C. S., Raphael, T. E., & Anderson, L. (1985). *Teaching cognitive strategies to the mildly handicapped: A classroom intervention study.* The Cognitive Strategy Instruction in Writing Project. Project funded by the U. S. Department of Education Office of Special Education Programs. East Lansing: Michigan State University.

Planning
- ☐ Who will read my paper?
- ☐ Why am I writing this?
- ☐ What do I know about this topic?
- ☐ How can I group/label my facts?

Organizing
- ☐ Which pattern guide do I use (why am I writing this)?
- ☐ Have I filled in the pattern guide completely and answered the questions being asked?

Writing
- ☐ I need to write a paper using the information from the pattern guide, using complete sentences.
- ☐ Have I followed the flow or organization of the pattern guide?

Editing
Self-evaluation
Did I . . .
- ☐ Tell what was being explained?
- ☐ Tell what things you need?
- ☐ Make the steps clear?
- ☐ Use key words?
- ☐ Make it interesting to the reader?
- ☐ Star the parts I like?
- ☐ Put question marks in the margins by things that are unclear?
- ☐ Prepare two questions for my peer editor?

Peer evaluation
- ☐ I need to summarize the paper.
- ☐ Can I pick out, and do I understand, the most important features of the paper?
Did the author . . .
- ☐ Tell what was being explained?
- ☐ Tell what things you need?
- ☐ Make the steps clear?
- ☐ Use key words?
- ☐ Make it interesting to the reader?
- ☐ Would revisions improve the quality or clarity of the paper? Where?
- ☐ I need to share suggestions with the writer.

Collaborative conference
- ☐ Have we decided on ways to make the paper better?

Revising
- ☐ Have I made the changes to improve my paper using my self-evaluation?
- ☐ Have I made changes to improve my paper using my peer's evaluation?
- ☐ Have I made the changes that we decided upon in our collaborative conference?
- ☐ Is my final draft clean and free of errors?

FIGURE 8.4. Example of a checklist for the POWER strategy.

COPS

Students need to focus on the content of their writing, yet still monitor the mechanical aspects of their writing. The University of Kansas Institute for Research in Learning Disabilities developed a strategy called COPS to assist students in making mechanical revisions (Table 8.2). Students are prompted through a series of questions to monitor and revise any mechanical errors in their papers. Students follow the mnemonic COPS. The *C* reminds them to ask themselves if they have capitalized the first words and proper names. The *O* stands for overall appearance. Students ask themselves, "How is the overall appearance?" This is where students check their handwriting and overall neatness of the paper. The *P* stands for punctuation. Students are prompted to ask themselves, "Have I put in commas and end punctuation?" This is aimed at basic mechanics; it helps students attend to end punctuation, as well as punctuation within sentences. The final step in the strategy is the *S*, which stands for spell. Students ask themselves, "Have I spelled all words correctly?" Students should be encouraged to identify any words that they suspect are spelled incorrectly. Those words need to be checked for accuracy in the same manner that other material in the text is corrected.

Mechanical revisions, or transcription revisions, are essential to composition; too many mechanical errors are distracting to the reader and take away from the intent of the composition. It is also essential for young authors to understand the purpose of writing and be aware that revisions should not only clean up their writing, but clarify their thoughts. There are several strategies that can assist students in revising the contents of their written work.

SCAN

Graham and MacArthur (1988) developed the SCAN revision strategy (Table 8.3). This strategy was developed for use with a word processor, but can be used on hard copy without a computer as well. The SCAN strategy facilitates students' ability to examine written compositions in terms of clarity and cohesiveness, add material where necessary, and correct mechanical errors (Harris & Graham, 1999). The SCAN strategy consists of six steps. Step 1 is to read your essay. Students need to read the first draft of their essay to reacquaint themselves with the substance of their paper. Step 2 is to find the sentence that tells what

---

TABLE 8.2. COPS Revision Strategy

C—Have I capitalized the first word and proper names?

O—How is the overall appearance?

P—Have I put in commas and end punctuation?

S—Have I spelled all the words right?

Note. Based on Schumaker, J. B., Deshler, D. D., Nolan, S., Clark, F. L., Alley, G. R., & Warner, M. M. (1981). *Error monitoring: A learning strategy for improving academic performance of LD adolescents* (Research Rep. No. 34). Lawrence: University of Kansas, Institute for Research in Learning Disabilities.

TABLE 8.3. SCAN Content Revision Strategy

Step 1:   Read your essay.

Step 2:   Find the sentence that tells what you believe—Is it clear?

Step 3:   Add two more reasons why you can believe it.

Step 4:   SCAN each sentence:
"Does it make <u>s</u>ense?"
"Is it <u>c</u>onnected to my belief?"
"Can I <u>a</u>dd more?"
<u>N</u>ote errors.

Step 5:   Make your changes on the computer and/or on a hard copy.

Note. Based on Graham, S., & MacArthur, C. (1988). Improving learning disabled student's skills at revising essays produced on a word processor: Self-instructional strategy training. *Journal of Special Education, 22*(2), 133–152.

you believe—Is it clear? This step encourages writers to reexamine their topic sentence and make sure it is stated clearly and accurately. Students also checks the topic sentence to ensure that it reflects the desired intent. If it does not, then it needs to be revised. Step 3 is to add two more reasons why you can believe it. This helps the writer to provide enough support to adequately defend his or her position. Step 4 is where the SCAN mnemonic comes in. In Step 4 students are to SCAN each sentence and ask themselves: "Does it make <u>s</u>ense?" "Is it <u>c</u>onnected to my belief?" "Can I <u>a</u>dd more?" Then, students <u>n</u>ote any errors. Each sentence is "scanned" to make sure the essay is (1) clear—will the reader understand it?; (2) useful—does it directly support the development of the argument?; (3) complete—do more details need to be added to make the sentence better?; and (4) error free—are there any mechanical errors that need to be corrected? Step 5 is the final step. During this step students make any necessary changes. This can be done on either the computer or on a hard copy.

IMPLEMENTATION PLANS

In this section, we provide partial examples of implementation plans for each of the writing strategies previously mentioned.

Stage 1 for WWW, What = 2, How = 2: Developing and Activating Background Knowledge

Prior to teaching the strategy, it is necessary to evaluate the students' background knowledge, attitudes, and beliefs about writing. Formal or informal assessments can be used to determine what skills the students possess and what skills they lack; doing a task breakdown will provide the information for identifying the skills necessary to successfully complete the strategy. Table 8.4 shows a sample task breakdown for the WWW, What = 2, How = 2 strategy.

TABLE 8.4. Sample Task Breakdown for WWW, W = 2, H = 2

Strategy	Skills	Assessment
Basic writing skills	Ability to write (print)	Given an informal assessment, the student will correctly produce letters.
	Ability to spell	Provided with a spelling test on common words in narrative prose, the student will be able to write and spell words correctly.
	Knowledge of basic grammar and punctuation	Given text with grammatical and mechanical errors, the student will be able to satisfactorily correct those errors.
Who is the main character? Who else is in the story?	Knowledge of story elements	Provide students with a written task, requiring them to include and develop a main character and supporting characters in a story.
	Knowledge of main character and how to develop a main character	
	Knowledge of other characters	
When does the story take place?	Knowledge of setting	Provide students with a written task prompting them to include setting, action, consequence, story ending, and emotion.
What does the main character do?	Knowledge of action	
What happens when he or she tries to do it?	Knowledge of consequence of action	
How does the story end?	Knowledge of story endings/resolutions	
How does the main character feel?	Knowledge of emotions and how to present them in text	

Stage 2 for POW + TREE: Discussing the Strategy

This is the first stage in "initiating" the strategy. In this stage it is important to stress the relevance of the strategy. An initial conference between the teacher and student is necessary. During this initial conference the teacher will discuss the student's current performance. In order for students to be successful and self-regulating they need to make a commitment to use the strategy, or "buy in." Thus, it is important for the teacher to stress the value of the strategy. Brainstorm with the students on situations where using this strategy or completing the given task accurately is important. For example, the following might be appropriate brainstorming ideas in response to the question "When would it be important for you to write a persuasive opinion paper?":

- Complaining to a company
- Debating or defending a position
- Letter to the editor
- Campaigning
- Trying to change someone's mind

[handwritten note: Conferences can be a critical component to aide in writing coherence]

A sample script for "selling" the strategy fo[r] ...

"The reason I wanted to talk with you is that we have been doing a lot of writing this year, and I know sometimes writing can be a difficult thing to do. Let's take a look at some of the papers that you wrote this month. You really did a nice job _____ [point out positives; focusing on topic sentences, reasons, explanations, and endings]. However, if I try and understand what your opinion is on _____ [topic of the paper], it is difficult for me. Earlier you had said that it would be important to make your opinion clear if you were _____ [focus on when they felt it would be important to write a persuasive opinion paper]. Right now your opinion is not as clear or persuasive as it could be. I have an idea how we can make your opinion clearer in your writing. You know how you use tools in shop class to make your projects better? I have a tool for you to use in writing that will make your papers better. The tool is a strategy called POW + TREE. The POW part of this strategy gives you power when you write, and the TREE part helps you to remember all the parts to a good opinion essay."

In this stage we also introduce the strategy steps, and any prompts that will be given (Figure 8.5).

Stage 3 for COPS: Modeling the Strategy

The teacher will need to use a think-aloud to demonstrate the use of the strategy. Here is an example of a think-aloud for the COPS strategy.

"OK, what is it I have to do here? I know, I have to edit my paper. Editing is hard for me, but I know that using my COPS strategy will help me do a good job. I can remember COPS because police 'clean up the neighborhood,' and I need to 'police up,' or clean up my paper by editing, and making sure I don't leave any errors (rule breakers). The COPS strategy can help me to remember what to do when I am editing. OK, I can do this if I try my best and use my strategy. I should write down the steps of my strategy so I don't forget any of them; OK, C stands for *capitalize*—Have I capitalized the first word and proper names? Next is O. What does O stand for? I can't remember. I know, I can just look at the wall chart . . . let's see . . . the chart says, 'Overall appearance—How is the overall appearance?' Oh yeah, I remember that now; I better write it down. Let's see, then is P, for *punctuation*—Have I put in commas and end

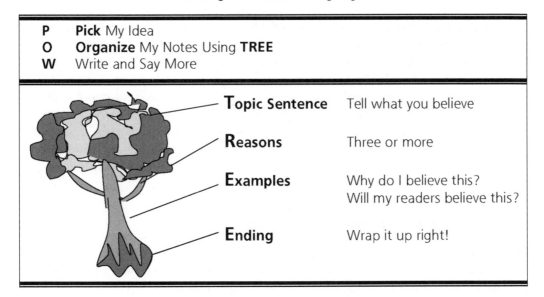

P	**Pick** My Idea
O	**Organize** My Notes Using **TREE**
W	Write and Say More

Topic Sentence Tell what you believe

Reasons Three or more

Examples Why do I believe this?
Will my readers believe this?

Ending Wrap it up right!

FIGURE 8.5. Example of a mnemonic chart for POW + TREE.

punctuation? Good, I'm remembering most of this; I can do this! Finally comes *S*, which stands for *spelling*—Have I spelled all the words right? Great, I got them all written down; I'm really doing well. OK, what do I do now? I need to start with the *C* and ask myself, 'Have I capitalized the first word and proper names?' Let's see . . . oops, here's a sentence that needs a capital letter at the beginning, and oooh, I forgot to capitalize the name of this town. Good thing I'm going over this! OK, that seems to be all of them. What's next? I have written down *O*. I need to ask myself, 'How is the overall appearance?' Well, I should clean up some of my handwriting; I can barely read it, and if I can't read it I'm sure no one else will either! Oh, there are quite a few extra marks, too. I need to erase those and clean up my paper; I want it to look good when I hand it in, maybe I will get a gold star. I would really like one of those gold stars on my paper! OK, all clean; it looks good. Now, what do I need to do? What's after *O*? *O* . . . *P*; I need to ask myself, 'Have I put in commas and end punctuation?' I need to remember where to use commas. OK, I use commas when I am listing things; here's a list . . . I remembered to use commas. Way to go! When else do I use commas? I use commas to break up sentences, where I want a pause. Let's see, do I have any long sentences? Yep, here's one that could use a comma! Are there any others? No, I don't see any; looks good! How about that end punctuation? Oops, forgot a period at the end of a sentence, and I really should change that to a question mark. That's an asking sentence, not a telling sentence. The rest of it looks really good. Wow, this is going really well! I like using this strategy, it's kind of fun, and I can't believe it, but I'm almost done! I'm up to the *S*, the last letter! I need ask myself, 'Have I spelled all the words right?' This is kind of tough for me, but I know I can do it; I've come this far. I can't quit now! OK, let me see . . . most of it looks OK, but there are a few words that I'm just not sure about. I better look those up in the dictionary. That's what we're supposed to do first if we're not sure how to spell a word. . . . OK, all done! I did a great job; using that strategy and sticking with it really helped me remember what to look for when I'm editing my paper."

Stage 4 for POWER: Memorizing the Strategy

Memorizing the strategy is extremely important! We want the students to be able to focus on the task and not on trying to remember the steps of the strategy. The specific activities used to help students memorize a strategy are not nearly as important. There are many appropriate activities. The important aspect of the activities is whether or not they facilitate memorization. However, you will need to plan and prepare the activities and monitor their effectiveness. Here are some examples of memorization activities for the POWER strategy.

Ball Toss Game

The teacher starts off with the ball and tosses it to a student. That student starts off and says, "P; P stands for planning. We need to plan what to write, remembering the audience for the paper, the purpose, and the background information necessary to write the paper." Then that student tosses the ball to another student of their choice. That student needs to say, "O; O stands for . . . " and so on. It is important that the students not only say the letter and what the letter stands for, but also what that means. That is, they need to know what to do at each step in the strategy.

Reciting the Strategy with a Partner

Students will be matched up in pairs. A student who struggles will be matched with a peer who can help with memorization of the strategy. These peers will be instructed on how to help their partners prior to the activity. The students will recite the POWER mnemonic and what they need to do at each step in the strategy. Students will take turns using the mnemonic chart to check if their partner can recite the steps of strategy and what must be done at each step.

Making Student Checklists

Students will be given a checklist for the POWER strategy (Figure 8.4). The checklists will list the steps of the strategy and what must be done at each step. Students will be able to use these to ensure all steps of the strategy are completed. These will be laminated for multiple uses and placed on students' desks to be readily accessible.

Stage 5 for SCAN: Supporting the Strategy

In this stage, scaffolding is important. With scaffolding it is possible for a gradual transfer of strategy ownership from teacher to student. Students need to be given adequate time and support to master the strategy. Here are examples of how to use content, task, and material scaffolding with the SCAN strategy.

Content Scaffolding

Provide students with a simple passage. The teacher and students then go over the passage and SCAN for revisions. The teacher directs the process and the students provide answers to teacher-directed questions (i.e., "Is this a complete sentence?" "Does this make sense here?" "Are the author's feelings clear?"). Next, students are given a passage that they had written during their baseline probes. They can use the SCAN strategy to evaluate and revise their compositions. Provide a chart to ensure every step is included.

Task Scaffolding

During collaborative practice the teacher prompts students to name the step that should be performed; then the teacher describes the step and models its use. In subsequent lessons the teacher asks students to name the steps in the SCAN strategy and describe each step, and then the teacher models the steps. Finally, the students name, describe, and model the steps of the SCAN strategy.

Material Scaffolding

Provide students with a mnemonic prompt card to be placed on their desk. Initially, this card lists the steps of the strategy and describes what to do at each step. Over time these cards will provide less direction, first fading the descriptions, and eventually fading the mnemonic and steps altogether. At this point students should have reached mastery of the strategy and be able to work independently.

Stage 6 for POWER: Independent Performance

At this stage the student is ready to use the strategy independently. The teacher's main task is to monitor students' performance and check on proper and consistent use of the strategy. If students deviate from the given POWER strategy, performance will be evaluated, and action will be taken only if performance is no longer improving.

Teachers also must evaluate whether or not the strategy is being generalized to other appropriate situations. Students will not always generalize strategies to appropriate situations; they will often need to be prompted and encouraged to do so. To promote generalization, students will be encouraged to use the strategy in other content areas where they are required to write expository papers. All team teachers will be informed about the use of the strategy, the prompts, and what is required at each step. All team teachers will be given a wall chart to hang up in their room as a reminder for students to use the POWER strategy when appropriate. Note that these activities can begin earlier in the instructional process.

Students will keep a writing portfolio; this will allow them to see the difference that the use of the strategy has made in the content of their writing. To create the portfolio:

1. Collect initial baseline probes—These probes will be used in the initial conference and as part of the scaffolding process. They will also serve to illustrate the development of the student's written compositions.
2. Take writing samples during strategy instruction. This is a way to demonstrate student progress through the use of the POWER strategy.
3. Take a final sample, which will be included once it is determined that the student has reached mastery of strategy use.

Portfolios serve many purposes; the main purpose is to provide evidence of improved academic performance. These portfolios will be evaluated by several people: students, teachers, parents, and administrators. After evaluating their own portfolio, students will be questioned to find out whether or not they see an improvement in their writing skill and if they see the strategy as valuable to them or not. The teacher will evaluate the portfolio to provide evidence of improved academic performance for grading purposes.

FINAL THOUGHTS

Writing is a complex task requiring attention to multiple processes. Negotiating and coordinating skills, knowledge, strategies, and conventions of written language can be difficult even for skilled writers. These processes are even more difficult for students with LD. Students with LD often lack the knowledge, skills, and strategies to be effective writers, and do not understand that writing is purposeful. They have difficulty expressing their ideas, focus on mechanical aspects of written communication, use unproductive strategies to facilitate their writing, and do not attend to critical elements of writing. It is also important to attend closely to prerequisite skills, particularly transcription skills and spelling. Students with LD also often lack the prerequisite skills necessary to effective writers. This makes the writing process even more difficult.

Despite the difficulties inherent in the writing process, the evidence is clear that, through strategy instruction, students with LD can be taught to attend to the critical elements of writing: planning, organizing, and revising, which can provide them with the knowledge, skills, and strategies to be effective writers.

REFERENCES

Berninger, V., Vaughan, K., Abbott, R., Abbott, S., Rogan, L., Brooks, A., Reed, E., & Graham, S. (1998). Early intervention for spelling problems: Teaching functional spelling units of varying size with a multiple-connection framework. *Journal of Educational Psychology, 90,* 587–605.

Berninger, V. W., Vaughan, K. B., Abbott, R. D., Rogan, L., Brooks, A., Reed, E., & Graham, S. (1997). Treatment of handwriting problems in beginning writers: Transfer from handwriting to composition. *Journal of Educational Psychology, 89*(4), 652–666.

De La Paz, S. (1999). Self-regulated strategy instruction in regular education settings: Improving outcomes for students with and without learning disabilities. *Learning Disabilities Research and Practice, 14*(2), 92–106.

De La Paz, S., & Graham, S. (1995). Dictation: Application to writing for students with learning disabilities. In T. Scruggs & M. Mastropieri (Eds.), *Advances in learning and behavioral disorders* (Vol. 9, pp. 227–247). Greenwich, CT: JAI Press.

Englert, C. S., & Mariage, T. V. (1991). Shared understandings: Structuring the writing experience through dialogue. *Journal of Learning Disabilities, 24*(6), 330–342.

Englert, C. S., & Raphael, T. E. (1988). Constructing well-informed prose: Process, structure and metacognitive knowledge. *Exceptional Children, 54,* 513–520.

Englert, C. S., Raphael, T. E., & Anderson, L. (1985). Teaching cognitive strategies to the mildly handicapped: A classroom intervention study. The Cognitive Strategy Instruction in Writing Project. Project funded by the U.S. Department of Education Office of Special Education Programs. East Lansing, MI: Michigan State University.

Graham, S. (1990). The role of production factors in learning disabled students' compositions. *Journal of Educational Psychology, 82,* 781–791.

Graham, S., Berninger, V. W., & Abbott, R. D. (1997). Role of mechanics in composing of elementary school students: A new methodological approach. *Journal of Educational Psychology, 89,* 170–182.

Graham, S., & Harris, K. R. (1989). Components analysis of cognitive strategy instruction: Effects on learning disabled students; compositions and self-efficacy. *Journal of Educational Psychology, 6,* 221–236.

Graham, S., & Harris, K. R. (1997). Self-regulation and writing: Where do we go from here? [Commentary]. *Contemporary Educational Psychology, 22,* 102–114.

Graham, S., & Harris, K. R. (2000). The role of self-regulation and transcription skills in writing and writing development. *Educational Psychologist, 35*(1), 3–12.

Graham, S., & Harris, K. R. (2003). Students with learning disabilities and the process of writing: A meta-analysis of SRSD studies. In H. L. Swanson, K. R. Harris, & S. Graham (Eds.), *Handbook of learning disabilities* (pp. 323–344). New York: Guilford Press.

Graham, S., Harris, K. R., & Mason, L. (2005). Improving the writing performance, knowledge, and self-efficacy of struggling young writers: The effects of self-regulated strategy development. *Contemporary Educational Psychology, 30,* 207–241.

Graham, S., Harris, K. R., & Sawyer, R. (1987). Composition instruction with learning disabled students: Self-instructional strategy training. *Focus on Exceptional Children, 20*(4), 1–11.

Graham, S., & MacArthur, C. (1988). Improving learning disabled students' skills at revising essays produced on a word processor: Self-instructional strategy training. *Journal of Special Education, 22*(2), 133–152.

Harris, K. R., & Graham, S. (1992). Self-regulated strategy development: A part of the writing process. In M. Pressley, K. R. Harris, & J. Guthrie (Eds.), *Promoting academic competence and literacy in schools* (pp. 277–309). San Diego, CA: Academic Press.

Harris, K. R., & Graham, S. (1999). Programmatic intervention research: Illustrations from the evolution of self-regulated strategy development. *Learning Disability Quarterly, 22,* 251–262.

Idol, L., & Croll, B. J. (1987). Story-mapping training as a means of improving reading comprehension. *Learning Disability Quarterly, 10, 214–230.*

MacArthur, C., & Graham, S. (1987). Learning disabled students' composing under three methods of text production: Handwriting, word processing, and dictation. *Journal of Special Education, 21*(3), 22–42.

Montague, M., Graves, A., & Leavell, A. (1991). Planning, procedural facilitation, and narrative composition of junior high students with learning disabilities. *Learning Disabilities Research and Practice, 6,* 219–224.

Newcomer, P. L., & Barenbaum, E. M. (1991). The written composing ability of children with learning disabilities: A review of literature from 1980 to 1990. *Journal of Learning Disabilities, 24,* 578–593.

Reynolds, C. J., Hill, D. S., Swassing, R. H., & Ward, M. E. (1988). The effects of revision strategy instruction on the writing performance of students with learning disabilities. *Journal of Learning Disabilities, 21*(9), 540–545.

Scardamalia, M., & Bereiter, C. (1987). Knowledge telling and knowledge transforming in written composition. In S. Rosenberg (Ed.), *Advances in applied psycho-linguistics: Vol. 2. Reading, writing, and language learning* (pp. 142–175). Cambridge, MA: Cambridge University Press.

Schumaker, J. B., Deshler, D. D., Nolan, S., Clark, F. L., Alley, G. R., & Warner, M. M. (1981). *Error monitoring: A learning strategy for improving academic performance of LD adolescents* (Research Rep. No. 34). Lawrence: University of Kansas, Institute for Research in Learning Disabilities.

Troia, G. A., & Graham, S. (2002). The effectiveness of a highly explicit, teacher-directed strategy instruction routine: Changing the writing performance of students with learning disabilities. *Journal of Learning Disabilities, 35*(4), 290–305.

Wong, B. Y. L. (2000). Writing strategies instruction for expository essays for adolescents with and without learning disabilities. *Topics in Language Disorders, 20*(4), 29–44.

Wong, B. Y. L., Wong, R., & Blenkinsop, J. (1989). Cognitive and metacognitive aspects of learning disabled adolescents' composing problems. *Learning Disability Quarterly, 12,* 300–322.

CHAPTER 9

Strategies in Reading Comprehension

Reading comprehension is considered the "essence of reading" (Durkin, 1993). If readers can read the words but do not understand what they are reading, they are not really reading. Reading, at some level, is involved in all academic courses. Students are expected to read a variety of texts and comprehend them in order to gain knowledge. While reading comprehension in schools usually involves understanding textbook assignments, reading comprehension skills can also influence a student's ability to understand written directions, homework assignments, and other literature. Comprehension of text is not exclusive to academic learning; it is also essential to being a lifelong learner. Thus, improving students' reading comprehension can positively impact both educational outcomes and other aspects of their lives.

Comprehension of text requires a wide variety of skills and cognitive processes. Students must be able to negotiate, manipulate, translate, and construct meaning from written language (King, 1994). Proficient readers not only read fluently, they also construct meaning through interactions with text (Durkin, 1993). There is a reciprocal interaction between the reader and the ideas or message presented in a particular text. Good readers continuously construct and reconstruct meaning while reading. They are able to activate background knowledge prior to reading (prereading strategies). They monitor comprehension while reading (during-reading strategies), and they check for understanding after reading (postreading strategies) (National Reading Panel, 2000). These strategies are automatic to good readers, however many of these concepts seem to elude struggling readers, including students with LD. Thus, instruction for struggling readers must address these deficits.

Research on text comprehension demonstrates that students with LD can be taught to use comprehension strategies (Bakken, Mastropieri, & Scruggs, 1997; Englert & Mariage, 1991; Gardill & Jitendra, 1999; Idol, 1987; Johnson, Graham, & Harris, 1997; Nelson, Smith, & Dodd, 1992). It is important that comprehension be addressed early on. Comprehension strategies should be taught in the primary grades; reading comprehension should be emphasized from the beginning rather than waiting until students have *mastered* the prerequisite skills of reading (National Reading Panel, 2000). Effective reading comprehension strategies should be taught explicitly, through direct explanation, modeling, and guided practice. Students should be made aware that the overall goal is improved reading comprehension, and understood the importance of the strategy to achieving that goal. The strategy should be demonstrated along with the metacognitive processes associated with it; students should be provided ample opportunities to practice using the strategy, and directed through the process until they have mastered it.

PROBLEMS FOR STUDENTS WITH LEARNING DISABILITIES

Students with LD have particular difficulty with many of the skills involved in comprehending text. By definition, students with LD experience unexpected failure to learn. The overwhelming majority of students with LD (at least 80%) experience serious difficulty learning to read (Gersten, Fuchs, Williams, & Baker, 2001). Clearly students with LD are not a homogeneous group; however there are some commonalities that can be noted. Many students with LD show specific deficits in the area of phonological processing (decoding—sound/symbol correlation) and fluency (decoding with speed, accuracy, and expression). These deficits affect their ability to comprehend text. However, many other children with LD are able to read reasonably fluently but do not understand what they have read because of specific cognitive processing difficulties (Williams, 2003). Thus, some students with LD possess the cognitive abilities necessary to effectively comprehend text; however, for some reason they do so inefficiently or ineffectively (Gersten et al., 2001).

Reading comprehension involves strategic processing of language and concepts; students must be able to take in information from written language, organize that information in a logical manner, and construct meaning from that information. Students with LD often have greater difficulty with this, and breakdowns often occur because they are unable to regulate their cognitive processes in a purposeful, reflective manner (Gersten et al., 2001). Swanson and Alexander (1997) identified four particular cognitive processes that pose difficulties for students with LD: (1) phonological processing (noted earlier), (2) orthographic and semantic processing, (3) metacognition, and (4) working memory.

Orthographic and Semantic Processing

Orthographic (spelling) and semantic (word meaning) processing difficulties directly impact a student's ability to comprehend text. If students are unable to negotiate spelling conventions or understand the meaning of words in text it is not likely that they will be able to comprehend the text. Orthographic processing difficulties are common among students with LD. It is often difficult for students with LD to understand or manipulate the conventions of written language such as correct and incorrect spellings (Swanson & Alexander, 1997). Semantic processing (understanding the meaning of words) presents difficulties for students with LD. They are often unable to create a meaningful representation of text; it is suggested that this is one reason for their reading difficulties (Swanson & Alexander, 1997). They have particular difficulty retrieving semantic information while reading. This inability to remember the meaning of words dramatically influences their ability to comprehend text.

Metacognition

Metacognition is essential to reading comprehension. The reader's awareness of and ability to regulate, monitor, and adjust cognitive actions are key components of comprehension (Swanson & Alexander, 1997). Good readers will focus their attention, realize when there is a breakdown in comprehension, and apply fix-up strategies to gain comprehension of text. Poor readers, including those with LD, often lack the awareness or ability necessary to regulate those various cognitive actions. Often, students with LD possess a degree of metacognition but lack strategies to properly utilize that knowledge. For example, they may be aware when a breakdown in comprehension occurs but lack the necessary fix-up strategies to achieve comprehension. Teaching students with LD procedures or strategies to enhance their metacognition can positively influence their text comprehension (Swanson & Alexander, 1997).

Working Memory

Working memory is the portion of memory used to process information (Swanson, 1996). Working memory is essential to text comprehension; while reading, it is necessary to briefly store incoming information while other information is being obtained or manipulated. This is how text begins to evolve into meaningful information (Swanson & Alexander, 1997). However, working memory is a processing resource of limited capacity. It is able to hold only a limited number of "chunks" of information at a time, and then only for a matter of seconds. We are consciously aware of the information in our working memory; however if we do not process the information, it will be lost. In other words, as soon as information is not being used it disappears. To effectively comprehend text, one must be able to hold a small amount of information in working memory for a short time while simultaneously processing that information (Swanson & Alexander, 1997).

PREREQUISITE SKILLS

A variety of skills are necessary to successfully comprehend written material. The National Reading Panel, the Partnership for Reading, the National Institute for Literacy, the National Institute of Child Health and Human Development, and the U.S.

Department of Education have identified five essential components to effective literacy instruction: (1) phonemic awareness, (2) phonological processing, (3) fluency, (4) vocabulary, and (5) text comprehension. These components are not independent of each other. A student's ability to manipulate sounds in spoken language (phonemic awareness) is a critical component, affecting the ability to understand that there is a predictable relationship between spoken and written sounds (phonics). Students must regulate those cognitive processes in order to read accurately and fluently (fluency). A student's ability to read fluently and to understand the meaning of novel words (vocabulary) directly affects his or her ability to comprehend text (text comprehension).

Effective instruction in each of these areas is crucial. Explicit, systematic instruction in early literacy skills has proven to be the most effective method for teaching these essential skills (National Reading Panel, 2000). Each skill builds on the next with the end goal of reading comprehension. Phonemic awareness is the ability to discern, reflect on, and manipulate the individual sounds in spoken words. Prior to learning to read print, children need to become aware of how the sounds in words work. Children who cannot discern and manipulate the phonemes of spoken words will have a difficult time learning how to relate these phonemes to graphemes (letters representing sounds) when they see them in written words (National Reading Panel, 2000). The ability to relate phonemes to written words is part of phonological processing. Phonological processing involves learning the alphabetic system; children must learn the letter–sound correspondences and spelling patterns, as well as be able to apply this knowledge to their reading. Phonological processing is consistently implicated in the ability of students with LD to successfully comprehend text. This is one of the most overt processes that present difficulties for students' success with reading comprehension (Swanson & Alexander, 1997).

Reading fluency is also highly correlated with reading comprehension. Fluent readers are able to decode text with speed, accuracy, and expression. Reading fluently is dependent upon word recognition skill. Students who are not fluent readers often have difficulty gaining the meaning of text (National Reading Panel, 2000). Meaning is often compromised by lack of fluency, resulting in unrewarding reading experiences, and reading is then avoided or done merely as a task to get finished with little cognitive involvement (Cunningham & Stanovich, 1998).

Vocabulary is a prerequisite of reading comprehension because readers must know what *most* of the words mean before they can understand what is being read. Vocabulary and reading comprehension are both related to the meaning of print. Vocabulary is linked to the specific meaning of words, while reading comprehension is thought of in larger units of meaning (i.e., themes or concepts). Vocabulary can be broken down into different categories: listening vocabulary, speaking vocabulary, reading vocabulary, and writing vocabulary (National Reading Panel, 2000). Each of these requires a different level of knowledge. Reading vocabulary requires that students recognize and understand various words or word parts in written text. A student's ability to recognize and understand words in text directly affects his or her ability to comprehend text (National Reading Panel, 2000). Struggling readers and students with LD typically bring less vocabulary knowledge to a reading task, and consequently their comprehension suffers.

PREREADING STRATEGIES

Students with LD often possess a limited understanding of various text structures (the way ideas in text are organized) and often have limited knowledge of subject matter (Garner, 1987). They have difficulties specifically with the difference between narrative (story structure) and expository text structures (textbook or formal writing structure).

Narrative Text Structure

Narrative text structure is usually the first structure that children are exposed to, and not surprisingly they are often more familiar with it than with other structures. Narratives are generally a sequence of events involving characters, actions, goals, and emotions. Skilled readers typically understand this series of events and expect the story to unfold in a certain way. This leads them to ask relevant questions about the story they are reading while they are reading it (Gersten et al., 2001). Less skilled readers often lack mastery of this schema and must be taught how text is structured and what relevant questions would be.

The Story Grammar Strategy

Short and Ryan (1984) taught students to use the Story Grammar strategy (see Figure 4.5 in Chapter 4), providing children with a strategic plan for selecting important aspects of the story information for further study. These students were taught to vocalize questions dealing with important story information, note questions in the margins, and underline story information answering the Story Grammar questions. The Story Grammar strategy has five questions:

1. Who is the main character?
2. Where and when did the story take place?
3. What did the main character do?
4. How did the story end?
5. How did the main character feel?

This strategy is an unstructured strategy; the procedural information is left out (i.e., exactly what steps the students will perform to use the strategy). Chapter 4 provides an example of how the Story Grammar strategy can be structured, as well as a sample implementation plan. When students were initially taught to use the Story Grammar strategy, they were given written text that could be marked on. This is not a luxury that is afforded to many classroom teachers; thus the sample implementation plan does not follow along exactly with Short and Ryan's (1984) study.

Expository Text Structure

As children progress through school, the demands change, with an increasing emphasis on comprehension of expository text. Typically, children are "learning to read" up through third grade. By fourth grade there tends to be a shift from "learning to read" to "reading to learn." Instruction for children in the primary grades relies heavily on reading stories for reading instruction. However, in fourth grade students are increasingly expected to work with expository text. Students with LD often have a difficult time gaining knowledge from expository text.

Often, difficulties are due to the fact that students with LD have limited knowledge of expository text structure. Unlike narrative text structures, children are not regularly exposed to expository text structures outside of the school environment. There are a number of text structures that provide useful information. Some are physical features such as headers, bold print, italics, tables, and figures. We discuss strategies that use text features in Chapter 11, which focuses on study skills. Anderson and Armbruster (1984) identified six major expository text structures (Table 9.1): (1) description, (2) temporal sequence of events, (3) explanation, (4) definition–example, (5) compare–contrast, and (6) problem–solution–effect. Good readers are aware of text structures and are able to make logical connections and create their own schema (representation) while reading text.

Research on expository text comprehension suggests that (1) awareness of text structure is acquired developmentally, (2) some text structures are more apparent and easier for readers to grasp, and (3) skill at discriminating text structure, and using it, appears to be central for comprehension of expository text (Gersten et al., 2001). If students are ill equipped to negotiate and strategically process expository text, it will be difficult for them to gain knowledge from the text. Teaching students strategies for negotiating and comprehending expository text can significantly improve their performance; knowledge of text structures leads students to ask themselves constructive questions about the text they are reading, and build the cognitive connections necessary for comprehension (Gersten et al., 2001).

TABLE 9.1. Examples of Expository Text Structures

Text structures	Explanation
Description	Text that illustrates a topic; a written account, representation, or explanation of something.
Temporal sequence of events	The time order in which things are arranged, actions are carried out, or events happen.
Explanation	A statement giving reasons for something or details of something.
Definition–example	Describing or stating something clearly and unambiguously, as well as providing an illustration that supports or provides more information.
Problem–solution–effect	A difficult situation, or matter, and how it is resolved, and how the change occurred as a direct result of the situation and resolution.

Note. See Anderson and Armbruster (1984) for more details.

The SCROL Strategy

The SCROL strategy was designed to improve student reading and learning from content-area texts (Grant, 1993). It is intended for students in middle and upper grades. The SCROL strategy (see Figure 4.2 in Chapter 4) includes five steps: (1) *Survey* the headings; (2) write down any key words from the heading that might provide *Connections* between them; (3) *Read* the text looking for words and phrases that express important information about the headings; (4) *Outline* the text using indentations to reflect text structure; and (5) *Look back* at the text and check the accuracy of the major ideas and details. This strategy is intended to help students read and understand a variety of texts. The strategy encourages students to use text headings to aid their comprehension and help them find and remember important information. Chapter 4 provides additional information and an example of an implementation plan for the SCROL strategy.

DURING-READING STRATEGIES

While reading new, unfamiliar text, students with LD often lack strategies to assist them when comprehension of text is disrupted. Monitoring comprehension is essential to the reading process. This requires that students be actively involved at a metacognitive level. Unfortunately, as we mentioned earlier, students with LD are not actively involved at metacognitive level. However, through strategy instruction, students can be taught to be more actively involved with the reading material and monitor their comprehension of the text.

Question Generation/Question Answering

The most common measure of a student's reading comprehension is answering questions at the end of a text (Graham & Wong, 1993). Answering questions after reading encourages students to focus on the important concepts in text; however, students with LD often have a difficult time with this. One way to bolster student performance in question answering is teaching students to generate their own think-type questions. By generating think-type questions, students become more cognitively involved with the text. Question generation promotes active engagement with text, as well as increasing students' ability to monitor comprehension.

Question-Generation Strategy

Davey and McBride (1986) taught upper elementary students how to generate two types of questions, those linking information across sentences and those related to the *most* important information (Table 9.2). First, students were taught the value of question generation while reading. Generating questions while reading promotes active involvement with text, cues the reader to focus on important concepts, and prompts the reader to think beyond what is provided in the text. Second, students were taught to differentiate between locate- and think-type questions. Locate-type questions merely

TABLE 9.2. Steps in Teaching Students a Question-Generation Strategy

Step 1. Provide rationale
- Explain why generation of think-type questions helps reading comprehension.

Step 2. Question type
- Explain the difference between locate- and think-type questions.
  - *Locate-type questions* can be answered directly from the text—for example, "What is the capital of Nebraska?"
  - *Think-type questions* require thinking beyond the text—for example, "Why did the author use a tunnel to describe her life?"

Step 3. Linking information
- Explain what a question stem is.
- Explain signal words for question stems: *What, Why, How.*
- Provide examples of question stems and what appropriate responses look like.
  Q: "What did the author say about _____ in the previous passage?"
  A: "The author said _____."
  Q: "Why did the author use _____ to explain _____ in the previous passage?"
  A: "The author used that as an example because _____."
  Q: "How does _____ relate to _____?"
  A: "_____ relates to _____ by _____."

Step 4. Self-monitoring
- Teach students how to self-monitor their performance of the question-generation strategy by using a checklist (Figure 9.1).

Note. Based on Davey, B., & McBride, S. (1986). Effects of question-generation training on reading comprehension. *Journal of Educational Psychology, 78,* 256–262.

pose a question that can be answered by directly restating information from the text (e.g., "What year was the first Nobel Peace Prize awarded?"). Think-type questions require additional cognitive and linguistic demands. Students are required to think beyond what is in the text, and state that as a question. Good think-type questions help you remember key information, help you know if you need to reread, and help you to anticipate test questions (e.g., "Why did the author use a graphic artist to describe ratios?"). Third, students were taught how to generate question stems for relating information from one part of the passage to information in another part (i.e., How did the author relate _____ to _____? Why did the author use _____ to describe _____?). Then, students were taught important signal words to use in question stems (*what, why,* and *how*) and what an appropriate response would look like. For example, "What did the author say about _____ in the previous passage? The author said _____." Finally, students were taught how to self-monitor their use of the question-generation strategy (Figure 9.1). Students also were presented with questions about how well they felt they did using question generation.

Graphic/Semantic Organizers

Graphic organizers, originally called structure overviews, provide readers with new approaches to reading that are different from traditional, linear text presentation (Horton, Lovitt, & Bergerud, 1990). In this approach, a graphic is used to illustrate the structure of the text and the interrelations between concepts, providing readers with a

How well did I identify important information?

5 = Excellent 4 = Good 3 = Satisfactory 2 = Somewhat 1 = Not at all

How well did I link information together?

5 = Excellent 4 = Good 3 = Satisfactory 2 = Somewhat 1 = Not at all

How well could I answer my question?

5 = Excellent 4 = Good 3 = Satisfactory 2 = Somewhat 1 = Not at all

Did my "think" question use different language from the text?

☐ Yes   ☐ No

Did I use good signal words?

☐ Yes   ☐ No

FIGURE 9.1. Question-generation strategy checklist.

clearer, more substantial understanding of what is being read (Chang, Sung, & Chen, 2002). Graphic organizers vary in structure and detail. Even though graphic representations of different texts will look different, the underlying principles and methods of application are very similar. They all convert linear information (text) into nonlinear graphic representations. Graphic organizers can be used with narrative or expository text.

The Story Map Strategy

Idol (1987) used a graphic organizer called the Story Map to improve students' reading comprehension. This technique was based on a schema-theoretic view of reading comprehension. This view emphasizes developing an improved association between the reader's prior knowledge structures (schemas) and written text. This approach helps students effectively apply story schemas to create a graphic representation. The Story Map (Figure 9.2) is a graphic representation of parts of a story, and how they are interrelated. This framework draws the student's attention to elements common among narrative prose.

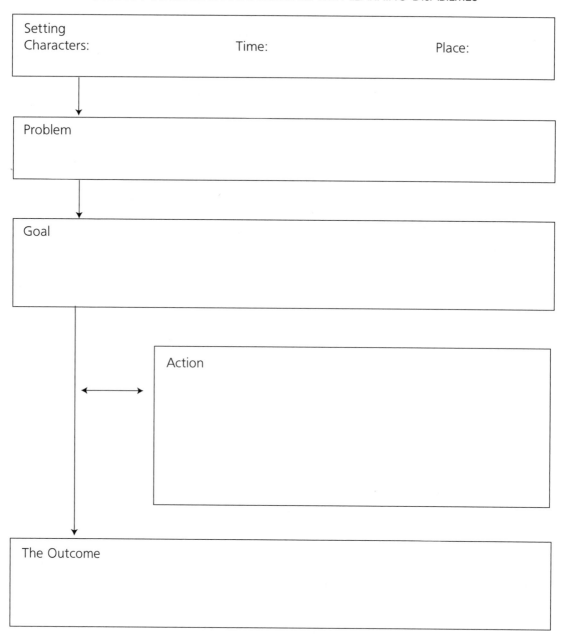

FIGURE 9.2. Example of a Story Map. From Idol, L. (1987). Group story mapping: A comprehension strategy for both skilled and unskilled readers. *Journal of Learning Disabilities, 20*(4), 196–205. Copyright 1987 by PRO-ED, Inc. Reprinted by permission.

Students are taught to read the story and note, in some manner, the elements in the story map: (1) the setting, including characters, time, and place, (2) the problem, (3) the goal, (4) the action, and (5) the outcome. As mentioned earlier, this is an unstructured strategy; the exact procedure, or structure to follow, will need to be determined by the teacher. We provide an example of how this could be done in Chapter 4.

POSTREADING STRATEGIES

Linking Comprehension Questions to Text

The ability to answer questions at the end of text *is* important; however the ability to successfully search for appropriate information within a text to find the correct answer is of equal importance (Raphael & McKinney, 1983). As noted earlier, question answering is one of the primary means by which we assess a student's ability to comprehend text. This makes a student's ability to access appropriate information within a text a key factor in successfully comprehending text. Knowledge of the relationship between comprehension questions and the text used to answer them is a critical comprehension skill (Raphael & McKinney, 1983). Explicit instruction on this relationship can improve comprehension skills and dramatically affect reading comprehension.

Question–Answer Relationship Strategy

Raphael and Wonnacott (1985) taught students to recognize the relationship between comprehension questions and the text answer sources; these question–answer relationships (QARs) were divided into three types (1) "right there" (text explicit), (2) "think and search" (text implicit), and (3) "on my own" (script implicit). A "right there" QAR is a question with an answer stated explicitly in the text within a single sentence. A "think and search" QAR is a question that requires the reader to integrate information across sentences or paragraphs. An "on my own" QAR is a question that requires the reader to draw from his or her own background knowledge to answer the question. Through a process of modeling and fading, students were taught to identify the type of QAR posed by particular questions. Students were led through examples and provided rationales for different QARs. Independent practice was increased once students had achieved mastery of the QAR strategy. Students were given passages and comprehension questions to assess their ability to identify the different QARs (Figure 9.3). For example, students would read a passage about early cowboys and then be given a question like "For cowboys, what particular dangers were associated with a cattle drive?" The student would determine what type of QAR the question represented, locate the answer in the text, and answer the question on the appropriate line.

Summarizing

Text summarization is merely generating a representation of the gist of a passage (Pressley & Harris, 1990). Text summarization prompts students to identify the main

What made Albert Einstein a great scientist?

RIGHT THERE _____

THINK AND SEARCH _____

ON MY OWN _____

What is he best known for?

RIGHT THERE _____

THINK AND SEARCH _____

ON MY OWN _____

What type of disability did he have?

RIGHT THERE _____

THINK AND SEARCH _____

ON MY OWN _____

FIGURE 9.3. QAR task example.

From Robert Reid and Torri Ortiz Lienemann (2006). Copyright by The Guilford Press. Permission to photocopy this figure is granted to purchasers of this book for personal use only (see copyright page for details).

idea of the passage, delete any unnecessary details, and run through the main points. This encourages students to build their own schema of concepts and ideas presented in text, and increases their understanding and memory of what was read (Nelson, Smith, & Dodd, 1992). Text summarization also prompts students to utilize metacognitive processes (awareness and control of the reading process) and cues them to attend to the structure of ideas within text, and how ideas relate to each other (Rinehart, Stahl, & Erickson, 1986). Improving students' metacognitive control enables them to better evaluate their reading and increases their awareness of the process necessary to comprehend text.

Summary Skills

The Summary Skills Strategy developed by Nelson, Smith, and Dodd (1992) can be used to guide students' summarization of expository text. The strategy consists of three main steps: (1) identify and organize the main idea and important information, (2) identify important things the writer said about the main idea, and (3) clarify and revise the summary. These steps are broken down further into nine self-directional prompts (Table 9.3). Students are prompted through the series of steps to identify and organize the main idea and important information in the text and put it into a summary. Students are further prompted to clarify and revise their summaries.

Eight of the nine steps shown in Table 9.3 are aimed at generation of summary material, while the ninth is directed toward clarification of the text summary. The "generation" steps identify and organize the main idea and important information. The first step is for students to ask themselves, "What was the main idea?" and write it down. Texts vary in their explicitness of main idea. Students must be taught how to identify a main idea, and the purpose of a main idea. A main idea is the central theme; all the other ideas support this main one. Next, students are prompted to ask themselves, "What important things did the writer say about the main idea?" and write down the important things that the writer said. Students are taught to identify supporting ideas.

TABLE 9.3. Summary Writing Guide

I. Identify and organize the main idea and important information.

Step 1. Think to yourself—"What was the main idea?" Write it down.

II. Identify important things the writer said about the main idea.

Step 2. Think to yourself—"What important things did the writer say about the main idea?" Write down the important things the writer said.

    1. _____

    2. _____

    3. _____

    4. _____

    5. _____

Step 3. Go back and check to make sure you understood what the main idea was and the important things the writer said about this.

Step 4. Think to yourself—"What is the main idea or topic that I am going to write about?" Write a topic sentence for your summary.

Step 5. Think to yourself—"How should I group my ideas?" Put a "1" next to the idea you want to be first, put a "2" next to the idea you want to be second, and so on.

Step 6. Think to yourself—"Is there any important information that I left out or is there any unimportant information that I can take out?"

Step 7. Write a summary about what you read.

Step 8. Read your summary and think to yourself—"Is anything unclear?" Rewrite your summary (if necessary).

III. Clarify and revise the summary.

Step 9. Ask your classmate to read your summary and tell you if there is anything that is not clear. Rewrite your summary (if necessary).

Note. Based on Nelson, J. R., Smith, D. J., & Dodd, J. M. (1992). The effects of teaching a summary skills strategy to students identified as learning disabled on their comprehension of science text. *Education and Treatment of Children, 15*(3), 228–243.

Supporting ideas help to further develop and support the main idea. The importance of information is determined by whether or not its exclusion would weaken the statement of the main idea.

Then, in Step 3, students are prompted to go back and check to make sure they understood what the main idea was and the important things were that the writer said about this. This step is to ensure that students check over what it is they identified as the main idea and supporting details. Through checking students may find that they did not have a clear idea of what the main idea was, or that the supporting ideas do not support what they thought was the main idea. At this point they may need to go back and restate the main idea. Step 4 prompts students to ask themselves, "What is the main idea or topic that I am going to write about?" and write a topic sentence for their summary. Students are instructed on how to create a topic sentence. Topic sentences are merely a restatement of the main idea in a complete sentence. In Step 5 students are taught to rank their supporting ideas; they are to ask themselves, "How should I group my ideas?" and put a 1 next to the idea they want to be first, put a 2 next to the idea they want to be second, and so on. By doing this they are organizing their summary, and possibly eliminating any unnecessary ideas.

In Step 6, students are prompted to ask themselves if there is any important information they left out or any unimportant information they can take out. Students must look through the text again and determine whether or not they have included all relevant information, as well as whether or not they have included unimportant information. In Step 7 students are told to write a summary about what they read. By this point they should have a summary well planned and organized for composition. Step 8 starts the revision process; students are prompted to read their summary and ask themselves, "Is anything unclear?" and rewrite the summary (if necessary). Students need to determine whether or not their summary is an accurate representation of the text, and whether it highlights all the important points. Step 9 is the final step; students are prompted to have a classmate read their summary and ask the classmate to tell them if there is anything that is not clear. This peer review process is an additional step to ensure the clarity of the students' summaries.

IMPLEMENTATION PLANS

In this section, we provide examples from various stages of implementation plans for the reading comprehension strategies previously mentioned.

Stage 1 for Question Generation: Developing and Activating Background Knowledge

Prior to teaching the strategy, it is necessary to evaluate the student's background knowledge. Formal or informal assessments can be used to determine what skills the student possesses and what skills may be lacking; doing a task breakdown will provide the information for identifying the skills necessary to successfully complete the strategy (Table 9.4).

TABLE 9.4. Sample Task Breakdown for Question-Generation Strategy

Strategy	Skills	Assessment
Basic skills	Ability to read at the level of text presented	Students will be given an assessment, to determine appropriate independent reading levels.
	Ability to write	Given an informal assessment, the student will produce complete sentences.
Self-monitoring		
"How well did I identify important information?"	Ability to pick out important information Ability to critique own work	Provide students with a written text, require them to pick out the important information, and check to see how well they thought they did.
"How well did I link information together?"	Knowledge of linking words and how to use them	An informal assessment on linking words and usage will be given.
"How well could I answer my question?"	Knowledge of how to answer a question completely	An informal assessment on answering sentences completely will be given.
"Did my 'think' question use different language from text?"	Knowledge of "think" questions	Students will be asked to define "think" question and provide an example.
"Did I use good signal words?"	Knowledge of signal words	Students will be asked to list signal words and explain their purpose.

Stage 2 for Graphic/Semantic Organizers: Discussing the Strategy

This is the first stage in "initiating" strategy instruction. In this stage it is important to stress the relevance of the strategy. An initial conference between the teacher and student is necessary. During this initial conference the teacher will want to discuss the student's current performance. In order for the student to be successful and self-regulating he or she needs to make a commitment to use the strategy, or "buy in." It is important for the teacher to stress the value of the strategy. Brainstorm situations where using this strategy or completing the given task accurately is important. For example, the following might be appropriate brainstorming ideas in response to the question "When would it be important for you to read and understand text?":

- For a test
- For an assignment
- Making an informed decision
- Learning more about something of interest to you
- Assembling something
- Operating equipment

As a last resort the teacher can use a behavioral contract, where the student tries the strategy and gets reinforcement.

A sample script for "selling" the strategy follows:

> "This year we are doing a lot of reading! Sometimes it is a little difficult to keep everything straight. When we take our comprehension test sometimes your memory of what was read is not too clear. Let's take a look at some of tests that we took this quarter. You really did a nice job _____ [point out the positives]. However, if I look at the questions, there are some that aren't answered completely, and some that you just didn't seem to be too sure about. Earlier we mentioned that it is important to be able to read and comprehend text for assignments or for learning more about something. It appears that we could improve on this. Part of the reason you are having trouble is that no one ever taught you the tricks of it. The good news is that I have a trick to teach you that can really help you with your reading comprehension. You know how when you go on a trip you use a map to guide you? Well, I have a 'map' to help guide you with your reading. It's called a 'semantic map,' or 'graphic organizer.' 'Semantic' means 'meaning'; this is a map to help you remember the important ideas in what you have read, and improve your reading comprehension."

Students need to "buy in" before you can move on. In this stage we also introduce the strategy steps, and any prompts that will be given (see Table 9.2).

Stage 3 for Summarization: Modeling the Strategy

Here is an example of a think-aloud for a summarization strategy.

> "OK, I just got done reading the section in my science book for class tomorrow. Ugh! I hope I can remember all of that information tomorrow when we have to answer questions. Sometimes it's hard for me to remember what I've read the night before. Hey, I know what I can do. My teacher just taught us how to use a summarization strategy to help us remember what we've read, and I can use my Summary Writing Guide to help me write a good summary; that will help me remember what I've read. OK, here goes! First, I need to think to myself, 'What is the main idea?' OK, I know that because the whole section was about invertebrates in the sea, and the different kinds. But what was the 'main idea?' I think the main idea was that there are millions of different kinds of animals that in the sea, and they can be divided into three groups: (1) plankton, (2) benthos, and (3) nekton. OK, on to Step 2. I need to think to myself, 'What important things did the writer say about the main idea?' and write down the important things the writer said.
>
> "OK, I already identified what I think is the main idea, now I need to write down some of the important things that the writer said about invertebrates in the sea. I know that I need to find the important ideas in the reading

so I can support my main idea, and that will help me remember better. Well, let's see . . . the author divided the invertebrates into three categories, plankton, benthos, and nekton. That's pretty important, because everything else follows those three categories. If I didn't mention that I wouldn't be able put the rest of the information into the right categories, and that's pretty important. OK, what else? Plankton live near the surface of the water, benthos live deep down on the seabed, and nektons swim between the top and bottom layers. Let's see, there are two kinds of plankton that live in the sea: (1) phytoplankton—plants, and (2) zooplankton—animals. Wow, some jellyfish are nearly 80 inches wide. That's cool, I'm going to write that down.

"Whew, this is going pretty well! I remember most everything that I have read, and *everything* that I wrote down! This should really help me answer questions tomorrow, and when it comes to the test I will be able to look at my summary to help me study! OK, what else? Let's see, I've talked about plankton, hmm . . . OK, now nekton. That's what's mentioned next in the text. I'm just going though the text and picking out the important details, and I don't want to miss any, so I will just start at the beginning, and stop at the end. OK, nekton; what about nekton? Most of them are vertebrates, but not all—squid and octopus are nektons, but they are invertebrates. Last category, benthos; what about benthos? I already know that they live at the bottom of the sea. What else? OK, some benthos are animals that stay in one place (like coral), and some walk or crawl on the sea floor. Wow, I'm all done, that wasn't difficult at all!

"Let's see, that was Step 2, what is Step 3? Oh yeah, I go back and check to make sure I understood what the main idea was and the important things the writer said about this topic. OK, I do understand the main idea, and important things. Good! What next? Step 4: OK, I need to write a topic sentence. Let's see, we talked about topic sentences in class. I know that a topic sentence needs to express the main idea, and *all* the important ideas need to support that topic sentence. Hmm, how can I say that? Well, I could just say, 'Invertebrates that live in the sea can be classified in three different categories.' That's true! Well, do all my important details support that? Kind of, but not quite. I should add the three different categories, plankton, benthos, and nekton. That would make a great topic sentence. 'Invertebrates that live in the sea can be classified in three different categories: plankton, benthos, and nekton.' Great! Now Step 5, grouping my ideas. OK, I'm going to rank them, 1, 2, 3 . . . that looks good.

"Step 6, I need to check my important information to see if I left any out, or need to take out any unnecessary information. Hmm, I think I have all the important information, but do I have any that is unnecessary? Yeah, I think that statement about the jellyfish is unnecessary; it's cool, but it doesn't really further develop the main idea. OK, good. Step 7—'Write a summary about what you read.' . . . That was easy; I just rewrote my topic sentence, and put my important details into complete sentences. Step 8, I read my summary and rewrite if necessary. OK, it sounds pretty good; I don't think I need to rewrite it. Step 9, ask a classmate to read it; I'll have Maci read it. She knows a lot about science. Wow, Maci thought it was good! That's great! I'm done, and I remember all the important parts of the reading. The summarization strategy really helped!"

Stage 4 for SCROL: Memorizing the Strategy

Memorizing the strategy is extremely important! As a student once said, "If you can't remember it you can't use it" (Harris, personal communication, 2005). We want the students to focus on the task and not on the steps of the strategy. Memorization also frees up working memory. The specific memorization activities themselves are not critical. There are many appropriate activities. The important aspect of the activities is whether or not they facilitate memorization. However, you will need to plan and prepare the memorization activities and monitor their effectiveness. Many strategies use acronyms that can help students memorize the strategy (e.g., SCROL); however, students must be able to do more than simply name the steps. They must know and understand what must be done at each step of the strategy. For example to memorize SCROL, students might pair up. Then one student can give the letter (e.g., S) and the other state the step and what must be done.

Stage 5 for Question–Answer Relationship: Supporting the Strategy

In this stage, scaffolding is important. With scaffolding it is possible for a gradual transfer of strategy performance from teacher to student. Students need to be given adequate time and support to master the strategy.

Content Scaffolding

Students will be provided with a simple passage. The teacher and students will then go over the passage and the comprehension questions at the end of the passage. Together they will determine what type of QAR each comprehension question represents and answer those questions on the appropriate line. The teacher will direct the process, and the students will provide answers to teacher-directed questions (i.e., "What type of QAR does this question represent? Is the information found directly in one sentence of the text? Do you need to look in more than one sentence or paragraph to find the answer? Is this a question that requires you to think on your own?").

Task Scaffolding

Students will be taught one question–answer relationship at a time. They will first be taught to locate information in text to answer "right there" questions, then how to locate information in text to answer "think and search" questions. Finally, students will be taught how to utilize the information in text to answer "on my own" questions.

During collaborative practice, the teacher will prompt students to use their QAR categories to answer comprehension questions. The teacher will demonstrate the use of the QAR categories though modeling. In subsequent lessons the teacher will ask the students to fill in the QAR categories and describe how they knew which category the question represented. Finally, students will be given comprehension questions and the QAR categories and expected to determine the category and answer the questions correctly.

Material Scaffolding

The student will be provided with a QAR prompt card (Figure 9.4) to use with the comprehension questions at the end of each reading passage given. Initially, this prompt will serve as a guide to remind students of the question–answer relationships and how those relationships can help them answer comprehension questions. Students will be provided multiple opportunities to practice using their QAR strategy until they are able to do so independently and successfully answer comprehension questions.

Stage 6 for Summarization: Independent Performance

At this stage the student is ready to use the strategy independently. The teacher's main task is to monitor the student's performance and check on proper and consistent use of the strategy. However, it is important to keep in mind that our main goal is improved academic performance. Teachers must evaluate whether or not the strategy is being used and whether or not academic performance has improved. Generalization may

---

QAR Helper

What type of question is this?

RIGHT THERE
Can the information be found in one sentence of the text?

THINK AND SEARCH
Can the information be found in two or more of the sentences or paragraphs in the text? Does it require me to put the information together?

ON MY OWN
Does this question require me to use my background knowledge of the subject?

FIGURE 9.4. QAR scaffolding example.

also be a concern. Students will not always generalize strategies to appropriate situations; they will need to be prompted and encouraged to do so. Note that activities to promote generalization should start very early in the process. For example, in the discussion stage (Stage 2) teachers and students will often list situations where a strategy could or should be used.

To promote generalization, students should be encouraged to use the strategy in other content areas where they are required to read. All team teachers should be informed about the use of the strategy, the language, the prompts, and what is required at each step. All team teachers should be given a wall chart to hang up in their room as a reminder for students to use the Summary Writing Guide strategy when appropriate.

Students should be assessed regularly using the comprehension questions at the ends of their texts. These scores should be recorded and tracked for trends in progress. The goal is improved academic performance, and if performance isn't improving a reteaching of the strategy may be necessary. Once students are successful using the strategy and answering comprehension questions their performance should be monitored periodically. Even when students have reached the independent performance stage, they should be monitored to ensure proper use of the strategy. If students deviate from the given summarization strategy, performance should be evaluated, but action should only be taken if performance is no longer improving.

FINAL THOUGHTS

Reading is one of the most important skills students gain in school. No student can succeed without well-developed comprehension skills. Improving a student's comprehension of text can have a positive and lifelong impact on learning outcomes. In closing, we should stress that instruction in comprehension strategies should begin early and continue through a student's academic career.

REFERENCES

Anderson, T. H., & Armbruster, B. B. (1984). Content area textbooks. In R. C. Anderson, J. Osborn, & R. J. Tierney (Eds.), *Learning to read in American schools* (pp. 193–226). Hillsdale, NJ: Erlbaum.

Bakken, J., Mastropieri, M., & Scruggs, T. (1997). Reading comprehension of expository science material and students with learning disabilities: A comparison of strategies. *Journal of Special Education 31*(3), 300–324.

Chang, K. E., Sung, Y. T., & Chen, I. D. (2002). The effect of concept mapping to enhance text comprehension and summarization. *Journal of Experimental Education, 71*(1), 5–23.

Cunningham, A. E., & Stanovich, K. E. (1998). What reading does for the mind. *American Educator, 22*(1–2), 8–15.

Davey, B., & McBride, S. (1986). Effects of question-generation training on reading comprehension. *Journal of Educational Psychology, 78*, 256–262.

Durkin, D. (1993). *Teaching them to read* (6th ed.). Boston, MA: Allyn & Bacon.

Englert, C. S., & Mariage, T. V. (1991). Making students partners in the comprehension process: Organizing the reading "POSSE." *Learning Disability Quarterly, 14*, 123–138.

Gardill, M. C., & Jitendra, A. K. (1999). Advanced story map instruction: Effects on the reading comprehension of students with learning disabilities. *Journal of Special Education, 33*(1), 2–17.

Garner, R. (1987). Strategies for reading and studying expository text [Special issue: Current issues in reading comprehension]. *Educational Psychologist, 22*(3–4), 299–312.

Gersten, R., Fuchs, L., Williams, J., & Baker, S. (2001). Teaching reading comprehension strategies to students with learning disabilities: A review of research. *Review of Educational Research, 71*(2), 279–320.

Graham, L., & Wong, B. Y. L. (1993). Comparing two models of teaching a question-answering strategy for enhancing reading comprehension: Didactic and self-instructional training. *Journal of Learning Disabilities, 26*(4), 270–279.

Grant, R. (1993). Strategic training for using text headings to improve students' processing of content. *Journal of Reading, 36*(6), 482–488.

Horton, S. B., Lovitt, T. C., & Bergerud, D. (1990). The effectiveness of graphic organizers for three classifications of secondary students in content area classes. *Journal of Learning Disabilities, 23*(1), 12–22.

Idol, L. (1987). Group story mapping: A comprehension strategy for both skilled and unskilled readers. *Journal of Learning Disabilities, 20*(4), 196–205.

Johnson, L., Graham, S., & Harris, K. R. (1997). The effects of goal setting and self-instruction on learning a reading comprehension strategy: A study of students with learning disabilities. *Journal of Learning Disabilities, 30*(1), 80–91.

King, A. (1994). Guiding knowledge construction in the classroom: Effects of teaching children how to question and how to explain. *American Educational Research Journal, 31*(2), 338–368.

National Reading Panel. (2000). *Teaching children to read: An evidence-based assessment of the scientific research literature on reading and its implications for reading instruction* (NIH Publication No. 00-4769). Washington, DC: National Institute of Child Health and Development.

Nelson, J. R., Smith, D. J., & Dodd, J. M. (1992). The effects of teaching a summary skills strategy to students identified as learning disabled on their comprehension of science text. *Education and Treatment of Children, 15*(3), 228–243.

Pressley, M., & Harris, K. R. (1990). What we really know about strategy instruction. *Educational Leadership, 48*, 31–34.

Raphael, T. E., & McKinney, J. (1983). An examination of fifth- and eighth-grade children's question-answering behavior: An instructional study in metacognition. *Journal of Reading Behavior, 15*(3), 67–86.

Raphael, T. E., & Wonnacott, C. A. (1985). Metacognitive training in question-answering strategies: Implementation in a fourth-grade developmental reading program. *Reading Research Quarterly, 20*, 286–296.

Rinehart, S. D., Stahl, S. A., & Erickson, L. G. (1986). Some effects of summarization training on reading and studying. *Reading Research Quarterly, 21*(4), 422–438.

Short, E. J., & Ryan, E. B. (1984). Metacognitive differences between skilled and less skilled readers: Remediating deficits through story grammar and attribution training. *Journal of Educational Psychology, 76*(2), 225–235.

Swanson, H. L. (1996). Information processing: An introduction. In D. K. Reid, W. Hresko, & H. L Swanson (Eds.), *Cognitive approaches to learning disabilities* (pp. 251–285). Austin, TX: PRO-ED.

Swanson, H. L., & Alexander, J. (1997). Cognitive processes and predictors of word recognition and reading comprehension in learning-disabled and skilled readers: Revisiting the specificity hypothesis. *Journal of Educational Psychology, 89*(1), 128–158.

Williams, J. P. (2003). Teaching text structure to improve reading comprehension. In H. L. Swanson & K. R. Harris (Eds.), *Handbook of learning disabilities* (pp. 293–305). New York: Guilford Press.

CHAPTER 10

Strategies in Mathematics

Mathematics is a core academic competency. Mastering basic mathematic skills (e.g., knowledge of basic facts, problem solving) is critical for successful functioning in society. We are constantly confronted with problems that involve mathematics skills. These might range from "Do I have enough money to pay for these three items I want to purchase?" to I have to go 30 miles to a meeting that takes place in 30 minutes. How fast do I have to drive to get there on time?" Mastering the skills and strategies necessary to solve these problems is critical for functioning effectively in society (Patton, Cronin, Bassett, & Koppel, 1997). Our level of mathematics achievement is a matter of national concern, as research suggests that American children have serious deficits in many areas (Jitendra & Xin, 1997; Xin & Jitendra, 1999).

For purposes of this chapter, we limit our discussion to three major areas of mathematics: basic facts, computation procedures, and word-problem solving. Knowledge of basic math facts is a foundational for more advanced operations. Fluency with mathematics requires students to learn and store basic facts (e.g., $3 + 5 = 8$; $9 \times 7 = 63$) in long-term memory, and then rapidly and accurately recall and apply them. Computational procedures are also fundamental. Students must master procedures involved in computations such as long division, place value, and regrouping. They must also remember and apply these procedures correctly while simultaneously recalling and utilizing basic facts. Finally, students are required to develop and utilize word-problem-solving skills. Here students are confronted with word problems that require them to identify important information, conceptualize how to solve the problem, define appropriate equations, and solve equations. Again, knowledge of basic facts and computational procedures must also be accessed and utilized.

PROBLEMS FOR STUDENTS WITH LEARNING DISABILITIES

Problems with underachievement in mathematics are particularly pronounced for students with learning disabilities (Geary, 2003). Studies suggest that 5 to 10% of all school-age children have some type of serious deficit in mathematics and that difficulties in mathematics are common among children with LD (Geary, 2003; Rivera, 1997). Difficulties experienced by children with LD span all three areas (basic facts, computation procedures, and problem solving). As we've noted previously, children with LD are extremely heterogeneous; however, there are some problems that commonly occur (Geary, 2003). These include:

- Poor understanding of concepts underlying mathematical procedures
- Problems with counting and using counting to solve problems
- Use of immature or inappropriate strategies
- Difficulty with fact retrieval
- Difficulty coordinating and monitoring steps in computation
- Difficulty in word-problem solving

On the whole, children with LD are only slightly behind typically achieving peers in terms of development of number concepts (Geary, Hamson, & Hoard, 2000). But some commonly occurring problems, such as difficulty with counting concepts, have been demonstrated (Geary, Bow-Thomas, & Yao, 1992; Geary, Hoard, & Hamson, 1999). For example, children may believe that nonsequential counting (i.e., skipping some items and counting them later) will result in an incorrect count (Geary, 2003). Another example would be failure to grasp the commutative principle. Students who did not understand this principle would not understand that 8×5 is the same problem as 5×8. Poor understanding of number concepts can inhibit the use of advanced strategies and may affect ability to detect procedural errors (Geary, 2003). Counting problems are a serious concern because counting serves as an important preskill in the mastery of basic addition facts. Difficulty counting can inhibit the development of basic addition facts. Children with LD may be developmentally delayed in the use of counting to solve arithmetic problems. They may also fail to perceive the link between counting and problem solving. Many see counting as simply a rote activity (Geary, 2003).

Use of appropriate strategies is also a concern. Many children either fail to develop or fail to utilize more advanced strategies. For example, many children with LD don't gradually switch from counting to direct retrieval of math facts (Geary, Widaman, Little, & Corimer, 1987). Thus, these children use an inefficient means of retrieval. Memory problems are a major factor in poor mathematic performance. Children with LD commonly produce more errors in math fact retrieval than their peers. Research suggests that children with LD may have problems in storing basic facts in long term memory and accessing them readily. Errors in retrieval may be due to problems inhibiting irrelevant information and/or associations (Geary et al., 2000). For example, with a problem such as $6 + 2$, many will answer 7, the next number after 6. For complex problems (i.e., those that involve a number of operations), children with LD frequently make procedural errors. They may omit steps (e.g., fail to regroup) or have difficulty performing steps in the correct sequence. Procedural errors in computation appear to be due to problems monitoring and coordinating the sequence of problem-solving steps (Russell & Ginsberg, 1984). Problems with working memory are thought to be related to procedural difficulties.

Solving word problems is often extremely difficult for children with LD. The difficulties with word-problem solving go well beyond problems with decoding. Parmar, Cawley, and Frazita (1996) found that students with disabilities had difficulties representing problems, identifying salient information, and choosing the appropriate arithmetic operations. Word problems may contain irrelevant information, and solving them may require multiple operations or steps that can also cause serious problems (Fuchs & Fuchs, 2003). Thus, word problems place a number of demands on children's cognitive processing. These problems are exacerbated by the fact that mathematics instruction for children with LD often is focused on memorization of facts and computation skills at the expense of application of mathematics in problem-solving situations (Bottge, 1999; Parmar, Cawley, & Miller, 1994).

PREREQUISITE SKILLS

A list of all the possible prerequisite skills for mathematics would be beyond the scope of this chapter. There are, however, three major areas of preskills that are extremely important for successful development of mathematical skills: number sense, basic mathematics principles, and mathematic basic facts rules. These prerequisites are critical to the development of skill with basic facts, computation procedures, and problem solving. In this section we discuss each preskill.

Number Sense

Number sense is a concept that refers to "a child's fluidity and flexibility with numbers, the sense of what numbers mean, and an ability to perform mental mathematics and look at the world and make comparisons" (Gersten & Chard, 1999, p. 20). Children with good number sense have a "feel" for math. They can see patterns in numbers and have mastered concepts such as greater than, less than, and equal to. Van de Walle (1998) lists five components of number sense:

1. Well-understood number meanings (i.e., 3 corresponds to a certain quantity)
2. Awareness of multiple relationships among numbers (i.e., a set of 6 objects can be made with 2 sets of 3 or a set of 4 plus a set of 2)
3. Recognition of the relative magnitude of numbers (i.e., 5 is larger than 2)
4. Knowledge of the effects of operations on numbers (i.e., adding makes the number bigger)
5. Knowledge that numbers refer to measure of things in the real world

One of the key components of good number sense is a well-developed counting ability. Counting involves the ability to produce number words, and the knowledge that the number words have a one-to-one relationship with the set being counted. Counting is also a critical preskill for the development of knowledge of basic addition facts. Mastery of basic addition facts depends upon counting-based strategies initially (Garnett, 1992). Children go through five stages in mastery of basic addition facts:

- *Count all*: Given 3 + 2, the student counts 1, 2, 3, 4, 5 to get the answer (i.e., counts all the numbers).
- *Count on*: Given 2 + 5, the student begins at one addend and counts 2, 3, 4, 5, 6, 7.
- *Count on from larger addend or short-cut sum*: Given 2 + 5, the student begins at the larger addend and counts 5, 6, 7.
- *Memory*: Given 2 + 5, the student just "knows" the answer.

Obviously children with impaired counting skills will have difficulty progressing to the memory level where knowledge is automatic. Counting skills are also used in strategies for teaching basic facts, as we discuss later. Garnett (1992) recommended frequent practice in counting. This includes counting by 1's, 2's, and 5's. After students can count forward fluently, teachers should also attend to counting backward. This provides groundwork for subtraction skills.

Basic Mathematics Principles

There are a number of critical principles that are considered foundational for mathematical understanding and apply to many different levels of mathematics. Harniss, Carnine, Silbert, and Dixon (2002) and his colleagues noted the following set of critical principles:

- *Place value*: The position of a number provides information about the value of the number.
- *Expanded notation*: Numbers can be reduced to their underlying units (e.g., the number 437 is equal to four 100's plus three 10's, plus seven 1's)
- *Commutative property*: The order of numbers in an equation does not affect the result (e.g., 8 + 7 = 7 + 8). This is true for addition and multiplication, but not subtraction and division.
- *Associative property*: The grouping of numbers in an equation can be changed without changing the result; for example, (8 + 7) + 4 = 8 + (7 + 4). Again, only addition and multiplication are associative.
- *Distributive property*: Numbers in an equation can be redistributed; for example, $7 \times (8 + 4) = (7 \times 8) + (7 \times 4)$.
- *Equivalence*: The quantity on one side of the = sign is equal to the quantity on the other.

These principles, which Harniss and his colleagues term "big ideas," cut across all of basic mathematics and are critical for understanding mathematics and solving equations. For example, the commutative principle means that 5×4 is the same as 4×5. This in turn means that rather than having to memorize 100 basic addition facts, it's only necessary to learn 50, which decreases the memory burden significantly. Many children with LD do not understand the commutative principle and would think that the two problems were actually different.

Basic Facts Rules

For each of the four operations (addition, subtraction, multiplication, and division) there is an underlying set of rules. These rules are helpful in mastering the basic facts because they serve to help "chunk" facts into groups that are related. This in turn can help to reduce the demands on working memory and enable long-term storage in memory. These chunks can also be utilized as the basis for strategies, as we show later. Figure 10.1 shows the basic facts rules for addition, subtraction, multiplication, and division.

INSTRUCTION IN MATHEMATICS

In the sections that follow, we present examples of strategies for basic facts, computation procedures, and word-problem solving. We selected basic facts because they are the foundation for all mathematics skills. Students must master basic facts if they are to progress in mathematics. Computation involves application of basic facts to solve more advanced problems. This requires student to learn and follow an effective procedure. Many children with LD have difficulty with this. Word-problem solving was selected because it is a problem area for many children, and it is a critical area because it can help children develop problem-solving skills for real-world problems.

BASIC MATH FACTS STRATEGIES

Addition

Addition facts are the first in a series of fact families that must be learned. Basic facts are often taught by rote repetition. This is an extremely inefficient method for several reasons. First, it requires learning 100 facts by rote, and thus ignores the commutative principle. Second, and more importantly, it does not provide any framework to help students organize information to be learned. As we noted earlier, facts that are organized and related are much easier to learn than unrelated facts. Thornton and Toohey (1985) developed a chunking strategy to simplify instruction in basic addition facts. Figure 10.2 shows the strategy. This is an unstructured strategy. The strategy takes advantage of basic facts rules and simple mnemonics to group math facts by the strategy needed for recall. Each strategy group is taught in turn. Different strategies are used for each group. The "doubles" are taught by linking facts to pictures (e.g., 4 + 4 is the "spider fact," 6 + 6 is the "dozen eggs" fact). The "1 facts" and "2 facts" rely on counting skills. Students are taught to "feel the count." The key to this strategy is that all fact groups use a similar strategy for retrieval. The strategy does not cover all addition facts (i.e., 7 + 5, 8 + 4, 8 + 5, 8 + 6). This small group of facts must be taught sepa-

Addition	Subtraction	Multiplication	Division
The Order Rule (or commutative principle)	*The 0 Rule*: any number minus 0 is the number.	*The 0 Rule*: any number times 0 equals 0.	*The 0 Rule*: 0 divided by any number is 0.
The 0 Rule: any number plus 0 is the number.	*The 1's Rule*: any number minus 1 is 1 less than the number (count backwards by 1).	*The 1's Rule*: any number times 1 equals the number.	*The 1's Rule*: any number divided by 1 is the number.
The 1's Rule: any number plus 1 is one more than the number.	*The Same Number Rule*: any number minus itself is 0.	*The 2's Rule*: any number times 2 is double the number. Thus 8 × 2 is equal to 8 + 8.	*The 2's Rule*: any number divided by 2 is half the number.
The 9's Rule: any single-digit number greater than 0 added to 9 results in the addend number minus 1 plus 10.	*The Addition/ Subtraction Relationship Rule*: in a subtraction problem, the answer added to the number being subtracted equals the top number. Thus to solve 12 – 9 teach the student "What number plus 9 equals 12?"	*The 5's Rule*: any number times 5 is equivalent to counting by 5's the number of times indicated by the multiplier. Thus 5 × 4 is counting by 5's four times.	*The 9's Rule*: when dividing by 9 the answer is one more than the number in the 10's column. For example, 54 ÷ 9 = 6 (6 is one more than the number in the 10's column)
The 10's Rule: any single-digit number added to 10 results in the 0 being changed to the number being added.		*The 9's Rule*: when multiplying by 9, the answers can be found by taking 1 from the multiplier to get the number in the 10's position, and then adding enough to that number to make 9. For example 9 × 5—take 1 from 5 to get the number of 10's (i.e., 4) then add enough to 4 to make 9 (i.e., 5), thus the answer is 45.	*The Multiplication/ Division Relationship Rule*: to solve for 32 ÷ 4, think what number times 4 equals 32? The quotient times the divisor equals the dividend.

FIGURE 10.1. Basic facts rules.

Fact group	Sample facts		Verbal prompt	Strategy
Count Ons	8 + 2	5 + 1	Start big and count on.	"Feel" the count.
Zeroes	6 + 0	0 + 3	Plus zero stays the same.	Show it.
Doubles	5 + 5	8 + 8	Think of the picture.	Use the pictures (e.g., 4 + 4 is the spider fact).
Near Doubles	6 + 5	8 + 7	Think of double to help.	Relate to doubles through pictures.
9's	9 + 3	6 + 9	What's the pattern?	Use the pattern.
10's	7 + 3	6 + 4	Use 10 sums.	Remember the 10 frame.
Near 10's	7 + 5	4 + 8	Use 10's to help.	Up from 10's.

FIGURE 10.2. Addition fact-chunking strategy. Adapted from Thornton, C. A., & Toohey, M. A. (1985). Basic math facts: Guidelines for teaching and learning. *Learning Disabilities Focus* 1(1), 44–57. Copyright 1985 by Blackwell Publishing Ltd. Adapted by permission.

rately. They can be approached as "10's plus extras," or simply as extra facts and taught through memorization.

Multiplication

Multiplication facts are another important fact family. Once again, these facts are amenable to an approach that utilizes a chunking strategy. Wood and her colleagues (Wood & Frank, 2000; Wood, Frank, & Wacker, 1998) have developed and validated an effective strategy for teaching multiplication facts. The strategy divides the multiplication facts into six families: 0's, 1's, 2's, 5's, 9's, and pegwords (see Chapter 12 for more on pegwords). Facts are taught in this order. Note that the pegword facts are used for the 15 facts that do not fall into any of the first five families. Figure 10.3 shows the multiplication fact charts. Each fact family has its own strategy. In the case of the 2, 5, and 9 families, the strategy is combined with a graphic designed to serve as a mnemonic. Pegword facts use keywords (i.e., the pegword) in sentences. Students are taught to associate the words with numbers (e.g., door = 4; gate = 8; dirty = 30; shoe = 2). Pegwords are put into sentences that combine illustrations to help the child learn and remember facts. For example the problem 4 × 8 = 32 is represented by the sentence "Door on gate by dirty shoe" combined with a representation of these images.

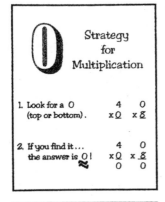
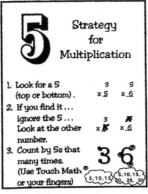

Strategy for Multiplication (0)

1. Look for a 0 (top or bottom).
2. If you find it... the answer is 0!

Strategy for Multiplication (1)

1. Look for a 1 (top or bottom).
2. If you find it... ignore the 1. The answer is... the other number!

Strategy for Multiplication (2)

1. Look for the 2 (top or bottom).
2. If you find it... ignore the 2... Look at the other number.
3. Remember the doubles picture for that number.

Strategy for Multiplication (5)

1. Look for a 5 (top or bottom).
2. If you find it... ignore the 5... Look at the other number.
3. Count by 5s that many times. (Use Touch Math® or your fingers)

Links for 9 Strategy

1 2 3 4 5 6 7 8

Strategy for Multiplication (9)

1. Look for a 9 (top or bottom).
2. If you find it... ignore the 9... Look at the other number.
3. Subtract 1 from that number. Put your answer in the 10's place.
4. Look at the number in the 10's place. Put the link to that number in the 1's place.

FIGURE 10.3. Multiplication strategy charts. From Wood, D. K., & Frank, A. R. (2000). Using memory-enhancing strategies to learn multiplication facts. *Teaching Exceptional Children, 32*(5), 78–82. Copyright 2000 by The Council for Exceptional Children. Reprinted by permission.

Students are taught each fact family in turn. After all fact families have been mastered students are taught to (1) scan a problem; (2) determine if one of the numbers is 0, 1, 2, 5, or 9; (3) if so, use the appropriate strategy; (4) if not, remember the pegword. When teaching the strategy self-instructions are modeled and stressed (e.g., "This problem has a 9 so I can use my 9's strategy"). As always, instruction should stress that successful use of the strategy will help the student to get the right answer. Note that this strategy would follow naturally from the addition facts strategy previously discussed. The procedures are quite similar, and one fact family from the addition strategy, the doubles, could be used for the 2's in the multiplication strategy.

COMPUTATION STRATEGIES

Many students with LD struggle with computational procedures. Solving problems such as 34 × 7, or 456 + 895, requires students to remember the necessary steps, the order of steps, and necessary basic facts. This can strain working memory for students with LD. As a result, they may forget the order of operation, regroup improperly, fail to regroup, or even develop improper algorithms. There are a number of strategies that are useful for helping students remember and follow computational procedures. Figure 10.4 shows sample computation strategies. These strategies typically consist of a mnemonic that serves to cue the student to remember and perform steps to correctly solve problems. It is often useful to combine these types of strategies with self-monitoring. The self-monitoring serves to cue the student to perform all steps of the strategy in the correct order. As the student gains fluency with the strategy, the self-monitoring can be faded. Note that it is also possible to develop customized strategies for students. The process for creating customized computational strategies developed by Dunlap and Dunlap (1989) was discussed in Chapter 7.

WORD-PROBLEM-SOLVING STRATEGIES

Many children with LD struggle with word problems. Word-problem solving requires students to apply basic facts and computational skills to novel situations. There are two components to word-problem solving (Jitendra, Hoff, & Beck, 1999): (1) *problem representation*, which entails translation of a problem from words into a meaningful representation, and (2) *problem solution*, which entails selection and application of appropriate mathematical operations based on the representation. Problem solution includes both solution planning and execution of appropriate mathematical operations. Research strongly suggests that two critical components for successful word-problem solving are explicit instruction in problem solving and the use of graphic representation of word problems (Jitendra et al., 1999; Xin & Jitendra, 1999).

SOLVE IT!

To solve word problems, students must read the problem, decide what to do, solve the problem, and check that the answer is reasonable. The SOLVE IT! strategy is designed to help students "understand the mathematical problems, analyze the information presented, develop logical plans to solve problems, and evaluate their solutions" (Montague et al., 2000, p. 111). SOLVE IT! is a structured strategy that uses explicit instruction in problem solving steps. SOLVE IT! features a structured series of steps, each of which incorporates self-instructions and self-monitoring (i.e., Say, Ask, Check). Students are taught to carefully read problems, paraphrase the problem, analyze the information, form a plan, solve the problem, and assess their solution. Figure 10.5 shows the steps in SOLVE IT! and the associated self-instructions and self-monitoring.

Schema-Based Strategies

The wide variety of possible word problems is one factor that makes them more difficult for students. The ability to organize word problems into a small number of groups

Subtraction Strategy

SUBTRACT. Remember the 4 B's:
Begin? In the 1's column.
Bigger? Which number is bigger?
Borrow? If bottom number is bigger I must borrow.
Basic Facts? Remember them. Use Touch Math if needed.

- Begin	- Begin	- Begin
- - - Bigger	- - - Bigger	- - - Bigger
- - - Borrow	- - - Borrow	- - - Borrow
- - - Basic Facts	- - - Basic Facts	- - - Basic Facts
8 7 6	6 2 3	5 6
− 3 9 8	− 1 5	− 3 5

Addition Strategy

ADD. Remember SASH:
Start in the 1s column.
Add together the numerals in each column.
Should I carry a numeral?
Have I carried the correct numeral?

- Start	- Start	- Start
- - - Add	- - - Add	- - - Add
- - - Should I carry	- - - Should I carry	- - - Should I carry
- - - Have I carried	- - - Have I carried	- - - Have I carried
1 2 7	3 5 7	6 4
+ 3 9 8	+ 1 2	+ 1 7

Multiplication Strategy

MULTIPLY. Remember MAMA:
Multiply the 1's column.
Across Do I need to go across to the 10's?
Multiply the bottom 1's digit with the top 10's digit.
Add any number that was carried in Step 2.

- Multiply	- Multiply	- Multiply
- - - Across	- - - Across	- - - Across
- - - Multiply	- - - Multiply	- - - Multiply
- - - Add	- - - Add	- - - Add
1 7	3 5	6 4
× 8	× 3	× 7

FIGURE 10.4. Examples of computation strategies. Subtraction and addition strategies adapted from Frank, A. R., & Brown, D. (1992). Self-monitoring strategies in arithmetic. *Teaching Exceptional Children, 24*(2), 52–53. Copyright 1992 by The Council for Exceptional Children. Adapted by permission. Multiplication strategy reprinted from Reid, R. (1992). *A brief multiplication strategy.* Unpublished manuscript, University of Nebraska–Lincoln.

Read (for understanding)

> *Say*:   Read the problem. If I don't understand, read it again.
>
> *Ask*:   Have I read and understood the problem?
>
> *Check*:   For understanding as I solve the problem.

Paraphrase (your own words)

> *Say*:   Underline the important information. Put the problem in my own words.
>
> *Ask*:   Have I underlined the important information? What is the question? What am I looking for?
>
> *Check*:   That the information goes with the question.

Visualize (a picture of a diagram)

> *Say*:   Make a drawing or a diagram.
>
> *Ask*:   Does the picture fit the problem?
>
> *Check*:   The picture against the problem information.

Hypothesize (a plan to solve the problem)

> *Say*:   Decide how many steps and operations are needed. Write the operation symbols (+, −, x, ÷).
>
> *Ask*:   If I do _____, what will I get? If I do _____, then what do I need to do next? How many steps are needed?
>
> *Check*:   That the plan makes sense.

Estimate (predict the answer)

> *Say*:   Round the numbers, do the problem in my head, and write the estimate.
>
> *Ask*:   Did I round up and down? Did I write the estimate?
>
> *Check*:   That I used important information.

Compute (do the arithmetic)

> *Say*:   Do the operations in the right order.
>
> *Ask*:   How does my answer compare with my estimate? Does my answer make sense? Are the decimals or money signs in the right place?
>
> *Check*:   That all the operations were done in the right order.

Check (make sure everything is right)

> *Say*:   Check the computation.
>
> *Ask*:   Have I checked every step? Have I checked the computation? Is my answer right?
>
> *Check*:   That everything is right. If not, go back. Then ask for help if I need it.

FIGURE 10.5. The SOLVE IT! strategy. From Montague, M., Warger, C., & Morgan, T. (2000). Solve It! Strategy instruction to improve mathematical problem solving. *Learning Disabilities Research and Practice, 15,* 110–116. Copyright 2000 by Blackwell Publishing Ltd. Reprinted by permission.

with common characteristics that can then be represented and solved simplifies the difficulty of word problems greatly. Schema-based strategies approach word problems from this perspective. Schemas are representations of word-problem structures. Schemas "capture both the patterns of relationships as well as their linkages to operations" (Marshall, 1995, p. 67). Thus, schema based approaches allow the student to both understand how to represent problems and identify the correct operations for solving them (Jitendra, DiPipi, & Perron-Jones, 2002). An advantage of schema-based approaches is that when one piece of information is retrieved other information that is linked to it will also be activated (Jitendra et al., 2002; Marshall, 1995). Major types of problem schemas are "change, equalize, combine, compare, vary, and restate." These are the most typical types of word problems in elementary and middle schools (Riley, Greeno, & Heller, 1983; Van de Walle, 1998). Figures 10.6 and 10.7 show examples of problem types for each schema.

Jitendra and her colleagues (Jitendra & Hoff, 1996; Jitendra et al., 1998, 1999, 2002) have developed and validated a schema-based approach to word-problem solving. The strategy requires students to learn the types of schemas to mastery and to match each schema with the appropriate diagram (developed by Marshall, 1998). The diagram serves to remind the student to record the important information and to cue the appropriate arithmetic operation. The steps in the strategy are:

- *Identify problem schemas*: Students are taught the types of schemas to mastery and how to differentiate between them through the use of several examples.
- *Create an appropriate diagram*: Students are then taught how to appropriately diagram the different types of schemas (Figure 10.8). The diagrams serve as graphic organizers that help students organize and remember important information.
- *Flag the missing element with a question mark*: The missing element, or the answer that the problem is requesting, is then flagged with a question mark. The question mark lets students know that they must use a mathematical operation to figure out the number to go in that box or circle (Figure 10.8).
- *Apply the appropriate operation to solve the problem*: The type of schema and diagram will dictate the operation to be used. Students will need to be taught which operation goes with which type of schema and diagram (Figure 10.8).
- *Ask if the answer made sense*: Once students have solved the problems, they are to check to see if the answers make sense (e.g., if the operation is addition then the answer should be greater than both the addends). Students could use estimating to determine if their answers are reasonable.
- *Check the work*: Students should be taught to "work the problem backwards." Working a problem backwards requires students to do the opposite operation to determine whether or not the answer is correct (e.g., subtraction $\rightarrow$ addition, and multiplication $\rightarrow$ division).

Note that all of these steps must be taught to a high degree of mastery. Figure 10.8 shows examples of how a graphic organizer could be used with the different types of story problems.

Change

Results unknown

Dr. Gerber has 6 golf balls. Dr. Lloyd gave him 8 more. How many golf balls does Dr. Gerber have?

Sue has 21 cats. She gave 11 to John. How many cats does Sue have left?

Change unknown

Reese had 7 baseballs. Chris gave him some of her baseballs. Now Reese has 23 baseballs. How many baseballs did Chris give Reese?

John has 12 slices of pizza. He gave some pizza to Stan. Now John has 3 slices of pizza. How many slices did John give to Stan?

Start unknown

Torri had some hamburgers. Then Wendy gave her 7 hamburgers. Now Torri has 18 hamburgers. How many hamburgers did Torri have at the beginning?

Trevor had some cows. He gave 6 cows to Maci. Now Trevor has 22 cows. How many cows did Trevor have before he gave some to Maci?

Equalize

Mike has 7 dollars. Ron has 14 dollars. How many dollars does Mike need to have as many as Ron?

Javon has 25 trading cards. Fred has 11 trading cards. How many cards would Javon have to give away to have as many as Fred?

Combine

Total set unknown

Melody has 5 flowers. Emma has 9 flowers. How many flowers do they have in total?

Subset unknown

Emma and Leigh have 28 rabbits altogether. Leigh has 13 rabbits. How many rabbits does Emma have?

Compare

Difference unknown

Alex has 11 books. Joe has 5 books. Alex has how many more books than Joe?

Laura has 17 pens. Ross has 11 pens. Ross has how many fewer pens than Laura?

Compared quantity unknown

Andy has 4 computers. Matt has 8 more computers than Andy. How many computers does Matt have?

Laura has 23 books. Ross has 6 fewer books than Laura. How many books does Ross have?

Referent unknown

Jorge has 10 DVDs. He has 3 more DVDs than Cindy. How many DVDs does Cindy have?

Nirbhay has 17 dollars. He has 9 dollars less than Alan. How many dollars does Alan have?

FIGURE 10.6. Addition and subtraction word-problem types.

Vary

   Size of groups unknown

   In Steve's basketball camp there are 5 balls for 25 players. How many players must share each ball?

   Whole unknown

   George worked picking up bottles for 6 days. He earned 54 dollars for each day he picked up bottles. How much did George earn?

Compare

   Referent unknown (compared is part of referent)

   Mike and Ron bought some cherries. Mike bought 4 pounds of cherries. Ron bought one-third as many cherries as Mike. How many cherries did Ron buy?

   Compared unknown (compared is part of referent)

   Stan and Michalla both got speeding tickets. The amount that Stan had to pay was one-half the amount that Michalla had to pay. Stan had to pay 40 dollars. How much did Michalla have to pay?

   Compared unknown (compared is multiple of referent)

   John has 20 doughnuts. Evie has 4 times as many doughnuts as John. How many doughnuts does Evie have?

Restate

   Susan and Lynette took a walk. Lynette walked half as far as Susan. If Susan walked 18 miles, how far did Lynette walk?

FIGURE 10.7. Multiplication and division story problem types.

From Robert Reid and Torri Ortiz Lienemann (2006). Copyright by The Guilford Press. Permission to photocopy this figure is granted to purchasers of this book for personal use only (see copyright page for details).

IMPLEMENTATION PLANS

In this section, we provide partial examples of implementation plans for the math strategies previously discussed.

Stage 2 for Computation Strategies: Discussing the Strategy

This is the first stage in "initiating" the strategy. In this stage it is important to stress the relevance of the strategy. During an initial conference the teacher will want to discuss the students' current performance. It is also important for the teacher to stress the value

Change Problem

Frank has 8 seashells. Edward gave him 8 more. How many sea shells does Frank have now?

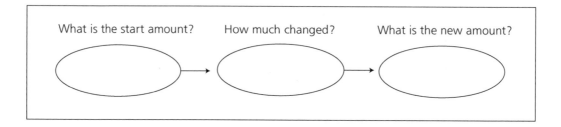

Vary Problem

In Steve's basketball camp there are 5 balls for 25 players. How many players must share each ball?

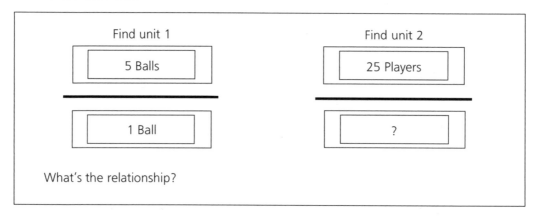

FIGURE 10.8. Examples of graphic organizers for word problems.

of the strategy. Brainstorm with the students on situations where using this strategy or completing the given task accurately is important. For example, the following might be appropriate brainstorming ideas in response to the question "When would it be important for you to make accurate math calculations?"

- Balancing your checkbook
- Trying to figure out if you have enough money to buy what you want
- Following a recipe

- Measuring anything
- Building a house
- Fixing your car
- Planning next year's crops
- For a test
- For an assignment

As we noted earlier some students may be unsure about or reluctant to try a strategy. If this occurs, we recommend the use of a behavioral contract. The student agrees to try using the strategy for a set period of time. In return, the student receives an agreed-upon reinforcer (e.g., extra computer time).

A sample script for "selling" the strategy follows:

"Math is everywhere! We came up with a lot of instances where it would be important to make accurate math calculations. We decided that it is really important when we are balancing our checkbook, and seeing if we have enough money to buy that new CD we want. Math is a very important part of our lives whether we like it or not. Sometimes it's difficult to remember all of the different steps in various math calculations, or our 'computational procedures.' One procedure we have been using a lot, and one that is giving many of us difficulties, is multiplication of multidigit numbers (i.e., 10's, 100's, 1,000's). We have been working on this for a while now in math, and I've noticed that many of you are having difficulty remembering the procedures. It's important to remember the procedures; if you don't follow the correct procedure you won't get the correct answer. This problem has been affecting your grades. Let's take a look at some of your recent quiz scores. You really did a nice job _____ [point out the positives]. However, there seems to be a breakdown in your procedural methods, because you are getting quite a few incorrect. Earlier we mentioned that it is important to be able to make correct math calculations in assignments, quizzes, or tests; it appears that we could improve on this. The good news is that I have a way that can really help you with your multiplication procedures. It's a 'trick' to help you remember the multiplication computation procedures. This 'trick' is a strategy called MAMA. Just like your mom's help, this strategy will help you! It should make multiplication easier for you, and your grades will improve."

In this stage we also introduce the strategy steps, and any prompts that will be given (Figure 10.9).

Stage 3 for SOLVE IT!: Modeling the Strategy

The teacher will need to use a think-aloud to demonstrate the use of the strategy. Here is an example of a think-aloud for SOLVE IT!

MAMA

Step 1:   Multiply the 1's column.

Step 2:   Across—Do I need to go across to the 10's?

Step 3:   Multiply the bottom 1's digit with the top 10's digit.

Step 4:   Add any number that was carried in Step 2.

FIGURE 10.9. Prompt sheet for the MAMA strategy.

From Robert Reid and Torri Ortiz Lienemann (2006). Copyright by The Guilford Press. Permission to photocopy this figure is granted to purchasers of this book for personal use only (see copyright page for details).

"OK, I am doing my math homework. Things are going just fine; I know how to do these subtraction problems with regrouping when they are written out in standard form. OK, but now I am up to the last section and they are *story problems*! Story problems always give me trouble! Ugh, what can I do? Oh yeah, the other day we talked about a trick that could help us with our story problems; it was called the 'SOLVE IT!' strategy. I'll try it now. OK, first I need to <u>Read</u> for understanding. Being able to read the problem is important, but it's even more important that I understand what I've read. If I don't understand it I'll never be able to pull out all of the necessary information to solve it.

"At each step in the SOLVE IT! strategy I am supposed to follow three steps: (1) Say, (2) Ask, and (3) Check. So, at this step I need to *say*: 'Read the problem. If I don't understand, read it again.' OK, so I'll read the problem. The problem says: 'Taylon has 427 head of cattle on his ranch. Sydni has 605 head of cattle on her ranch. How many more cattle does Sydni have than Taylon?' All right, I read the problem, now what? I need to *ask* myself, *Have I read and understood the problem?' Well, I read the problem; did I understand it? I think so. Now I can just go to the next step and check* for understanding as I solve the problem. I double-check to make sure I understood the problem while I'm attempting to solve it. Now what do I need to do? The next step is to <u>Paraphrase</u> the problem in my own words, so I *say*: Underline the important information. Put the problem in my own words. Well, I know that the number of cattle is important. I know that because the question asks me 'how many more?' Numbers in story problems are usually important.

"OK, now I need to put the problem in my own words. Sydni has more cows than Taylon. She has 605, and he has 427. How many more does she have? This is going pretty smooth; now I need to *ask*: 'Have I underlined the important information?' Yes, I underlined the number of cattle each rancher had. Those are the numbers I need to work with. Good. Now, 'What is the question? What am I looking for?' The question is, 'How many more head of cattle does Sydni have than Taylon?' So, I'm looking for how many MORE. OK, now I need to *check* that the information goes with the question. So, the question asks how many head of cattle? That's the information that I underlined; that's right then. It's helpful to do these checks to make sure I'm not messing up or leaving out important steps along the way.

"What's next? <u>Visualize</u> a picture of a diagram. I know what a diagram is. That's like a graph, or a web. OK, I need to *say*: 'Make a drawing or diagram.' All right, I've drawn my graphic representation. Now I need to *ask*: 'Does the picture fit the problem?' Well, it shows Sydni's ranch with her cattle, and Taylon's ranch with his cattle; yes, it does fit the problem! Let's keep going! Next, I need to <u>Hypothesize</u> a plan to solve the problem. What does 'hypothesize' mean? I know in science it means to make an educated guess, so I think this step means I need to make an educated guess at a plan to solve this problem. I'm now supposed to *say*: 'Decide how many steps and operations are needed. Write the operation symbols (+, −, x, ÷). This problem has only one step.' I need to find the difference between Taylon's herd and Sydni's herd. I already know how many cattle each of them has; all I need to do is find the difference. I know that difference almost always means subtraction, so I will write down a −. Now, I need to *ask*: If I do subtraction, what will I get? Well, I will get a number smaller than my largest number, but I don't know what that will be until I actually solve the problem.

"OK, so I know that I only need to perform one operation, and that operation is subtraction. This sounds like a reasonable plan. Now, I need to *check* that the plan makes sense. Well, I already said that it sounds reasonable. That means I think my plan makes sense. How will I know? Let's see, what's my next step? My next step is to <u>Estimate</u>, and predict my answer. That will help me to make sure my plan makes sense. All right, on to the next step; I need to *say*: 'Round the numbers, do the problem in my head, and write the estimate.' OK, so if I round the larger number, 605, I get 600. I round the larger number first because I know with subtraction the larger number is always on top. All right, now the other number, 427, and I get 400. Now I need to do the problem in my head (600 − 400 = 200), and write the estimate, so I'll write down 200. Now, I need to *ask*: 'Did I round up and down?' Well, I only rounded down, but that's because I know when I round if a number is less than 5 I round down, but if a number is 5 or greater I round up. In both of the numbers that I was rounding, the second digit was less than 5, so I rounded down. I still need to *ask*: 'Did I write the estimate?' Yes, I wrote it on the board.

"Now, I need to *check* that I used important information. Yes, I did! I used the information that I underlined. I didn't even realize it at first, but having the numbers underlined really helped me find the correct information. Wow, this is going very well; this strategy is really helping me with my story problem. What's next? Compute, or do the arithmetic. I'm finally ready to solve the problem. I feel very confident that I'm going to be able to SOLVE IT! Let's see, 605 – 427 = ? OK, I got it, 178. Now, I need to *ask*: 'How does my answer compare with my estimate? Does my answer make sense? Are the decimals or money signs in the right place?' Well, my answer is very close to my estimate; if I rounded my answer I would get my estimate! I think I did it, my answer definitely makes sense. There are no decimals or money symbols, so I don't need to worry about that. Almost done, only one more step! I need to Check to make sure everything is right. So, I *say*: 'Check the computation.' OK, I used the correct operation, and my estimate is close to my answer, but I'm not sure if it's completely accurate. How can I make sure my answer is correct? Well, we usually check our work by performing the opposite operation; even though this is a story problem this should still work, all I'm doing is subtraction! OK, so I can do addition to check. I will add my answer to the number I subtracted, and I should get the larger number. I already know how to do this! All right, so 178 + 427 = 605; yes, I got it right! Next, 'Have I checked every step? Have I checked the computation? Is my answer right?' Yes, I checked every step (I only had one), I checked my computation by doing the opposite operation, and I determined that I had the correct answer! Finally, I need to *check* that everything is right. If not, go back. Then ask for help if I need it. Well, I already asked myself these questions, and I determined that I got the right answer, so I don't need to go back, or ask for help. I did it! I did it, and I know I got it all right. Wow, when I try, and use the appropriate strategy story problems aren't so bad! That was actually kind of fun!"

Stage 5 for Schema-Based Strategies: Supporting the Strategy

Students will need to automatically recognize the various types of schemas used. They will need to be able to identify the features of the semantic relations in the problem and check the salient element of the chosen problem schema. Based on Jitendra's (Jitendra et al., 1998) procedures, scaffolding should include the following:

1. Teachers model collaboratively with students. Students help identify critical elements or constraints of the word problems.

- Students practice identifying the different problem types in the story situations (e.g., Change, Group, and Compare).
- Students translate the information (i.e., read and understand the word problem).
- Students map the features of the situation onto the schema diagrams (Figure 10.8).

2. Teachers review the problem schemas through collaborative modeling. Any student misconceptions should be addressed immediately, and explicit feedback provided along with additional modeling.

- Equations, instead of word problems, are presented; however, teachers still *read* a word problem to the students.
- Teachers should use a facilitative questioning procedure for students to identify the semantic features of the problem.
- Teachers then demonstrate how critical elements of the specific problem are translated and mapped on the schema diagrams (Figure 10.8).
- The missing element is flagged with a question mark.

3. Instruction is given on the second strategy step. During this stage, students should be provided with explicit feedback on their ability to synthesize the steps of the strategy. Teachers should use guided practice and modeling, and provide immediate corrective feedback at each step in the instructional process.

- The teacher explains how to find the total amount in the word problem by focusing on the specific information in the problem. For example:
  - *Change problem*: Students will need to determine if the problem ends with more or less than the beginning amount.
    - ending state = total when the change results in an increase
    - beginning state = total when the change results in a decrease
  - *Compare problem*: Students compare the value of the referent and compare objects to determine the greater quantity, or the total.
  - Students must read the comparison or difference statement in the word problem.
  - Students are taught a generalizable rule based on the part–whole concept for determining the operation to be used. They must examine the part of the situation that is unknown and whether it represents the "whole" or "part" to be solved.
    - If whole is *not* known, then add to find total
    - If whole is known, then subtract to the other (part) amount

Initially, students should only be given one type of problem; after they are able to successfully use the strategy with that type of problem, others should be introduced one at a time.

Stage 5 for Basic Multiplication Strategies: Supporting the Strategy

In this stage, scaffolding is important. With scaffolding it is possible for a gradual transfer of strategy performance from teacher to student. Students need to be given adequate time and support to master the strategy.

Content Scaffolding

Students will be provided with simple multiplication problems. The teacher and students will then go over the problems and the use of the different strategies. Together they will determine what type of multiplication strategy is appropriate, and solve the problem together. The teacher will direct the process and the students will provide answers to teacher-directed questions (i.e., "What type of multiplication strategy does this problem represent? What do we need to remember to solve this problem?").

Task Scaffolding

Students will be taught one multiplication strategy at a time. Students will first be taught the "0 strategy" for multiplication to mastery, then students will taught each additional strategy as listed in Figure 10.3.

During collaborative practice the teacher will prompt students to use their various multiplication strategies to solve problems. The teacher will demonstrate the use of the various multiplication strategies though modeling. In subsequent lessons the teacher will ask the students to identify the strategy necessary to solve the problem, and ask how they knew which strategy to use (the teacher will direct the process). Finally, the student will be given a set of multiplication problems and expected to choose the appropriate multiplication strategy and answer the questions correctly.

Material Scaffolding

The students will be provided with multiplication strategies prompt cards (Figure 10.3) to use with their independent math work. Initially, this prompt will serve as a guide to remind them of various multiplication strategies, and the cues that go with each. Students will be provided multiple opportunities to practice using their multiplication strategies until they are able to do so independently and to successfully solve basic multiplication problems.

Stage 6 for Computational Strategies: Independent Performance

At this stage the student is ready to use the strategy independently. The teacher's main task is to monitor the student's performance and check on proper and consistent use of the strategy. However, it is important to keep in mind that our main goal is improved academic performance. Teachers must evaluate whether or not the strategy is being used, if it is being generalized to other appropriate situations, and whether or not academic performance has improved. Students will not always generalize strategies to appropriate situations; they will need to be prompted and encouraged to do so.

To promote generalization, students will be encouraged to use the strategy in other content areas where they are required to compute mathematical calculations. All team teachers will be informed about the use of the strategy, the language, the prompts, and what is required at each step. All team teachers will be given a wall chart to hang up in their room as a reminder for students to use the computational strategies when appropriate.

Students will be assessed regularly with independent work, quizzes, and tests, specifically in math class. These scores will be recorded and tracked for trends in progress. The goal is improved academic performance, and if performance isn't improving a reteaching of the strategies may be necessary. Once students are successful using the strategies their performance should be monitored periodically. Even though they have reached the independent performance stage, they will be monitored to ensure proper use of the strategy. If students deviate from the given computation strategies, performance will be evaluated, and action will be taken only if performance is no longer improving.

FINAL THOUGHTS

There is good evidence that strategies can be effective for all the levels of mathematics included in this chapter. In fact, because it is often highly procedural and rule based, mathematics is a natural area for strategy instruction. Still, there are some areas (e.g., algebra, geometry) that have not been well studied or have not been studied in groups with LD. In these cases, teachers would need to construct their own strategies using a task analysis as a guide. An accurate task breakdown combined with the SRSD model should be helpful where there are no existing strategies.

REFERENCES

Bottge, B. A. (1999). Effects of contextualized math instruction on problem solving of average and below-average achieving students. *Journal of Special Education, 33,* 81–92.

Dunlap, L. K., & Dunlap, G. (1989). A self-monitoring package for teaching subtraction with regrouping to students with learning disabilities. *Journal of Applied Behavior Analysis, 22,* 309–314.

Frank, A. R., & Brown, D. (1992). Self-monitoring strategies in arithmetic. *Teaching Exceptional Children, 24*(2), 52–53.

Fuchs, L. S., & Fuchs, D. (2003). Enhancing the mathematical problem solving of students with mathematical disabilities. In H. Swanson, K. R. Harris, & S. Graham (Eds.), *Handbook of learning disabilities* (pp. 306–322). New York: Guilford Press.

Garnett, K. (1992). Developing fluency with basic number facts: Intervention for students with learning disabilities. *Learning Disabilities Research and Practice, 7,* 210–216.

Geary, D. C. (2003). Learning disabilities in arithmetic: Problem solving differences and cognitive deficits. In H. Swanson, K. R. Harris, & S. Graham (Eds.), *Handbook of learning disabilities* (pp. 199–212). New York: Guilford Press.

Geary, D. C., Bow-Thomas, C. C., & Yao, Y. (1992). Counting knowledge and skill in cognitive addition: A comparison of normal and mathematically disabled children. *Journal of Experimental Child Psychology, 54,* 372–391.

Geary, D. C., Hamson, C. O., & Hoard, M. K. (2000). Numerical and arithmetical cognition: A longitudinal study of process and concept deficits in children with learning disability. *Journal of Experimental Child Psychology, 77,* 236–263.

Geary, D. C., Hoard, M. K., & Hamson, C. O. (1999). Numerical and arithmetical deficits in learning disabled children: Relation to dyscalculia and dyslexia. *Aphasiology, 15*, 635–647.

Geary, D. C., Widaman, K. F., Little, T. D., & Cormier, P. (1987). Cognitive addition: Comparison of learning disabled and academically normal elementary school children. *Cognitive Development, 2,*249–269.

Gersten, R., & Chard, D. (1999). Number sense: Rethinking arithmetic instruction for students with mathematical disabilities. *Journal of Special Education, 33,* 18–28.

Harniss, M. K., Carnine, D. W., Silbert, J., & Dixon, R. C. (2002). Effective strategies for teaching mathematics. In E. Kame'enui, D. Carnine, R. Dixon, D. Simmons, & M. Coyne (Eds.), *Effective teaching strategies that accommodate diverse learners* (pp. 121–148). Columbus, OH: Merrill.

Jitendra, A., DiPipi, C. M., & Perron-Jones, N. (2002). An exploratory study of schema-based word-problem-solving instruction for middle school students with learning disabilities. *Journal of Special Education, 36,* 23–38.

Jitendra, A. K., Griffin, C. C., McGoey, K., Gardhill, M. K., Bhat, P., & Riley, T. (1998). Effects of mathematical word-problem solving by students at risk or with mild disabilities. *Journal of Educational Research, 91,* 345–355.

Jitendra, A. K., & Hoff, K. (1996). The effects of schema-based instruction on the mathematical word-problem solving performance of students with learning disabilities. *Journal of Learning Disabilities, 29*(4), 422–431.

Jitendra, A. K., Hoff, K., & Beck, M. M. (1999). Teaching middle school students with learning disabilities to solve word problems using a schema-based approach. *Remedial and Special Education, 20,* 50–64.

Jitendra, A. K., & Xin, Y. P. (1997). Mathematical word-problem-solving instruction for students with mild disabilities and students at-risk for math failure: A research synthesis. *Journal of Special Education, 30,* 412–438.

Marshall, S. P. (1995). *Schemas in problem solving.* New York: Cambridge University Press.

Montague, M., Warger, C., & Morgan, T. (2000). Solve It! Strategy instruction to improve mathematical problem solving. *Learning Disabilities Research and Practice, 15,* 110–116.

Parmar, R. S., Cawley, J. F., & Frazita, R. R. (1996). Word problem solving by students with and without mild disabilities. *Exceptional Children, 62,* 415–429.

Parmar, R. S., Cawley, J. F., & Miller, J. H. (1994). Differences in mathematics performance between students with learning disabilities and students with mild retardation. *Exceptional Children, 60,* 549–563.

Patton, J. R., Cronin, M. E., Bassett, D. S., & Koppel, A. E. (1997). A life skills approach to mathematics instruction: Preparing students with learning disabilities for the real-life math demands of adulthood. *Journal of Learning Disabilities, 30,* 178–187.

Reid, R. (1992). *A brief multiplication strategy.* Unpublished manuscript, University of Nebraska–Lincoln.

Riley, M., Greeno, J., & Heller, J. (1983). Development of children's problem solving ability in arithmetic. In H. Ginsburg (Ed.), *The development of mathematical thinking* (pp. 153–196). New York: Academic Press.

Rivera, D. P. (1997). Mathematics education and students with learning disabilities: Introduction to the special series. *Journal of Learning Disabilities, 30,* 2–19.

Russell, R. L., & Ginsburg, H. P. (1984). Cognitive analysis of children's mathematical difficulties. *Cognition and Instruction, 1,* 217–244.

Thornton, C. A., & Toohey, M. A. (1985). Basic math facts: Guidelines for teaching and learning. *Learning Disabilities Focus, 1*(1), 44–57.

Van de Walle, J. A. (1998). *Elementary and middle school mathematics: Teaching developmentally* (3rd ed.). New York: Longman.

Wood, D. K., & Frank, A. R. (2000). Using memory-enhancing strategies to learn multiplication facts. *Teaching Exceptional Children, 32*(5), 78–82.

Wood, D. K., Frank, A. R., & Wacker, D. P. (1998). Teaching multiplication facts to students with learning disabilities. *Journal of Applied Behavior Analysis, 32,* 323–338.

Xin, Y. P., & Jitendra, A. K. (1999). The effects of instruction in solving mathematical word problems for students with learning problems: A meta-analysis. *Journal of Special Education, 32,* 207–225.

CHAPTER 11

Study Skills Strategies

The term "study skills" refers to a wide variety of skills necessary to be successful in any academic setting. These skills include note taking, test taking, homework completion, and general school "survival skills" (e.g., coming to class prepared, being organized, and paying attention in class) (Smith & Smith, 1989). These skills become more important as the student progresses through school and are particularly critical at the secondary level, where teachers expect students to display these "responsible behaviors" (Snyder & Bambara, 1997). Effective study skills can be the difference between academic success and academic failure, and can often lead to positive outcomes across multiple academic settings (Gettinger & Seibert, 2002).

As they mature, successful learners display appropriate, self-directed behavior in order to gain information (Schumaker & Deshler, 1988). This information comes from a wide variety of source books, as well as material presented in class. Successful learners are strategic in gaining information; they devise plans and gather information in a systematic fashion (deBettencourt, 1987). For example, they listen while the teacher is delivering instruction, take notes, ask questions, answer questions, and contribute to the discussion. When given an assignment, successful students use class time efficiently, consult textbooks and other appropriate sources of information to answer questions, and complete assignments in a timely manner. These skills are essential to academic success. Unfortunately, many students with LD lack efficient and effective study skills strategies.

When compared to normally achieving peers, students with LD have trouble with note-taking skills, error monitoring, knowledge of test-taking strategies, and ability to scan a textbook for information (Carlson & Alley, 1981). Teaching study skills strategies such as note-taking strategies, test-taking strategies, time management, and assignment completion can help students become more successful and independent (Olson & Platt, 2000). Effective study strategies can represent the key to independent learning for students with LD, and can be the difference between academic success and academic failure (Bos & Vaughn, 2002).

PROBLEMS FOR STUDENTS WITH LEARNING DISABILITIES

Because of current inclusive practices students with LD generally spend all or most of their day in the general education classroom. However, the general education classroom is often not set up for students with LD to succeed. From around fourth grade and up, most instruction is delivered in a lecture format. This delivery style demands effective note taking, adequate writing skills, and rapid and efficient information processing. Students must be able to focus on salient information, accurately remember important details, and retrieve this information for assessments or examinations. This type of learning puts students with LD at a definite disadvantage. Without the necessary cognitive skills, background knowledge, and appropriate strategies they may flounder. Thus it is important that students with LD be taught strategies to focus and enhance their efforts. Students with LD have several characteristics that negatively affect their study skills.

Lack of Coordinated Strategies

Learning is an active process. Study skills, such as taking notes, completing homework, or taking a test, require a student's active engagement both cognitively and meta-cognitively. Successful students are actively involved in academic tasks and understand that their success is due to their effort and use of effective strategies. In contrast, as we discussed in Chapter 1, students with LD are likely to lack appropriate strategies and background knowledge, and to possess a negative belief about their academic abilities. In order to be successful in the general education classroom, students must be actively engaged in learning activities and utilize effective strategies.

Focus on Irrelevant Information

Gaining information in the general education classroom is based largely on a student's ability to focus on important information. Study skills require students to differentiate between relevant and irrelevant information. For example, when taking notes from a lecture or text, students must be able identify and to write down key information. This puts students with LD at a disadvantage; they do not often *devote* attention to learning. They may not be able to identify what information is important or they may focus on irrelevant information, distractions in the classroom, or other elements that are not related to a learning task. They also may need to focus attention on receiving information (i.e., decoding text, understanding lecture language), rather than processing the information relevant to the task (Kops & Belmont, 1985).

Working Memory Deficits

Research indicates students with LD have smaller working memories than their normally achieving peers (Swanson & Trahan, 1992). This affects their ability to encode, organize, and process information. It also puts students with LD at a distinct disadvantage in terms of study skills, because study skills can place extreme demands on working memory. For example, note taking requires a student to attend to information presented verbally and/or visually in a lesson, focus on important information, remember the information, organize the information, and condense or synthesize information, all the while accessing basic skills such as transcription, spelling, and outlining.

Inability to Make Appropriate Generalizations

Students are often expected to use information or skills previously learned and generalize them to appropriate situations. This is often necessary in order to gain new information. For example, a common strategy for reading a chapter in a textbook is to skim the headings, note charts, graphs, or figures that may be important, ask yourself questions about the material, and activate prior knowledge before reading. Successful students know that this strategy will be useful for a wide variety of tasks, and they can appropriately generalize this strategy. Students with LD are not likely to make these appropriate generalizations; if they do know strategies they often do not generalize these strategies to other appropriate situations. Students must be taught generalization of skills and strategies to other appropriate situations.

Poor Writing Skills

Many academic activities require students to turn information known, heard, or read into intelligible written language (e.g., taking tests, taking notes, and completing assignments). Englert and Raphael (1988) noted that students with LD experience greater difficulties than their nondisabled peers with the demands of writing. They experience difficulties with planning, organizing, and revising their writing, as well as with basic transcription skills. Transcription skills, which include handwriting and spelling, are often overlooked but can be critical (Graham & Harris, 2000). Because of poor transcription skills, many students with LD exhibit writing that is practically indecipherable—even to the student!

Lack of Organization

Students with LD often approach complex tasks in a disorganized fashion. The lack of a planful, step-by-step approach to academic tasks means that the students may waste time or use ineffective or inefficient approaches to task completion. This is especially important in the case of tasks that involve multiple steps (e.g., doing a book report).

PREREQUISITE SKILLS

When teaching students study skills strategies it is critical to consider the prerequisite skills necessary for students to be successful. Study skill prerequisites include (1) recording, (2) organizing, (3) remembering, and (4) using information (Gettinger & Seibert, 2002).

Recording

Recording includes writing/transcription skills. It is necessary for students to be able to successfully record information; if information is written incorrectly it will be difficult for the student to successfully complete the academic task. For example, students are required to record their assignments (i.e., assignments given verbally or posted in the classroom, generally on the board); an incorrect recording of the assignment would most likely result in an incomplete assignment. If the student is lucky, the teacher will allow him or her to redo the assignment; however this will often result in a loss of points, and a very frustrated student. Students are also required to write/record while gaining and demonstrating knowledge. Writing is commonly used for test taking, assignment completion, and note taking.

Organizing

Organization of information is crucial to a student's success in the general education classroom. The ability to organize incoming information, from text or lecture, is a make-it or break-it skill in the inclusive classroom. If students are unable to organize incoming information in a meaningful fashion, they will not be able to understand that information. If they are not able to relate what they have learned in an organized fashion they will not be able to demonstrate their knowledge on assignments or examinations.

Remembering

The ability to recall information is essential to a student's academic success. Assessments and examinations are designed to test a student's ability to recall previously learning material. If a student is unable to remember or recall information, then it is difficult to say that he or she has "learned" that information. There are many mnemonic strategies that are extremely effective at improving memory for academic material. Because this area is so important, we will deal with strategies designed to help with information storage and retrieval in the next chapter.

Appropriate Use

Gaining information, understanding it, and remembering it are all necessary skills in the classroom, but the ability to appropriately use the information is arguably the most important. Students must be able to use information to demonstrate their knowledge, as well as develop additional skills. Being able to use information appropriately is the reason for learning it in the first place.

INSTRUCTION IN STUDY SKILLS

Olson and Platt (2000) made the following recommendations for planning study skills instruction for students with LD:

1. The study skills should be functional and meaningful, determined by the needs of the students.
2. Students need to be convinced that the study skills are useful, necessary, and effective in solving problems.
3. The instruction should be direct, organized, and sequential, with instructor modeling, many examples presented, difficult points explained, and student progress monitored.
4. Instruction should show what study skills can be used, how they can be used, and when and why they are beneficial.
5. The instructional materials used with the students should be motivating, meaningful, relevant, and easy to understand.

In the sections that follow, we focus on four major areas of study skills: (1) note-taking skills, (2) homework (task) completion, (3) test-taking strategies, and (4) classroom survival strategies.

NOTE-TAKING STRATEGIES

Taking notes is an important means of organizing information, and accurate note taking is essential in most content-area classrooms (Deshler, Ellis, & Lenz, 1996). Students who record and review their personal lecture notes perform better on tests than do students who just listen to lectures (Kiewra, 1987). Taking notes requires students to receive information and process it simultaneously. This places demands on working memory and decreases the cognitive processing abilities available for organizing and storing information (Kiewra, 1987). The effective note taker uses working memory capacity to simultaneously attend to, store, and manipulate information selected from the lecture, while also transcribing ideas just previously presented and processed (Kiewra & Benton, 1988).

In order to manipulate information for note taking, students must be able to hold information and process it at the same time. The more information they are required to process in working memory, the less space they have left to hold information to transcribe. Awareness of demands on working memory is important in note taking. Humans are probably able to deal with only two or three items of information at a time, when required to process rather than merely hold information (Sweller, Van

Merrienboer, & Paas, 1998). Thus, it becomes important to reduce demands on working memory for students with LD, who already may have difficulties in this area.

Note taking involves more than just writing. It also involves comprehension of the lecture or text, and the organization and production of intelligible text. Students must be able to select relevant information from a lecture or text, maintain that knowledge while integrating it with new and old ideas, and then select the information to be transcribed (Kiewra, 1987). Typically, students with learning disabilities try to take notes verbatim (Suritsky, 1992). These students' inability to process information in a timely manner makes the task of note taking laborious and extremely frustrating. Students with lower information-processing ability record fewer notes and tend to have lower achievement; one possible reason for their lower achievement is their somewhat terse note taking (Kiewra, 1987).

Teachers will often allow students to tape-record lectures or use copies of peers' notes, but neither strategy helps students compensate for comprehension deficits or distinguish subtle differences among similar concepts (Deshler & Graham, 1980). Using another student's notes is usually not as effective as using those generated by the student, but can be done to compensate for note-taking deficiencies. However, providing students with notes during a lecture can be beneficial. When students are provided with complete and organized notes (rather than being required to review their own notes) they will perform better (Kiewra, 1984). Notes should be available for the students during the lecture to act as an effective retrieval cue later (Benton, Kiewra, Whitfill, & Dennison, 1993). While it is effective to have students listen to lectures and review a set of provided notes, this is not best practice. Students are able to recall more information from well-done personally recorded notes than from notes provided to them (Kiewra, 1984). Thus, it is highly beneficial to assist students in improving the notes they generate themselves.

Lazarus (1988, 1991) taught students to used guided notes to improve the content of their notes. Guided notes are a skeleton outline containing the main ideas and related concepts of a lecture, with designated spaces for students to complete as the lecture proceeds. The type and amount of information can vary depending on the subject matter and the student's skill level. One of the key aspects of guided notes is providing for maximum student response, meaning that students have numerous opportunities to fill in blanks and to receive feedback. Figure 11.1 provides an example of a skeleton outline containing only the most fundamental information (main ideas and key concepts) that provides students with several opportunities to fill in the rest (Lazarus, 1996). Notes will vary depending upon students' needs.

Note the review tally in the upper right-hand corner of the sample notes. Students can put check marks in the boxes to keep track of how many times the notes are used or reviewed. This will allow them to monitor their efforts in learning the material. Reviewing notes is important, because it promotes mastery of the content. However, be realistic and don't provide too many boxes, as students may see that as one more requirement and get frustrated (Lazarus, 1996). Lazarus (1996) provided some practical tips for developing skeleton outlines: (1) Use existing lecture notes, (2) use a consistent format, and (3) provide for maximum student response.

Review Tally

Chapter 20
Cell Reproduction

I. All life starts out as a _____ _____.

    A.   - - - - - - - - - - - - -

    B.

II. _____ _____ are formed by _____ _____

III. Types of cell division.

    A. Mitosis—DEFINITION:

        1. Mitosis is used for replacement of:

           a.

           b.

           c.

           d.

           e.

        2.

        3.

FIGURE 11.1. Example of a student copy of the guided notes with cues and review tally. From Lazarus, B. D. (1996). Flexible skeletons. *Teaching Exceptional Children, 23,* 34–40. Copyright 1996 by The Council for Exceptional Children. Reprinted by permission.

Use Existing Lecture Notes

Guided notes are most effective if created from existing lecture notes (Lazarus, 1996). Creating guided notes from existing lectures notes helps students follow both the lecture and the notes; each provides a cue for the other. If students get lost in the lecture they should be able to find their place by using the guided notes, and vice versa. Using existing lecture notes is easier for the teacher and provides students with a comprehensive outline of the lecture. The amount of information provided will vary depending on a particular student's level of need. Guided notes should, at the least, contain the main ideas covered in the lecture. It may also be beneficial to include key phrases, definitions, related issues, and contrasting viewpoints to avoid confusion (Lazarus, 1996).

Use a Consistent Format

Using a consistent format that corresponds with the structure of the lecture helps students use guided notes efficiently (Lazarus, 1996). If the notes follow the lecture format students are able to focus on the information being provided instead of figuring out where they are in their notes. In fact, the format should parallel the sequence of the lecture. It should correspond with the structure and content of the course. This will organize information to facilitate note taking and aid in comprehension and retention of the material. Providing a consistent format will also help in review. The consistency of the notes will assist students in recalling information presented in the lecture; if the notes mirror the lecture, then students will have a much easier time remembering the information presented in the lecture.

Provide for Maximum Student Response

Students should be given numerous opportunities to respond and receive feedback while using the guided notes (Lazarus, 1996). The more opportunity students have to use the guided notes the more effective and efficient they will become. Lazarus (1996) noted several ways in which students and teachers can use guided notes.

1. During lectures, show transparencies of completed copies of the guided notes on an overhead projector (see Figure 11.2). By covering the transparency and revealing each related phrase as it is discussed, teachers give students access to accurate information in a way that helps them keep their place.

2. Visual cues such as blanks, alphabet letters, and labels (see Figure 11.1) on the students' copies of the notes convey the amount and type of information to record. For example, the letters *a* through *e* under numeral 1 ("Mitosis is used for the replacement of") alerts students that five related concepts will be presented.

3. Although a chapter in a textbook may take a week or more to cover in class, give the students copies of the guided notes for the entire chapter before you give them their reading assignment. Students may then use the guided notes as a reading guide while reading the assignment.

4. Holding a 5- or 10-minute supervised review period at the end of each class gives you an opportunity to evaluate students' guided notes and provide corrective feedback and reinforcement. This not only gives students review time, but also provides them with the opportunity to clarify any confusing information in their notes before the notes are reviewed.

5. Provide guided notes for all students in the class. All students benefit and the student with LD is not singled out.

Guidelines for Making Guided Notes

Lazarus (1996) provided some tips for making guided notes. To create guided notes, first highlight information from existing lecture notes to create the skeleton for students to use. Then copy the highlighted information. Highlight the additional information using a marker in a second, transparent shade so you can simply add the information to the original guided notes. Use this to make transparencies. These tips work nicely when you are working from existing lecture notes; however, if you are just creating lecture notes it may be easier to start with a skeleton outline and let that guide your lec-

Chapter 20
Cell Reproduction

I. All life starts out as a <u>single</u>   <u>cell</u>   .

    A.   Single cells - - - - - - - - - - - - - - - - millions of cells

    B.   Humans have millions of cells.

II. <u>New</u>   <u>cells</u>   are formed by <u>cell</u>   <u>division</u>   .

III. Types of cell division.

        A. Mitosis—DEFINITION: process of cell division in which two cells are formed from one cell.

           1. Mitosis is used for replacement of:

               a. red blood cells

               b. skin cells

               c. muscle cells

               d. root tips

               e. leaf cells

           2. Before cells divide, the cell parts are copied so the result is two identical cells.

           3. Mitosis is a series of steps.

FIGURE 11.2. Example of a transparency with completed guided notes. From Lazarus, B. D. (1996). Flexible skeletons. *Teaching Exceptional Children, 23*, 34–40. Copyright 1996 by The Council for Exceptional Children. Reprinted by permission.

ture. Initially, preparing guided notes takes about 1–2 hours per chapter; however, they can be used repeatedly.

HOMEWORK/TASK COMPLETION

Homework provides students with opportunity to practice skills learned in the classroom (Polloway, Epstein, & Foley, 1992). Homework is one of the most efficient ways to improve a student's academic performance (Cancio, West, & Young, 2004). However, for students with LD, homework may produce mixed outcomes (Hughes, Ruhl, Schumaker, & Deshler, 2002). In order for students to benefit from homework, teachers must assign appropriate tasks, and students must complete those tasks. Teachers must be mindful of the students' level of independent functioning or provide them with the support necessary to complete their homework successfully; students must actually complete the homework. Students with LD have a number of problems with homework. They frequently misunderstand what has been assigned. Because of organizational deficits they often fail to gather the necessary materials to complete the assignment (Polloway et al., 1992). They also have difficulty recording assignments, managing their time, focusing on homework, monitoring progress, and maintaining effort if the task becomes difficult (Hughes et al., 2002).

Glomb and West (1990) taught high school students to use a homework completion strategy. This strategy was designed to teach students how to plan assignments and monitor their academic work for (1) completeness of assignment, (2) how accurately they followed all of the directions or performance standards for the assignment, and (3) neatness. Students were first taught to identify what to do before starting homework and after completing homework, particularly in regard to completing independent seatwork or homework assignments. Important steps before homework completion included understanding the requirements of the given assignment, preparing to complete the assignment (i.e., gathering all necessary materials), and determining how the assignment would be completed (i.e., time frame, any additional resources). Steps after completing homework included reviewing for accuracy and completeness, making any necessary changes, and handing it in on time.

The WATCH strategy (Figure 11.3) consists of four steps: (1) Write down an assignment when it is given and write the due date; (2) Ask for clarification or help on the assignment if needed; (3) Task-analyze the assignment and schedule the tasks over the days available to complete the assignment; and (4) Check all work for completeness,

---

☐ **W**rite down an assignment, and **W**rite the due date
☐ **A**sk for clarification or help on the assignment if needed
☐ **T**ask—analyze the assignment and schedule the tasks over the days available
☐ **C**heck all work for **C**ompleteness, **A**ccuracy, and **N**eatness

"Do I understand the assignment?"
"Do I need help?"

Class: Social Studies   **Date:** 8/13

Assignment: Read Chapter 12 and answer the comprehension questions
                   at the end.

Task Analysis:
   ➤ **Date:** 8/13—Survey the chapter/questions; read pages 38–43 and take notes
   ➤ **Date:** 8/14—Read pages 44–49 and take notes
   ➤ **Date:** 8/15—Answer questions
   ➤ **Date:**
   ➤ **Date:**

Due Date: 8/16   Before turning in Check for:
                                         ☐ **C**ompleteness
                                         ☐ **A**ccuracy
                                         ☐ **N**eatness

FIGURE 11.3. Example of a completed WATCH sheet.

accuracy, and neatness. The first three are taught first. Students can use an assignment planner that can assist them to carry out each step; planners are an excellent way to monitor students' use of the strategy. The planner can also prompt students with the questions, such as "Do I understand the assignment?" and "Do I need help?" These cues are part of the self-instruction component of the strategy.

Expectations vary for different classes, and different teachers. The monitoring component of this strategy includes checking for completeness, accuracy, and neatness of assignments. This means that teachers will need to teach students performance standards for completeness, accuracy, and neatness of their assignments, and how to evaluate their work according to each standard. Performance standards will vary depending on the content area and the teacher's expectations. Performance standards should reflect expectations the teacher has established for the class. The assignment planner can have the acronym CAN on it to cue students to check tasks for completeness, accuracy, and neatness (Figure 11.3).

TEST-TAKING STRATEGIES

For middle and high school students, tests generally make up the majority of a student's grade in a content-area class. Students with LD have particular difficulty with the skills required to take a test. Preparing for tests is often problematic because of these students' difficulties with organization, comprehension, memory, task completion within time limits, self-doubt, and "test-wiseness" (Olson & Platt, 2000).

Ritter and Idol-Maestas (1986) noted that text anxiety, carelessness, poor use of time, and confusion are serious problems for test takers. The additional pressures of time limits, different forms of response, recalling previously learned information, and putting it into an understandable answer pose problems for many students; students are expected to work independently and read the directions, read the questions, remember the correct response, and write the correct response. Each of these tasks requires a unique set of skills and is essential to performing well on a test (Ritter & Idol-Maestas, 1986).

Teaching students test-taking strategies can dramatically improve their test-taking abilities, as well as their scores on tests. One approach to improving students' test scores is to help them become "test-wise." Test-wiseness is described as a student's capacity to use the characteristics and formats of a test and/or the test-taking situation to receive a high score (Scruggs & Mastropieri, 1988). Skills involved in test-wiseness include time-use strategies, error-avoidance strategies, guessing strategies, and deductive reasoning strategies (Scruggs, Bennion, & Lifson, 1985). Test-wiseness is independent of subject-matter knowledge; the focus is on adapting oneself to the test structure (i.e., if the test is a multiple choice test one needs to be prepared to discriminate between correct and incorrect information) (Ritter & Idol-Maestas, 1986).

Simmonds, Luchow, Kaminsky, and Cottone (1989) designed the SPLASH (Table 11.1) test-taking strategy for taking multiple choice tests. This is a preparation strategy as well as an actual test-taking strategy that helps student become more test-wise. The SPLASH acronym stands for:

TABLE 11.1. The SPLASH Strategy

<u>S</u>—Skim the test.

<u>P</u>—Plan your strategy.

<u>L</u>—Leave out tough questions.

<u>A</u>—Attack questions you know.

<u>S</u>—Systematically guess.

<u>H</u>—House cleaning; leave a few minutes to fill in all
      answers, check computer forms, clean up erasures.

Note. Based on Simmonds, E. P. M., Luchow, J. P., Kaminsky, S.,
& Cottone, V. (1989). Applying cognitive learning strategies in
the classroom: A collaborative training institute. *Learning Disabilities Focus, 4,* 96–105.

1. *Skim the entire test*—Students skim the test to get a general idea of what will be required of them (i.e., how many questions, what types of questions, areas of proficiency and deficiency). This will help them make a plan for attacking the test.

2. *Plan your strategy*—Once students have a general idea of the test they must plan their strategy. This generally includes time constraints, knowledge, and where to begin. Students should first answer all questions that they are sure of.

3. *Leave out difficult questions in a planned manner*—Omitting difficult questions in a planned manner means that students have an idea of which questions they will come back to first.

4. *Attack the questions you know immediately*—This focuses students' attention on information that they understand. Once they have answered all the questions that they immediately know they should move on to any questions they were unsure of.

5. *Systematically guess*—After exhausting other strategies (i.e., skimming for areas of proficiency, answering all questions that they are sure of, and planning how to attack the skipped questions) students should take their best guess at an answer.

6. *House cleaning*—Finally, students should leave 5 to 10% of their time to ensure that they have filled in all answers, checked computer forms, and cleaned up erasures.

Subjective or essay/short answer tests require different skills than objective tests. Often students with LD approach essay questions in a haphazard manner (Simmonds et al., 1989). Students with LD tend to jump right into writing without doing any sort of planning; Scardamalia and Bereiter (1987) termed this "knowledge telling." Little attention is directed toward the goal of answering the question; students will simply write down whatever it is they may know about the topic, and not take into consideration the goal of answering the question. Mapping can provide a more strategic approach, and can be introduced as an effective strategy to facilitate appropriate responses to essay questions (Marshak, 1984). The organization of a map provides a graphic representation of the essay's flow. Figure 11.4 shows a graphic organizer (map) for answering essay questions. Students using this map must be taught what an acceptable essay answer looks like. This strategy can be used to demonstrate that structure and organization influence the content and cohesiveness of essays (Simmonds et al., 1989). The

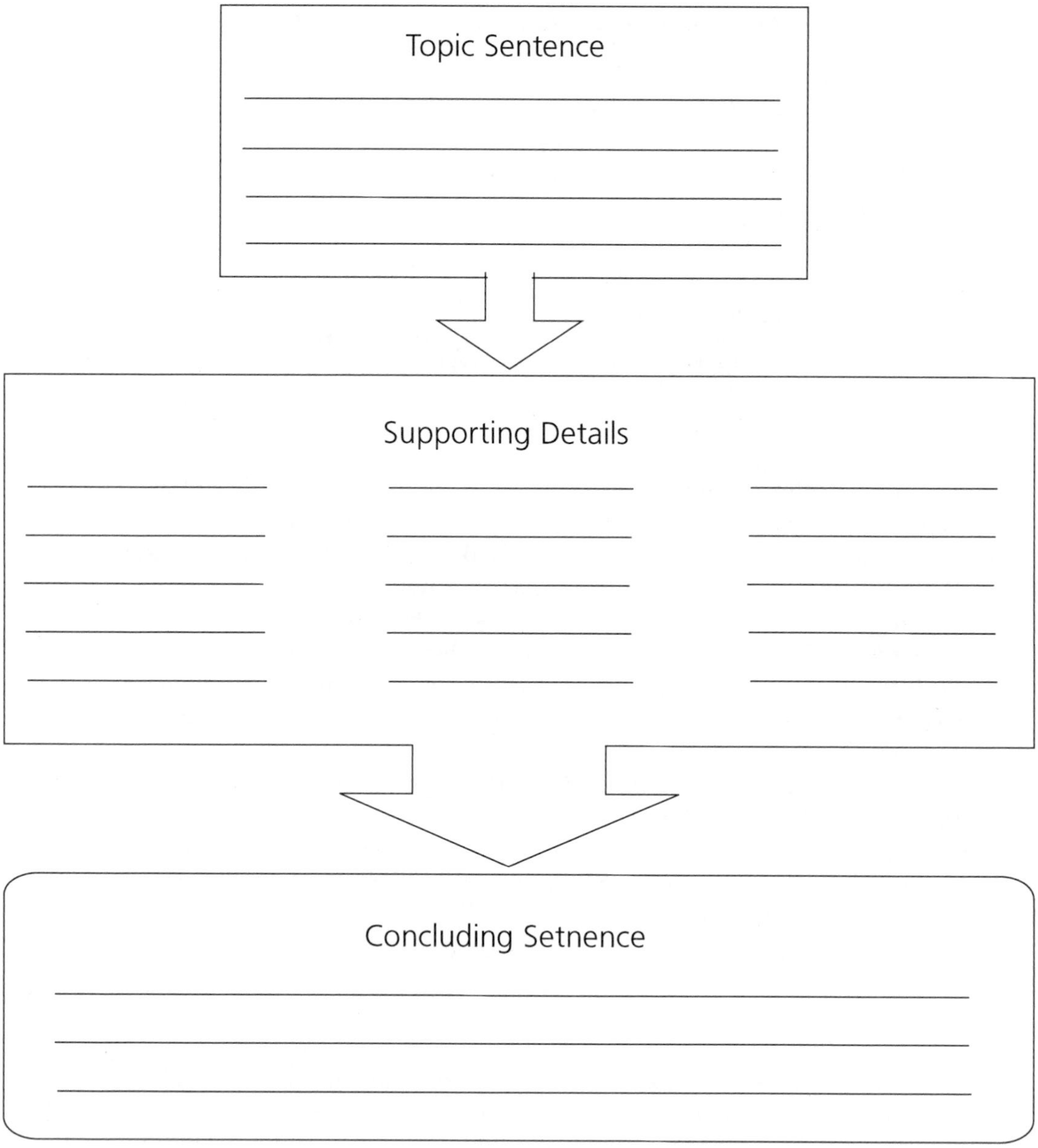

FIGURE 11.4. Example of a graphic organizer for answering essay questions.

first sentence in any essay is the topic sentence. The topic sentence states what the essay is about; all subsequent sentences should reflect the topic sentence. Subsequent sentences are called supporting sentences. Supporting sentences elaborate, explain, and defend the position of the topic sentence. The final sentence in any essay answer is a concluding sentence; this sentence wraps it all up, and brings the focus back to the topic sentence.

CLASSROOM SURVIVAL STRATEGIES

Up till now all of our strategies have dealt with academics. However, in the general education classroom it is sometimes necessary to provide students with a "survival strategy" that addresses organization and motivation. We have already discussed several monitoring strategies (i.e., strategies students can use to monitor their progress toward a goal). This final study skills strategy is a combination of a monitoring strategy and a *motivational* strategy; motivational strategies are designed to maintain motivation and minimize negative thoughts or feelings (Ellis & Lenz, 1987). Students with LD do not generally use monitoring or motivational strategies, which can lead to much frustration, as well as failure.

The PREPARE strategy (Table 11.2) (Ellis & Lenz, 1987) was designed as a classroom survival strategy to help students mentally prepare for class. Students can use the PREPARE strategy to monitor their class preparation behaviors; the PREPARE strategy also includes a motivational substrategy, PSYC. The PREPARE strategy contains six main steps: (1) Plan locker visits, (2) Reflect on what you need, and get it, (3) Erase personal needs (personal issues that do not have to do with class), (4) PSYC yourself up (P—Pause for an attitude check, S—Say a personal goal related to the class, Y—Yoke in negative thoughts, C—Challenge yourself to good performance), (5) Ask yourself where class has been, and where class is going (a brief review of what you have

TABLE 11.2. The PREPARE Strategy

Plan locker visits.

Reflect on what you need, and get it.

Erase personal needs.

PSYC yourself up.

    P—Pause for an attitude check.
    S—Say a personal goal related to the class.
    Y—Yoke in negative thoughts.
    C—Challenge yourself to good performance.

Ask yourself where the class has been, and where the class is going

Review notes and study guide

Explore meaning of teacher's introduction

Note. Ellis, E. S., & Lenz, K. (1987). A component analysis of effective learning strategies for LD students. *Learning Disabilities Focus, 2,* 94–107. Copyright 1987 by Blackwell Publishing Ltd. Reprinted by permission.

learned, and what you will be learning), (6) <u>R</u>eview notes and study guide, and (7) <u>E</u>xplore the meaning of teacher's introduction.

IMPLEMENTATION PLANS

As with previous chapters, we provide partial examples of implementation plans for each of the strategies previously presented.

Stage 1 for Guided Notes: Developing and Activating Background Knowledge

Prior to teaching the strategy, it is necessary to evaluate the students' background knowledge. Formal or informal assessments can be used to determine what skills the students possess and what skills they lack; doing a task analysis will provide the information for identifying the skills necessary to successfully complete the strategy (Table 11.3).

TABLE 11.3. Example of Task Breakdown for Guided Notes

Strategy	Skill	Assessment
Basic skills	Writing/copying	Given a spelling test using terms from the given content area, the student will be able to spell the words correctly with 80% accuracy.
	Reading from the board (transparency projection)	
	Spelling	Given the task of copying a passage from the board, the student will be able to copy everything with 100% accuracy.
Guided notes (format)	Knowledge of main ideas, key phrases, definitions, related issues, and contrasting viewpoints	Given a familiar passage from the student's textbook, the student will highlight main ideas, key phrases, definitions, related issues, and contrasting viewpoints using specific colors to identify each, with 100% accuracy.
	Understanding standard outline format (i.e., I for major headings, A for main ideas under major headings, and so on)	Given a standard outline format, students will be able to fill in each blank with the correct title (i.e., major heading, main ideas, and so on).
	Knowledge of lecture format	Given a simple lecture on familiar material, the student will be able to follow along and note major concepts with 90% accuracy.
Using the guided notes	Distinguishing relevant information	Given a familiar passage with a task that the student can perform, students will be able to highlight all information relevant to completing the task, with 90% accuracy.
	Writing and listening at the same time	Given a list orally, the student will be able to listen and write the correct list at the same time with 100% accuracy.
	Ability to put information into an organized format (guided notes).	Given a skeleton outline and a simple passage, students will be able organize the information in the passage.

Stage 2 for WATCH: Discussing the Strategy

This is the first stage in "initiating" the strategy. In this stage it is important to stress the relevance of the strategy. An initial conference between the teacher and student is necessary. During this initial conference the teacher will want to discuss the students' current performance. In order for students to be successful and self-regulating they need to make a commitment to use the strategy, or "buy in." It is important for the teacher to stress the value of the strategy. Brainstorm with the students on situations where using this strategy or completing the given task accurately is important. For example, the following might be appropriate brainstorming ideas in response to the question "When would it be important for you to complete an assignment?":

- To pass a class—and get to use the car
- At work when you're given something to do
- So your parents will be proud of you
- So you can play sports

A sample script for "selling" the strategy follows:

"The other day, we came up with a list of instances when it would be important to complete an assignment. Since we are here in school the obvious one was to pass a class. Passing a class provides other motivations: getting to use the car, being able to play in the big game on Friday night, not having to take the class over, or maybe even getting on the honor roll. There are lots of reasons to complete your assignments, but sometimes it's hard to get it all done! I used to have a difficult time with this too, but now I have secret weapon. It's a strategy called WATCH! This strategy helps me organize myself so I can get my work turned in on time. Yes, as teachers we still have work! This strategy has really helped me, and I would like to teach it to you to help you too. I would hate it if any of you had to miss something important just because you didn't get an assignment done."

Stage 3 for SPLASH: Modeling the Strategy

The teacher will need to use a think-aloud to demonstrate the use of the strategy. Note how self-statements are used to focus attention and to redirect maladaptive thoughts.

"OK, here goes another science test. I always have such a hard time taking these tests! I just don't even know where to begin. Wait a minute, in class we've been working on this test-taking strategy called SPLASH; I think I'll use that to help me. Let's see, what do I need to do first? SPLASH . . . oh yeah, the *S* in SPLASH stands for 'skim the entire test.' OK, I'll skim the test . . . it looks like there are 50 questions, 40 multiple choice, and 10 true/false. I like true/false questions; I usually seem to know those answers right away. I also saw some keywords that I know; I'm sure I'll know those answers, but I also saw some words whose meaning I can't remember right now. *Great*, now what am I going to do? I know there are some of those questions that I *can't* answer!!! Well, no need to focus on that; that won't help me! What's next in my strategy? That *may* help me! OK, S . . . P–the next step in the SPLASH strategy is to 'Plan my strategy once I have a general idea of the test.' Well, I know I have the whole hour to take the test, but some questions may take me longer than others (like those ones I'm not sure about), so I should start with the ones that I know for sure! I think I'll start with the true/false questions, since I like those. Then, I'll answer the multiple choice ones. The next step in my SPLASH strategy is L–'Leave out any difficult questions.' That will be easy, I already saw a few that I don't know; I'll leave those out. I like that step! OK, on to the next step. OK, what's next? I've S–skimmed, P–planned, and L–left out the hard ones; now, I need to A–'Attack the questions I know immediately.' OK, I will start with the true/false ones . . . OK, done, I knew most of those, but there was that one that I left out, because I'm just not sure about it. That's ok, according to my SPLASH strategy I'm supposed to leave out the difficult ones! I sure did that! OK, I've answered all the questions that I'm sure about, but I still have about 10 left! Now what? OK, back to SPLASH, S . . . P . . . L . . . A . . . S–stands for 'Systematically guess.' Well, I have a pretty good idea about most of these; answering all the questions that I was sure about helped me to remember some of the other things that I had forgotten, but there is still that true/false one that I have no idea about. I will just have to guess; I have a 50/50 chance at getting the right answer; I like those odds! OK, now what? SPLAS . . . H–stands for 'House cleaning'; I need to make sure my paper is clean, and I have all of my answers marked clearly. Wow, I'm done! That was so much easier using my SPLASH strategy; I don't feel like I wasted any time, and I feel pretty good about how I did!"

Stage 4 for PREPARE: Memorizing the Strategy

Memorizing the strategy is extremely important! We want the students to focus on the task and not on the steps of the strategy. The specific activities themselves are not nearly as important. There are many appropriate activities. The important aspect of the activities is whether or not they facilitate memorization; however, you will need to plan and prepare the activities and monitor their effectiveness. Previous chapters have provided examples of how to instruct effectively at this stage. Memorization of the PREPARE strategy could be promoted in a similar fashion.

Stage 5 for Guided Notes: Supporting the Strategy

In this stage, scaffolding is important. With scaffolding it is possible for a gradual transfer of strategy performance from teacher to student. Students need to be given adequate time and support to master the strategy.

Content Scaffolding

Students will be provided with completed guided notes and a skeleton outline. The teacher and students will go over the notes and discuss the components of the skeleton outline. The teacher will direct the process and the students will provide answers to teacher-directed questions (e.g., "What is the first major heading?" "Where would this definition go?" "What is the key concept here?").

Students will be given a skeleton outline and some simple, familiar, text. They will be asked to fill in the skeleton outline. The teacher will post the completed guided notes on the overhead and students will be able to check their outlines against the completed outline. The teacher will provide any support necessary in order for the students to be successful.

Task Scaffolding

During collaborative practice the teacher will question the students while lecturing as to what part of their skeleton outline they should fill in. The teacher will then fill in the outline and explain why the information should be in that particular location. In subsequent lessons the teacher will ask the students where information from lectures should go, and have them fill in the appropriate space, then the teacher will explain why that information needs to be in that particular location. Finally, the students will say where the information should go, fill in the skeleton outline, and explain why that information should be in that particular location.

Material Scaffolding

The students will be provided with several skeleton outlines. Initially, students will be provided with outlines containing most of the information (Figure 11.2). Over time outlines will provide less information but still provide the structure and key information (Figure 11.1). Eventually the skeleton outlines will be faded completely; at this point students should have reached the mastery level of taking notes and being able to work independently.

Stage 6 for SPLASH: Independent Performance

At this stage the student is ready to use the strategy independently. The teacher's main task is to monitor the student's performance and check on proper and consistent use of the strategy. With our main goal being improved academic performance, it is necessary to monitor student progress with the strategy. Teachers must evaluate whether or not the strategy is being used, if it is being generalized to other appropriate situations, and whether or not academic performance has improved. Records of student achievement on tests will be kept and monitored.

Teachers need to keep in mind the fact that students will not always generalize strategies to appropriate situations; they will need to be prompted and encouraged to do so. To promote generalization, students will be encouraged to use the strategy in other content areas where they are required to take tests (i.e., most all of them). All team teachers will be informed about the use of the strategy, the language, the prompts, and what is required at each step. All team teachers will be given a wall chart to hang up in their room as a reminder for students to use the SPLASH strategy when appropriate.

Even though students have reached the independent performance stage, they will be monitored to ensure proper use of the strategy. If students deviate from the given SPLASH strategy, performance will be evaluated, but action will be taken only if performance is no longer improving.

FINAL THOUGHTS

Study skills are an important part of any student's repertoire. The need for well-developed study skills becomes progressively greater as the student moves from elementary, to middle, to high school settings. Although these skills are critical for academic success, in our opinion they are too often overlooked because of the focus on basic academic skills at the elementary level, and the focus on content areas at the middle and high school levels. We would urge teachers to consider teaching organization, study skills, and test taking strategies as early as possible. These strategies will be useful then and will only become more important over time. Unfortunately, there was not space here to present many excellent study skill strategies. For more information on study skills strategies, we refer the reader to Davis, Sirotowitz, and Parker (1996) and Levine (1990).

REFERENCES

Benton, S. L., Kiewra, K. A., Whitfill, J. M., & Dennison, R. (1993). Encoding and external-storage effects on writing processes. *Journal of Educational Psychology, 85,* 267–280.

Bos, C. S., & Vaughn, S. (1998). *Strategies for teaching students with learning and behavior problems* (5th ed.). Boston: Allyn & Bacon.

Cancio, E. J., West, R. P., & Young, K. R. (2004). Improving mathematics homework completion and accuracy of students with EBD through self-management and parent participation. *Journal of Emotional and Behavioral Disorders, 12*(1), 9–22.

Carlson, S. S., & Alley, G. R. (1981). *Performance and competence of learning disabled and high-achieving high school students in essential cognitive skills* (Research Report No. 53). Lawrence: University of Kansas Institute for Research in Learning Disabilities.

Davis, L., Sirotowitz, S., & Parker, H. (1996). Study strategies made easy. Plantation, FL: Specialty Press.

deBettencourt, L. U. (1987). Strategy training: A need for clarification. *Exceptional Children, 54,* 24–30.

Deshler, D. D., Ellis, E. S., & Lenz, B. K. (1996). *Teaching adolescents with learning disabilities: Strategies and methods* (2nd ed.). Denver, CO: Love.

Deshler, D. D., & Graham, S. (1980). Tape recording educational materials for secondary handicapped students. *Teaching Exceptional Children, 12,* 52–54.

Ellis, E. S., & Lenz, K. (1987). A component analysis of effective learning strategies for LD students. *Learning Disabilities Focus, 2,* 94–107.

Englert, C. S., & Raphael, T. E. (1988). Constructing well-formed prose: Process, structure, and metacognitive knowledge. *Research and Instruction in Written Language, 54,* 513–520.

Gettinger, M., & Seibert, J. K. (2002). Contributions of study skills to academic competence. *School Psychology Review, 31,* 350–365.

Graham, S., & Harris, K. R. (2000). The role of self-regulation and transcription skills in writing and writing development. *Writing Development: The Role of Cognitive, Motivational, and Social/ Contextual Factors (Special Issue), 35,* 3–12.

Hughes, C. A., Ruhl, K. L., Schumaker, J. B., & Deshler, D. (2002). Effects of instruction in an assignment completion strategy in the homework performance of students with learning disabilities in general education classes. *Learning Disabilities Research and Practice, 17,* 1–18.

Kiewra, K. A. (1984). Acquiring effective notetaking skills: An alternative to professional notetaking. *Journal of Reading, 27,* 299–302.

Kiewra, K. A. (1987). Notetaking and review: The research and its implications. *Instructional Science, 16,* 233–249.

Kiewra, K. A., & Benton, S. L. (1988). The relationship between information-processing ability and notetaking. *Contemporary Educational Psychology, 13,* 33–44.

Kops, C., & Belmont, I. (1985). Planning and organizing skills of poor school achievers. *Journal of Learning Disabilities, 18,* 8–14.

Lazarus, B. D. (1988). Using guided notes to aid learning disabled students in secondary mainstream settings. *The Pointer, 33,* 32–36.

Lazarus, B. D. (1991). Guided notes, review, and achievement of secondary students with learning disabilities in mainstream content courses. *Education and Treatment of Children, 14,* 112–127.

Lazarus, B. D. (1996). Flexible skeletons. *Teaching Exceptional Children, 23,* 34–40.

Levine, M. (1990). Keeping a head in school. Cambridge, MA: Educators Publishing Service.

Olson, J. L., & Platt, J. M. (2000). *Teaching children and adolescents with special needs* (3rd ed.). Upper Saddle River, NJ: Prentice Hall.

Polloway, E. A., Epstein, M. H., & Foley, R. (1992). A comparison of homework problems of students with learning disabilities and nonhandicapped students. *Learning Disabilities Research and Practice, 7,* 203–209.

Ritter, S., & Idol-Maestas, L. (1986). Teaching middle school students to use a test-taking strategy. *Journal of Educational Research, 79,* 350–357.

Scardamalia, M., & Bereiter, C. (1987). Knowledge telling and knowledge transforming in written composition. In S. Rosenberg (Ed.), *Advances in applied psycholingustics: Vol. 2. Reading, writing, and language learning* (pp. 142–175). Cambridge, UK: Cambridge University Press.

Schumaker, J. B., & Deshler, D. D. (1988). Implementing the Regular Education Initiative in secondary schools: A different ball game. *Journal of Learning Disabilities, 21,* 26–31.

Scruggs, T. E., Bennion, K., & Lifson, S. (1985). Analysis of children's strategy use of reading achievement tests. *Elementary School Journal, 85,* 479–484.

Scruggs, T. E., & Mastropieri, J. (1988). Are learning disabled students "test-wise": A review of recent research. *Learning Disabilities Focus, 3,* 87–97.

Simmonds, E. P. M., Luchow, J. P., Kaminsky, S., & Cottone, V. (1989). Applying cognitive learning strategies in the classroom: A collaborative training institute. *Learning Disabilities Focus, 4,* 96–105.

Smith, G., & Smith, D. (1989). Schoolwide study skills program: The key to mainstreaming. *Teaching Exceptional Children, 21,* 20–23.

Snyder, M., & Bambara, L. (1997). Teaching secondary students with learning disabilities to self-manage classroom survival skills. *Journal of Learning Disabilities, 30,* 534–544.

Suritsky, S. K. (1992). Notetaking approaches and specific areas of difficulty reported by university students with learning disabilities. *Journal of Postsecondary Education and Disability, 10,* 3–10.

Swanson, H. L., & Trahan, M. R. (1992). Learning disabled readers: comprehension of computer mediated text: The influence of working memory, metacognition, and attribution. *Learning Disabilities Research and Practice, 7,* 74–86.

Sweller, J., van Merrienboer, J. J. G., & Paas, F. G. W. C. (1998). Cognitive architecture and instructional design. *Educational Psychology Review, 10,* 251–296.

CHAPTER 12

Mnemonics

W[hat's] the capital of Bolivia? What are the parts of the nucleus of an atom? What's the fourth planet from the sun? Name three reasons for the start of the Civil War? Students will commonly be called upon to answer questions such as these in classes, assignments, and examinations. This means that students must be able to efficiently and effectively store information in long-term memory and retrieve it on demand. As with other academic tasks, using strategies can help with storing and retrieving information. However, as we've previously discussed, students with LD do not spontaneously use appropriate and effective strategies that could help them remember. Thus, teachers should be aware of the need to not only teach content, but to also provide students with strategies to help them store and retrieve important information. One very effective type of memory strategy is a mnemonic.

A mnemonic is a strategy designed to help students store and retrieve information. Most students have, at one point, have learned a mnemonic strategy, although they may not have heard the term "mnemonic" (Scruggs & Mastropieri, 2000). For example, many students have learned the acronym ROY G. BIV to help them remember the colors of the rainbow. Each letter in the acronym represents one of the colors of the rainbow (i.e., red, orange, yellow, green, blue, indigo, violet). Another example that would be familiar to music students is the phrase "Every good boy does fine," used to help students remember the notes on the lines of the treble clef: *e, g, b, d,* and *f.* These are examples of how mnemonics can be used to remember factual or detailed information. Mnemonics can also be used to help us remember the order of steps in a process. For example, Please Excuse My Dear Aunt Sally is a first-letter mnemonic used to remember the order of operations in algebraic problems (Parenthesis, Exponents, Multiply, Divide, Add, and Subtract) (Mastropieri & Scruggs, 1991).

Mnemonic strategies have been used for thousands of years. The ancient Greeks used a form of mnemonics, the method of loci, to help orators remember their speeches. This strategy involves remembering a series of very familiar places or locations, such as the route taken from school to home, and pairing images of one piece of information with each place. For example, to remember a shopping list of hot dogs, ice cream, and cat food, you might pair up images of (1) hot dogs rolling down your driveway, (2) ice cream melting on the stoplight at the first intersection, and (3) a hungry cat in a shopping cart in the grocery store parking lot. The shopping list information can then be easily retrieved by mentally retracing one's route and recalling each of the items placed on the "mental map" (Schoen, 1996). Though this may sound strange, the method of loci is actually highly effective. This unconventional method illustrates an important point; the method is not what is important, what is important is how well it facilitates the different memory processes (i.e., encoding, storage, and retrieval) (Schoen, 1996).

There's a good reason why mnemonic strategies have been used for so long. Research clearly demonstrates that mnemonic techniques are superior to traditional methods of instruction when teaching the acquisition and recall of highly factual information (e.g., science and social studies information). For example, Mastropieri, Sweda, and Scruggs (2000) reported that using mnemonic strategies for social studies raised the average test scores of students with LD from 36 to 75%. Similarly, Mastropieri, Scruggs, Bakken, and Brigham (1992) found that mnemonics were effective in teaching U.S. states and capitals. Finally, Scruggs, Mastropieri, Levin, and Gaffney (1985) found that mnemonics could be used to teach multiple attributes of minerals (e.g., hardness scale, color, and their uses), and that mnemonic instruction was more effective than direct instruction or free study. On the whole, mnemonics have proven to be highly effective in improving retention of information in specific content areas for students with LD (Mastropieri & Scruggs, 1998; Scruggs & Mastropieri, 1990, 1992). Scruggs and Mastropieri (2000) reviewed the research in mnemonics and found that instruction that utilized mnemonics led to a nearly 2 to 1 improvement in learning. Moreover, the majority of the studies reviewed by Scruggs and Mastropieri were done with students with LD.

There are many different types of mnemonic strategies, each of which can be used for multiple purposes. In this chapter we present examples of the five main types of mnemonic strategies based on the classification developed by Mastropieri and Scruggs: (1) acronyms and acrostics, (2) mimetics, (3) symbolics, (4) keywords, and (5) pegwords.

PROBLEMS FOR STUDENTS WITH LEARNING DISABILITIES

As you will recall from Chapter 1, one of the most salient characteristics of students with LD is a problem with memory. Many students with LD do not efficiently encode and retrieve information from long-term memory. Memory is critical to intellectual functioning and learning (Swanson & Saez, 2003). The ability to recall information is directly linked to a student's ability to learn, and therefore obviously a key component to academic success. Swanson and Saez (2003) identified two reasons why memory is a critical area of focus for students with LD.

1. *Memory reflects applied cognition; that is, memory functioning reflects all aspects of learning* (p. 182). In schools, measures of learning are generally measures of memory (i.e., basic math facts, vocabulary, and reading comprehension). The way we measure whether or not students have learned content is to assess their memory of the information. If a student is unable to apply or recall new information it is difficult to determine whether or not learning has occurred.

2. *Several studies suggest that the memory skills used by students with LD do not appear to exhaust, or even tap, their abilities; therefore, we need to discover instructional procedures that can capitalize on this underdeveloped potential* (p. 182). The problems with recall of factual information for students with LD are probably not due to a deficient memory. Rather they are due to the failure to use strategies, or the use of ineffective or inefficient strategies. Students with LD have the potential to learn; however, unless they are taught how to recall information and use their cognitive abilities effectively they will never reach their full academic potential.

According to Mastropieri and Scruggs (1991), learning occurs most efficiently when new information can be linked to previously acquired information. That is, learning is a knowledge-based process that requires the active involvement of the learner to make connections between known information and to-be-learned information. Students with LD often fail to make these important mental "connections" between known and unknown information. This inability often results in school failure, poor performance on tests, and a general loss of information in content areas (Scruggs & Mastropieri, 2000). Because gaining knowledge requires learners to possess some knowledge, students must not only understand the new information presented to them, but must continually test, modify, and build upon or replace existing knowledge (Gaskins & Elliot, 1991). This presents problems for students with LD; many times they do not possess the prerequisite knowledge required to make learning meaningful and lasting. Research indicates that students who have a firmly established knowledge base will be able to easily assimilate and apply new information. This puts students with LD at a distinct disadvantage. Mastropieri and Scruggs (1991) called this phenomenon the "Matthew Effect," whereby the "informationally rich" become richer, and the "informationally poor" (students with LD) become poorer. This is a vicious cycle; the best way to break it is to provide students with LD a solid knowledge base, as well as strategies to promote the acquisition of future information.

ACRONYMS AND ACROSTICS: THE "FIRST LETTER" STRATEGIES

Acronyms

Most of us are familiar with acronyms. Acronyms are formed by taking the first letters of the words in a title or list of facts and combining them into a word. Each letter in an acronym represents the first letter of a word on a list of information to be learned or remembered. Acronyms serve as convenient shorthand representations of information. For example, it's much easier to say NASA than National Aeronautics and Space Administration, or KFC as opposed to Kentucky Fried Chicken. Generally, this type of mnemonic is most helpful when the items to be remembered are familiar and concrete. With only the first letter as a prompt, students must be familiar enough with the responses for that to serve as an adequate cue (Mastropieri & Scruggs, 1991). For example, a highly effective acronym for people studying U.S. geography would be HOMES. It represents the five Great Lakes. Each letter in the acronym HOMES represents a different lake: Huron, Ontario, Michigan, Erie, and Superior.

This strategy is highly effective, but *only* for people who are familiar with the names of the Great Lakes. Here, the first letter is typically enough to evoke the correct response. If students were not familiar with the names they would need to be taught them first, so that the first letter could serve as an adequate cue. Students would also need to be taught a way to associate the acronym HOMES with the names of the Great Lakes so they could retrieve it for later use (Mastropieri & Scruggs, 1998). This process is similar to the *keyword* process of recoding, relating, and retrieving (discussed in detail later on in the chapter). For this example, students could be taught to relate the acronym HOMES to the Great Lakes by visualizing "homes" built around the edges of the Great Lakes (providing a picture of this would be even better). For retrieving the names, the students would need to remember the visual image of homes built on the edge of the lakes, come up with the acronym HOMES, and use the first-letter cues to come up with Huron, Ontario, Michigan, Erie, and Superior (Mastropieri & Scruggs, 1998).

Acronyms are an excellent way to organize information; you've probably noticed that many of the strategies we have presented use acronyms in the name. For example:

- SCROL—Textbook reading strategy
- WWW, What = 2, How = 2—Narrative writing strategy
- FAST DRAW—Solving word problems
- POW + TREE—Expository writing strategy
- COPS—Mechanical revision strategy
- SCAN—Content revision strategy
- WATCH—Homework completion strategy
- SPLASH—Test-taking strategy
- PREPARE—General classroom survival strategy

There's a good reason for this. The acronym serves to help organize the steps in the strategy, stimulate memory of the strategy steps, and cue the order of steps.

Acrostics

An acrostic is a sentence in which the first letter of each word doubles as part of a mnemonic that represents the information to be learned and remembered. An example of this was provided at the beginning of this chapter for the notes on the lines of the treble clef, Every Good Boy Does Fine. Another example would be "Queen Hannah Gave Mr. Potter Every CD Collected." This assists in remembering the step in the scientific method of experimental research: Question, Hypothesis, Gather Materials, Perform Experiment, Collect Data, and Conclusion. Acrostics can also be used to remember the spelling of difficult words (e.g., "A rat in the house may eat the ice cream!" for the word *arithmetic*). Acrostics are sometimes used to help cue the steps in a strategy. For example, "Does McDonald's Sell CheeseBurgers?" can be used to help remember the steps in long division:

- Does _____ go into _____?
- Multiply to find out
- Subtract
- Check to make sure the result is smaller
- Bring down

When an acronym or an acrostic alone is not effective or practical, the two can be combined. For example, when remembering the order of the planets from the sun a combination can be used: "My Very Exciting Man, JSUN, Plays!" for Mercury, Venus, Earth, Mars, Jupiter, Saturn, Uranus, Neptune, and Pluto. Students would need to be able to remember which part of the sentence was an acronym, and which part was an acrostic; however, this would not be difficult if the students were familiar enough with the information to be remembered (the planets).

MIMETICS

The term "mimetic" literally means imitating or mimicking something. In the case of mnemonic strategies, a mimetic is simply a pictorial representation of the information that is to be learned. Many content areas require students to learn content that is concrete and that can easily be depicted in an illustration (Mastropieri & Scruggs, 1991). If the content is already familiar and meaningful to the student, then a mimetic is likely to be effective. For example, in social studies content introduced is often familiar and meaningful to students. For instance, students studying the Industrial Revolution would be familiar with the technology in 1800s that changed life in the United States (i.e., textile mills, mass production, the Erie Canal, the national road, and steamboats and railroads) (Figure 12.1). To teach this content, the teacher would present the picture and note how the mill was by the national road and the steamboats and steam engines were bringing goods for mass production. The teacher would remind the students that when they needed to remember something about technology in the 1800s they should remember the picture of how the steamboat and steam engines brought material along the national road to the textile mills. By reconstructing this information mimetically they would achieve greater recall of the information. We should stress that it is critical for the students to already be familiar with the content. For example, Mastropieri and Scruggs (1991) described the use of a mimetic showing convoys protecting U.S. oil

FIGURE 12.1. A mimetic representation of the Industrial Revolution. This picture depicts the major innovations of the 1800s leading to the Industrial Revolution: (1) textile mills, (2) assembly lines, (3) interchangeable parts, (4) steam engines, (5) the Erie Canal, and (6) the national roadway.

tankers in the Persian Gulf. However, because the students were unfamiliar with the term "convoy" the mimetic was not effective.

SYMBOLICS

Symbolics are similar to mimetics. Both use illustrations to represent information. Symbolics differ in that they are used to depict abstract information. Political cartoons are an excellent example of symbolics. Symbolics are used in the same manner as mimetics. As with mimetics, students must be familiar with the content. This is a serious concern because of the abstract nature of the content of symbolics. For example, most of us are familiar with the symbols used for the Republicans (an elephant) and the Democrats (a donkey). However, students with LD do not always know this association (Mastropieri & Scruggs, 1991). Symbolics are used in much the same manner as mimetics. Figure 12.2 provides an example of a symbolic mnemonic for the three branches of government, and what each branch represents. Again, it is important to remember that students *must* be familiar with the symbols used to represent each branch in order for this particular mnemonic to be effective. If these symbols are unfamiliar it would be necessary to teach these associations.

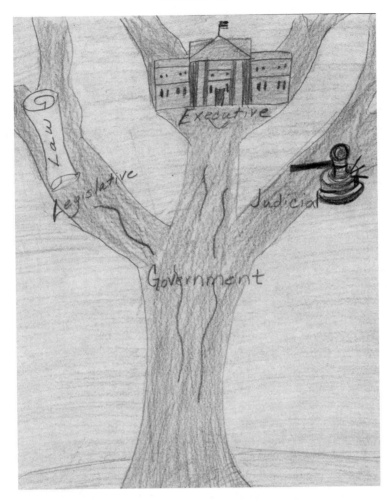

FIGURE 12.2. A symbolic representation of the three branches of government

KEYWORDS

The keyword method was initially developed as a technique for foreign vocabulary learning. It is rooted in the elaboration of unfamiliar vocabulary words or concepts (Atkinson, 1975). This is accomplished by making information to be recalled more concrete through association with visual images (mental pictures or actual illustrations) in which the keyword and target word or concept are interacting in a meaningful way (Foil & Alber, 2002; Scruggs & Mastropieri, 2000). Keywords are first chosen by examining terms for any salient or prominent acoustic characteristic they may hold in common, and then linking or integrating the keyword with the to-be-learned word or concept via an interactive mental image (Smith, 1985; Pressley, Levin, & Delaney, 1982). The keyword method can be described as a chain with two links connecting a new word to its definition (Atkinson, 1975). This is facilitated through a three-step process involving (1) recoding, (2) relating, and (3) retrieving new information (Levin, 1988).

1. *Recoding:* Teachers must choose a keyword that sounds like the vocabulary word to be learned. The word should be acoustically similar, familiar to the students, and concrete enough to be easily pictured.
2. *Relating*: Once a keyword has been chosen, it must be related, or linked, to the response, or to-be-learned information. This can be done in a sentence, a visual mental image, or, better yet, in a picture in which you can see the keyword interacting with the to-be-learned information.
3. *Retrieving*: After "recoding" the vocabulary word into a keyword, and relating it to the information to be learned through a sentence, visual image, or picture, students will need to be taught how to retrieve the definition.
   a. Have students think of the keyword when they are asked for the definition of the vocabulary word.
   b. Students then need to think back to the interactive picture with the keyword and definition.
   c. Finally, students retrieve the definition from the information in the picture (Mastropieri & Scruggs, 1991).

For example, suppose that the student needed to remember that *caballo* means horse in Spanish. One might select "cab" for a keyword, because it is acoustically similar to *caballo*. Then the teacher would create a picture relating the keyword (*cab*) to the target word (*caballo*). For example, here the obvious choice might be a picture of a horse driving a cab (Figure 12.3). Finally, the teacher would help the child construct a retrieval path to help remember the meaning of *caballo*. The teacher would tell the child, "When you hear the word *caballo* remember the keyword *cab*. Then remember the picture of the cab with the horse driving. This will help you remember that *caballo* means horse." The student would practice this sequence a few times to ensure that he or she was able to follow the three steps (i.e., recode, relate, retrieve). Remember that mnemonic strategies involve more than just pictures. Teachers need to teach students a retrieval path for information. Figure 12.4 shows additional examples of keywords.

The keyword method can also serve as the basis for a strategy. The LINCS strategy (Ellis, 1992) is a keyword vocabulary strategy. It is designed to assist students to independently generate keywords for target vocabulary. LINCS is an acronym for the following steps:

1. List the parts. Write the word on a study card and list the most important parts of the definition on the back (Figure 12.5).

Example: If the vocabulary word is "chrysalis," the student would write the word "chrysalis" on the front of the card and write "pupa of a moth or butterfly enclosed in a cocoon" on the back.

2. Imagine a picture. Create a mental picture and describe it.

Example: For the word "chrysalis" the student may think of a crystal ball with cocoon and a butterfly in it.

Caballo (cab) = horse

Recoding: *Caballo* sounds like the familiar, concrete word *cab*.
  (1) *Cab* sounds like *caballo*
  (2) A *cab* is familiar to most students.
  (3) A *cab* is concrete enough to be easily pictured.

<u>Relating</u>: Depict the information to be remembered (*horse*) interacting with the keyword (*cab*).

<u>Retrieving</u>:   1. Have students think of the keyword *cab,* when they are asked for
                the definition of *caballo*.
             2. Students then need to think back to the interactive picture of the
                horse driving the cab.
             3. Finally, students retrieve the definition from the information in
                the picture.

FIGURE 12.3. A keyword mnemonic example.

3. *Note a reminding word*. Think of a familiar word that sounds like the vocabulary word.

Example: For the word "chrysalis" the student may think of the familiar words "crystal ball" and write them on the bottom half of the front side of the card.

4. *Construct a LINCing story*. Make up a short story about the meaning of the word that includes the reminding word.

Example: The fortuneteller looked into her crystal ball and saw a pupa in a cocoon turning into a butterfly.

5. *Self-test*. Test your memory forward and backward.

Example: Look at the words "chrysalis" and "crystal ball" on the front of the card and say what is on the back of the card ("pupa of a moth or butterfly enclosed in a cocoon"): "The fortuneteller looked into her crystal ball and saw a pupa in a cocoon

Ocho = eight

The keyword to remember is *ouch!* When you hear *ocho* think of the figure 8 hurting its foot and yelling out the word "Ouch!"

Zapatos = shoes

The keyword to remember is *pot.*

When you hear the word *zapatos*, think of a bunch of shoes being used as flowerpots.

Beringia = land bridge that connected Asia and North America

The keyword to remember is *bear.*

When you hear *beringia*, think of a bear stretching over the water to make a bridge connecting Asia and North America.

FIGURE 12.4. Additional examples of keyword mnemonics.

turning into a butterfly." The student should also look at the back of the card to self-test the vocabulary word and the keyword.

A slight variation on this strategy would be to have students not only create a LINCing story, but to also create a LINCing picture. Students can create their own LINCing picture and put it next to their LINCing story on their word cards (see bottom of Figure 12.5). The picture can then serve as an additional cue to the meaning of the

---

Chrysalis

Fold here

Crystal ball

---

pupa of a moth or butterfly enclosed in a cocoon

The fortuneteller looked into her crystal ball and saw a pupa in a cocoon turning into a butterfly.

---

pupa of a moth or butterfly enclosed in a cocoon

The fortuneteller looked into her crystal ball and saw a pupa in a cocoon turning into a butterfly.

FIGURE 12.5. An example of the LINCS strategy.

---

word. Note that the Association for Supervision and Curriculum Development (2002) has a video that shows examples of how the LINCS strategy would be taught.

PEGWORDS

The pegword method uses "peg" words, or rhyming proxies, for numbers (e.g., one—bun, two—shoe, three—tree). Here are some commonly used pegwords for the numbers 1 through 10.

- One = bun, or gun, or sun
- Two = shoe
- Three = tree
- Four = door or floor

Pegword–Keyword Combination

Part of the eye	Recode–Keyword	Relate	Pictorial recoding
Cornea	Corn	The sun makes the corn grow.	
Iris	Iris (flower)	There is an iris in the shoe.	
Pupil	Pupil (student)	The pupil is under the tree.	
Lens	Lens (glasses)	There are lenses on the door.	

FIGURE 12.6. Combining pegwords and keywords.

- Five = hive
- Six = sticks
- Seven = heaven
- Eight = gate
- Nine = vine, line, or lion
- Ten = hen

Figure 12.6 shows an example of pegword–keyword combinations.

Pegwords can be helpful in remembering virtually any numbered or ordered sequences of information (e.g., the order of the U.S. presidents; the kingdom, phylum, and class of living organisms; causes or factors leading up to world conflicts). The pegword method is particularly useful in remembering the specific location of an item within a sequence (see Mastropieri & Scruggs, 1991). This method is often used with the keyword method to facilitate the recall of information that is ordered or numbered (Scruggs & Mastropieri, 1991). For example, when learning the periodic table of elements, remembering that the atomic number for carbon is 6 is much easier when one visualizes a car (keyword of carbon) made of sticks (the pegword for 6) (Figure 12.7). This helps make the association between carbon and its place in the periodic table. The pegword method is particularly useful in the social and physical/life sciences, which typically require classification, organization, and hierarchical categorizations of oftentimes seemingly unrelated information and events.

Research has shown that the combination of keywords and pegwords can be extremely effective. For example, Mastropieri and Scruggs (1991) showed that the combination of pegwords and keywords could be used to help students remember a mineral's place on the hardness scale along with major uses. An example would be the mineral wolframite, which is number 4 on the hardness scale. The researchers used a

Carbon (car) = atomic number 6 (sticks) – a "car" made of "sticks."

FIGURE 12.7. A pegword mnemonic example.

picture of a wolf (the keyword for wolframite) on a floor (the pegword for 4), turning on a light bulb (a major use for wolframite).

A keyword–pegword combination can be used if numbered or sequential information is associated with unfamiliar names of things (Mastropieri & Scruggs, 1991). For example, students learning about the five early Western philosophers Epicurus, Socrates, Plato, Xeno, and Aristotle, could use a combination of keywords and pegwords (see Figure 12.8 for examples) to remember the major philosophers. After they have been taught the keywords (recoded names to be learned), and the sentences for relating the information in order, students would need to be taught how to retrieve the information. It is important to practice all the steps in the retrieval process so students can tell you the correct answer as well as how they arrived at the correct answer (Mastropieri & Scruggs, 1991). This is an important link; if there is an interruption in the retrieval process the information is likely to be forgotten (i.e., students will not know how to retrieve the information).

FINAL THOUGHTS

Mnemonic strategies can be a valuable tool for teachers. However, it is important to realize their limitations. They are intended to assist with factual learning. Thus, the range of application may be somewhat limited. Still, as we noted earlier, recall of factual information is extremely important in its own right. Factual information is more than rote learning. Without a sound factual informational base it is incredibly difficult to progress academically.

In closing, we present some frequently noted comments/questions about mnemonics and their application in the schools taken from Mastropieri and Scruggs (1991).

• *"Making all those mnemonics is so much work; teachers don't have the time."* The key here is to remember to start small. One teacher we know had a problem with a health class that required memorizing a great deal of vocabulary. She decided to develop one set of mnemonics a year. She started with the 20 terms that caused the most problems. After 3 years she had addressed most of the problem terms, and her students with LD were doing much better in the course. Remember also that in the long run mnemonics will actually save you time because they will reduce the time spent in teaching that content. Think of the time spent developing mnemonics as an investment!

• *"I can't draw well enough to make the pictures."* Luckily the quality of the picture doesn't matter much. So long as the picture is recognizable mnemonics will be effective. It's also possible to use clip art or cut out pictures from magazines to help make the pictures. Drawing on the skills of students in art classes is another possibility.

• *"Won't all those pictures confuse students?"* Not really. The brain's capacity for storing information is virtually unlimited. The problem is in retrieving it and this is what makes mnemonics so effective. They provide a retrieval path that makes recalling

Philosopher	Recode–Keyword	Relate	Pictorial recoding	Retrieve
Socrates	Socks	I wear **socks** with my **shoes**.		To remember the second major philosopher, my pegword for *two* is *shoe*. I remember the shoe with a sock in it. *Sock* is my keyword for *Socrates*. That helps me remember that Socrates is the second major philosopher.
Plato	Plate	Why is that **plate** up in the **tree**?		To remember the third major philosopher, my pegword for *three* is *tree*. I remember the tree with a plate stuck in it. *Plate* is my keyword for *Plato*. That helps me remember that Plato is the third major philosopher.
Aristotle	Airplane	The **airplane** was flying so low it hit a bee **hive**.		To remember the fifth major philosopher, my pegword for *five* is *hive*. I remember the airplane that flew so low it hit a beehive. *Airplane* is my keyword for *Aristotle*. That helps me remember that Aristotle is the fifth major philosopher.

FIGURE 12.8. Combining keywords and pegwords.

information much easier. It is possible to put too much content in a lesson. So teachers do need to be sensitive to how much information to present in a lesson.

- *"Mnemonics stress pictures. What about 'auditory learners'?"* The notion that there are different types of learners is quite common. However, there is little if any research to support the notion that some students learn best via visual or auditory teaching. What research has shown is that mnemonics are universally beneficial for students who lack strategies to help with recall of information.

- *"Shouldn't students learn to make their own mnemonics?"* Students can learn to make their own mnemonics. We discussed one strategy—LINCS—in which students do exactly that. The question is not whether students can make their own mnemonics, but whether there is any *advantage* to having them do so. When students make their own mnemonics it takes much more time than when teachers create the mnemonics. This should be considered. However, it is also possible that for some students creating their own mnemonic could be more effective.

REFERENCES

Association for Supervision and Curriculum Development. (2002). Teaching students with learning disabilities in the regular classroom: Tape 2 (using learning strategies). Retrieved October 28, 2005, from http://shop.ascd.org

Atkinson, R.C. (1975). Mnemonic techniques in second-language learning. *American Psychologist, 30*, 821–828.

Ellis, E. (1992). *LINCS: A starter strategy for vocabulary learning.* Lawrence, KS: Edge.

Foil, C. R., & Alber, S. R. (2002). Fun and effective ways to build your students' vocabulary. *Intervention in School and Clinic, 37*, 131–139.

Gaskins, I., & Elliot, T. (1991). *Implementing cognitive strategy instruction across the school: The benchmark manual for teachers.* Cambridge, MA: Brookline Books.

Levin, J. R. (1988). Elaboration-based learning strategies: Powerful theory = powerful application. *Contemporary Educational Psychology, 13*, 191–205.

Mastropieri, M. A., & Scruggs, T. E. (1991). *Teaching students ways to remember: Strategies for learning mnemonically.* Cambridge, MA: Brookline Books.

Mastropieri, M. A., & Scruggs, T. E. (1998). Enhancing school success with mnemonic strategies. *Intervention in School and Clinic, 33*, 201–208.

Mastropieri, M. A., Scruggs, T. E., Bakken, J., & Brigham, F. J. (1992). A complex mnemonic strategy for teaching states and capitals: Comparing forward and backward associations. *Learning Disabilities Research and Practice, 7*, 96–103.

Mastropieri, M. A., Sweda, J., & Scruggs, T. (2000). Teacher use of mnemonic strategy instruction. *Learning Disabilities Research and Practice, 15*, 69–74.

Pressley, M., Levin, J. R., & Delaney (1982). The mnemonic keyword method. *Review of Educational Research, 52*, 61–91.

Schoen, L. M. (1996). Mnemopoly: Board games and mnemonics. *Teaching of Psychology, 23*, 30–32.

Scruggs, T. E., & Mastropieri, M. A. (1990). Mnemonic instruction for students with learning disabilities: What it is and what it does. *Learning Disability Quarterly, 13*, 271–280.

Scruggs, T. E., & Mastropieri, M. A. (1992). Classroom applications of mnemonic instruction: Acquisition, maintenance, and generalization. *Exceptional Children, 58*, 219–229.

Scruggs, T. E., & Mastropieri, M. A. (2000). The effectiveness of mnemonic instruction for students with learning and behavior problems: An update and research synthesis. *Journal of Behavioral Education, 10,* 163–173.

Scruggs, T. E., Mastropieri, M. A., Levin, J. R., & Gaffney, J. S. (1985). Facilitating the acquisition of science facts in learning disabled students. *American Educational Research Journal, 22,* 575–586.

Smith, S. M. (1985). A method for teaching name mnemonics. *Teaching of Psychology, 12,* 156–158.

Swanson, H. L., & Saez, L. (2003). Memory difficulties in children and adults with learning disabilities. In H. L. Swanson, K. R. Harris, & S. Graham (Eds.), *Handbook of learning disabilities* (pp. 182–198). New York: Guilford Press.

Index

It is important to note that too many strategies can overwhelm anyone & that students need practice, time, & guidance to become successful in transferring their newly found skills.